2000

YOUR FIRST
OF TEACHING AND
BEYOND

**THIRD
EDITION**

ELLEN L. KRONOWITZ

California State University, San Bernardino

 LONGMAN

An Imprint of Addison Wesley Longman, Inc.

New York • Reading, Massachusetts • Menlo Park, California • Harlow, England
Don Mills, Ontario • Sydney • Mexico City • Madrid • Amsterdam

Editor-in-Chief: Richard Wohl
Acquisitions Editor: Virginia L. Blanford
Marketing Manager: Renee Ortballs
Project Manager: Ellen MacElree
Design Manager: Wendy Ann Fredericks
Cover Design and Illustration: Joseph DePinho
Prepress Services Supervisor: Valerie A. Vargas
Electronic Production Specialist: Joanne Del Ben
Print Buyer: Denise Sandler
Electronic Page Makeup: UG
Printer and Binder: Maple-Vail Book Manufacturing Group
Cover Printer: Coral Graphics Services, Inc.

Library of Congress Cataloging-in-Publication Data

Kronowitz, Ellen. L.
    Your first year of teaching and beyond/Ellen L. Kronowitz.—3rd ed.
       p.   cm.
    Includes bibliographical references and index.
    ISBN 0-8013-3069-6
    1. First year teachers—Training of—United States. 2. Teacher ori-
entation—United States. 3. Teaching—Vocational guidance—United
States. I. Title.
LB2844.1.N4K766   1998
371.102—DC21   98-26708
                                           CIP

Please visit our website at http://longman.awl.com

ISBN 0-8013-3069-6

1 2 3 4 5 6 7 8 9 10—MA—01009998

For Gary, my foundation

Help, I'm Drowning

It was my first year of teaching
And I was buried alive
Under lesson plans and dittos
Not sure I'd survive.

My ed profs were experts
And so was the staff
To get their help in my classroom
I'd have cut my paycheck in half.

The parents were older than I was
They'd have run to the school board real fast
If they found out this five foot rookie
Was in charge of her very first class.

It wasn't the frequent bathroom breaks
The bonuses and exorbitant pay
It wasn't the two hour lunches
That brought me back each and every day.

Today gray haired grandmas and grandpas you'd see,
But in memory, third graders they will always be.

ELLEN KRONOWITZ

Contents

Preface

PURPOSE OF THE BOOK

Research on beginning teachers and their concerns often concludes that teacher education programs need to focus more on the first year of teaching and especially on the critical period preceding and following the first day of school. The high teacher dropout rate within the first five years makes clear that preservice and novice teachers must have help making the transition to the realities and practicalities of classroom life in their first years of teaching and beyond.

BALANCING RESEARCH AND PRACTICE

Your First Year of Teaching and Beyond, Third Edition, has a solid needs assessment base. In a study conducted at California State University, San Bernardino, preservice candidates, student teachers, and interns in the Department of Elementary and Bilingual Education were asked to generate an exhaustive list of questions about conducting the first day and weeks of school and surviving the first year of teaching. These questions were consolidated and compiled into a questionnaire that subsequently was sent to experienced teachers. It is their responses, an expanded commentary, and incorporated research findings that constitute the substance of this text. The study was recently updated to include responses from teachers at the Hillside-University Demonstration School, a public professional development school in partnership with California State University, San Bernardino.

TOPICS AND CONTENTS

Each chapter in this book addresses a documented concern of first-year elementary school teachers, such as curriculum planning, gathering materials, organization, discipline, authentic assessment, diversity, working with parents, working with school personnel, and the actual first day of classroom teaching. The introductory chapter establishes the research-based rationale for the book and a reflective orientation, and the concluding chapter offers some final advice on maintaining a reflective and professional mind in a healthy and stress-free body.

SPECIAL FEATURES

Worksheets and checklists are included at the back of the book on perforated pages. The worksheets enable readers to interact with the material presented and to move toward reflective practice. This interactive approach encourages readers to adapt the information to their own projected teaching situations and, thus, to make the information more meaningful and useful. Instructors may want to have the students work in cooperative groups to discuss the material and complete the worksheets; the book also lends itself to a workshop format should instructors prefer that instructional mode. Each worksheet or checklist is referred to at the appropriate place in the text and is symbol coded with the logos that appear below:

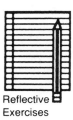
Reflective Exercises

Checklists

Duplicating Forms

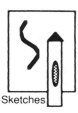
Sketches

Also included are reflection boxes that encourage the reader to interact with the material. The reflection boxes, identified with the light bulb logo, appear at the beginning and end of chapters. Each contains sentence stems that the reader can complete before and after reading and then again during the first year of teaching. It is recommended that readers use a blank journal to record responses to the sentence stems.

Beginning of Each Chapter

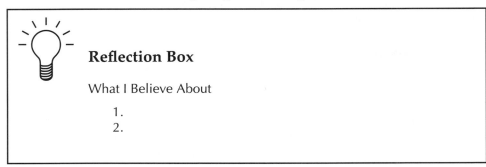

Reflection Box

What I Believe About

1.
2.

End of Each Chapter

Reflection Box

In what ways, if any, has the chapter changed my beliefs?

Questions I Still Have . . .

Reflection Box

What practices actually worked for me in my first year?

You will not be able to do everything this book suggests—even some experienced teachers may not get to everything.

NEW TO THE THIRD EDITION

Your First Year of Teaching and Beyond, third edition, is an expanded version of the second edition of the same title, published in 1996. The first edition, titled *Beyond Student Teaching,* was published in 1992. The title change in the second and third editions reflects a greater emphasis on the first year of elementary school teaching instead of just the initial days and weeks. The title change also reflects a broader potential audience. No longer exclusively addressed to student teachers, the second and now the third edition can be utilized by interns, novice teachers, school mentors for use with mentorees, principals, and district inservice coordinators. *Your First Year of Teaching and Beyond,* third edition, can serve as a refresher for more experienced teachers in urban or suburban school districts who want to reflect on their current practice.

To offer an improved balance of theory and practice, the content of the third edition has been expanded with additional references to individual differences and diversity, including second language, bilingual, special education, and multicultural populations. New to the third edition are unique anecdotes from first-year experiences in "Notes from the Teacher" boxes. The third edition offers expanded information on using technology in the classroom while it retains all of the unique features of the second edition, including:

- greater emphasis on reflection through the use of reflection boxes
- updated references, chapter summaries, and bibliographies

- interactive worksheets with space for reflective thinking and notations
- Spanish translation worksheets for parents (Worksheet 7.3B and 7.4B)
- a job search checklist in the Appendix (Worksheet 1.1) that includes information on résumé writing, interviewing, and sample interview questions

ACKNOWLEDGMENTS

A text such as this relies on input from school-based consultants, university colleagues, and a publishing team like Longman's. I would like to mention and thank those of you who have contributed to this effort. Your suggestions have been invaluable.

From Hillside-University School, I would like to thank the following contributors: Martha Pinckney, principal, Ann Kocher, Becky Monroe, Elsie Ramsey, Art Gallardo, Vic Zupancich, Shirley Clark, and Jan Christian. I would also like to thank others who submitted their unique anecdotes: Cathy McDowell, Michael Peterson, Anne Petrie, Laura Graham, Kris Ungerer, Dion Clark, Christina Jones, Don Gillman, Lena Bennett, Terri Hong, Nanette Williams, Heidi Thompson, Kim Ciabattini, and Ivania Martin. I would like to acknowledge Dion Clark and Laura Graham for their research assistance. I would also like to thank the following university colleagues and the expert reviewers who reviewed the manuscript:

Evonne F. Blakey, Chicago State University
Roger Brindley, University of South Florida
Jennifer P. Cochran, Monmouth University
Patricia J. Schindler, Tulane University
Alonzo H. Sosa, Texas A & M University—Commerce
Roberta Strosnider, Hood College
Walter H. Yoder, Jr., University of Akron

And last, I would like to thank the Longman team: Ginny Blanford, an insightful editor and friend; Allison Wolcott, her efficient assistant; Ellen MacElree, project manager; Wendy Fredericks, design manager; and Renee Ortbals, marketing manager.

ELLEN L. KRONOWITZ

chapter

1

Introduction

"What do I actually do during the first days, weeks, and year of school?" This question, posed by students in the last segment of the teacher credential program, stopped this instructor in her tracks.

"What do you mean?" I asked, although I had a fuzzy suspicion that I knew exactly what my students meant. They were anxious and scared, fearful that what they had learned and were learning didn't add up to a feeling of competence and confidence in light of an upcoming first day in a classroom solo. These future teachers went on to explain that after all of the educational psychology, the methods courses, and the student teaching experience, they had no idea what to do once they landed a job. These same anxieties burdened intern teachers and even some novice teachers, those who had survived the first year and wanted to reflect on and seek alternative solutions to the unique challenges of the first years of teaching.

These articulated concerns about the first years of teaching brought back memories of sleepless weeks prior to my own first teaching assignment. I was a cook with all the ingredients and many methods courses under my belt; yet I had not the vaguest idea how to combine instructional ingredients for the best possible effect. I stumbled through that first year and survived, but I knew back then—and current studies confirm—that there must be more to learn about the complexity of induction into the teaching profession.

I lead a workshop on the first year of teaching for all new elementary school teachers in the local school district. As a first task, I ask them to draw their classroom on the first day of school and write a word or phrase describing the room. You might want to take paper and pencil and do the same before reading further.

Typically, their drawings include desks and a chalkboard and tables and even bookshelves and bulletin boards. The words the new teachers use to describe their environments include *exciting, nurturing, inviting, supportive, warm, friendly,* and *organized.* Most teachers are embarrassed when moments later I ask, "How many of you drew in the kids?" Invariably, they have forgotten to include the children in their drawings. All agree with a nervous chuckle that the first day of school would be much less stressful without the children!

THE INDUCTION YEAR

Who wouldn't be nervous? Right out of a credential program or intern program you must assume more roles than you ever imagined during teacher education and practicum. Then, many of your responsibilities were shouldered by the supervising teacher, who had established organizational and management foundations long before you arrived on the scene.

During initial preparation, there is always a safety net. The supervising teacher can catch you when you fall and cheer you on over the rough times. The curriculum has been set, and you are responsible for pieces of the patchwork quilt but rarely for the whole thing. During your practicums, the ultimate accountability lies with the teacher. But once you have your credential in hand, the buck stops with you. Intern teachers are learning while teaching, and guidance may be sporadic and less intense than you need during your first year.

Lortie (1975) describes the abruptness with which teachers assume total responsibility as one of the major challenges of the first year. In what seems like a flash, *you* are accountable for the planning, organization, instruction, and assessment of students. *You* are responsible for your room environment and the routines that keep it operating efficiently. When you arrive at your own school, *you* will be asked to assume nonteaching duties from which student teachers are often excused, such as lunch, yard, and bus duty; social committees; and so forth. *You* need to meet new colleagues and explore a new community. *You* need to establish and maintain communication with the parents and perhaps supervise an aide. It's *your* paperwork now, and the record keeping and ongoing diagnosis are up to *you*!

Additionally, you may be assigned a challenging group of youngsters or find that some of the children have been "deselected" into your room by other grade-level colleagues. Compound this with an unfamiliar grade level and curriculum and you begin to understand why first-year teachers spend many sleepless nights before that first day of school.

All teachers have to be cheerleaders, interior decorators, artists, systems analysts, efficiency experts, performers, nurturers, assessors, judges, lion tamers, diagnosticians, psychologists, communicators, bookkeepers, managers, and friends—to name a few of the subspecialties of teaching. The list is endless. Teaching is one of the most complex professions in the world, and while I turn a sympathetic ear to preservice teachers who are perpetually sleepy and overwhelmed, I am silently saying to myself, "You don't know how easy you have it now!"

RESEARCH AND PRACTICE

New teacher induction is a growing field of inquiry among educational researchers. In some areas of the country there is a severe teacher shortage resulting from growing pupil populations, retirements, and/or competition from other fields that are draining the pool of candidates who traditionally have entered elementary school teaching. To complicate this situation, the beginning teacher dropout rate is alarmingly high. School districts increasingly realize that the effort to recruit new teachers needs to be combined with an effort to retain and support new teachers in the first years, when the going gets a little rough. The president of the United States, in his State of the Union Speech (1997), recognized the problems of recruitment and attrition: "We should reward and recognize our best teachers. And as we reward them, we should quickly and fairly remove those few who don't measure up, and we should challenge more of our finest young people to consider teaching as a career."

If current trends continue, approximately 50 percent of you will leave the profession of teaching within five years, 80 percent after ten years (Morey, 1990). Some 15 percent typically depart after the first year, another 15 percent after the second year, and about 10 percent after the third year; by the fourth year the turnover rate levels out to about 6 percent annually. In many hard to staff schools, reports the California Commission on Teacher Credentialing's Advisory Panel for the Comprehensive Review of Teaching Credential Requirements (1997), half of all beginning teachers leave after the first three years, and the attrition rate soars to two-thirds among underprepared teachers.

Why do teachers who have studied so hard, endured student teaching, and even survived the first year leave the field? There are a number of explanations, including unrealistic expectations (Nemser, 1983); lack of physical and mental conditioning (Ryan et al., 1980); isolation (Lortie, 1975); and value conflicts (Freedman, Jackson, & Boles, 1983). In addition, beginning teachers are often assigned to teach the most disruptive and least academically able students (Huling-Austin, 1989). Yee (1990) reports that teacher commitment affects attrition rates. Some enter the profession as a career, while others become teachers with the intent of leaving after a few years. But a large factor, according to Fineman-Nemser (1996), is the differential between beginning teacher salaries and the first-year salaries of other college graduates in their induction year as engineers, computer programmers, and health professionals.

Teaching is not easy. The introduction to the Association of Teacher Educators (ATE)'s publication, *Assisting the Beginning Teacher* (1989), concisely articulates the challenge: "Teaching is a highly complex series of acts. It is not learned easily. Further, it cannot be done by formula or recipe." Nemser (1983) suggests that teachers entering classrooms for the first time often bring with them idealistic and unrealistic expectations and are overwhelmed by the realities of their responsibilities. They panic, and they feel unprepared by their teacher education programs to deal with actual classroom life. Almost invariably, new teachers engage in stressful trial-and-error periods during which they figure out what works; they often count survival as their primary goal. Ryan and colleagues (1980) add that new teachers are not mentally or physically conditioned for the demands of their jobs and quickly fall prey to exhaustion. This physical fatigue can lead to psychological fatigue and eventually depression.

In addition, schools can be lonely places. Lortie's classic study of the culture of schools (1975) describes the physical isolation (one teacher in each classroom) that can lead to a sense of social isolation and discouragement that new teachers find difficult to overcome.

New teachers may also suffer value conflicts as they face schools that do not exemplify in practice what their teacher education programs have preached (Freedman, Jackson, & Boles, 1983). Schools often require teachers to behave in ways that are not consistent with the reasons they went into teaching in the first place. Lack of control over scheduling, emphasis on formal and technical assessment, and a mandated curriculum are a few of the challenges child-centered teachers must endure.

What can you do to confront—and not be discouraged by—these kinds of pressures in your first year as a teacher? At the outset, you should know that recent experiments and research in school-based management and teacher empowerment hold promising remedies to these conditions. But most important, you can, on a personal level, be prepared. Recognize and identify your own concerns, and then address them—before you begin teaching. These problems and others can be substantially reduced by appropriate preparation—the kind of analysis of what actually works, which is the focus of this book.

While some researchers are seeking answers by redesigning teacher education programs and some are championing school reforms, others are simply listening to new teachers and seeking ways to address their most pressing concerns right now. A review of 91 studies related to new teacher concerns (Veenman, 1984) identified problems that new elementary teachers perceived as most serious. These include:

- discipline
- dealing with individual differences
- motivating students
- relations with parents
- organization of class work
- assessment
- insufficient materials and supplies
- dealing with individual student problems
- heavy teaching loads
- insufficient preparation time
- relationships with colleagues
- planning and preparing for the day
- awareness of school policies and rules

Odell (1986) recorded the types of assistance requested most often by 86 elementary teachers during their first year of teaching. In the first semester, their requests included resources and materials, emotional support, instructional support, help with management, information about the school system, help with establishing a classroom environment, and demonstration teaching. During the second semester, instructional needs moved to the top of the list, followed by resources and materials, emotional support, and management assistance. This suggests that only *after* teachers have control of things like resources and materials are they ready for assistance with instruction. More recently, Brock and Grady (1996) note that both principals and beginning teachers, elementary and secondary, rank classroom management and discipline as the number one problem.

Lidstone and Hollingsworth (1992) identified two patterns of learning to teach among beginning teachers—those who are subject centered and those who are child centered. The first group needs help in routines and management, attending to student learning, and encouragement to reflect on their practice and rely on themselves for answers. The latter group, already focused on the students, needs support in management and curriculum, encouragement to balance idealism and pragmatism, and support to avoid excessive self-criticism.

In its report on the California New Teacher Project, *Success for Beginning Teachers* (1992), the Commission on Teacher Credentialing echoes the challenges others have reported and adds lack of assistance and lack of orientation to the list of "problems" confronting new teachers. The commission recommends that all beginning teachers in the state participate in programs of training assistance and support that should include seminars and opportunities to benefit from the advice of experienced teachers.

Daunting challenges face new teachers—but help is available. New school settings almost always provide many avenues of assistance, if you know the right questions to ask. Mentor and buddy teacher programs help ease the way in more and more districts, and in-service sessions are sometimes scheduled for new teachers. Your principal and other administrative and instructional personnel are there to help. Moskowitz and Stephens (1997) report that in the three teacher induction programs they studied (Australia, Japan, and New Zealand), new teachers had many of the same concerns as U.S. "inductees." While teaching wasn't any easier for beginners in these three countries, there were significant differences in the amount of mentoring and in the timing of the mentoring across the entire first year. Teachers also reported feeling more like professionals and more supported by others at their site. Importantly, new teachers did not perceive that they were assigned to the difficult classes and, in fact, they were given lighter loads and fewer administrative duties to facilitate their induction process.

Most important, help is available *before* you begin teaching. Griffin (1985) suggests that teacher education programs should include not only research findings but also the collected wisdom of experienced teachers—in other words, what works. What works is the essence of this text.

After reviewing the literature on first-year teachers some years ago, I was convinced that the preservice and intern teachers I worked with had the same concerns these studies list. Rather than wait until these beginners were already out there, I wanted to address

their first-year questions and concerns *before* they actually started teaching—during the preservice phase of their training. I began asking student teachers in methods classes to present the things that concerned or worried them about the first days and weeks of school. Not only were these concerns real, down-to-earth, and specific, they also reflected sincerely and openly the same concerns as those expressed by first-year teachers.

I first responded by inviting practicing elementary teachers to class to share their perspectives and ideas. It soon became apparent, however, that my students needed more—and more varied—input, and they needed it in a form that could be preserved and reviewed. To me, it seemed clear that advice from practicing teachers should be tapped and disseminated as early as possible—certainly before teachers stepped into their classrooms.

As a result, questions generated by 33 preservice teachers were compiled into a questionnaire that was distributed to 27 experienced teachers. Respondents were asked to assume that their advice would be read by teachers soon to enter the profession, not by other experienced teachers. The responses were practical, experienced-based answers that reflect what teachers do to set up an environment conducive to learning. The questionnaire was updated and recirculated as I wrote this book. The advice and guidelines provided in this text, then, reflect not only a review of the available literature on the first-day and first-year experience but also the invaluable ideas of resourceful and experienced teachers.

USING THIS BOOK

The chapters address the most daunting challenges of the first year of teaching in an elementary school classroom. These include curriculum planning, gathering of materials and supplies, classroom organization and management, pupil assessment and record keeping, and communicating with school-based personnel and parents. The final chapters focus on two extremely important areas, one on a single day and one on the rest of your professional life. Chapter 9 addresses the day that frightens beginning teachers more than any other: the first day of school. Specific suggestions about organizing and behaving on that all-important day are included. Finally, Chapter 10 speaks to professionalism and reflective practice—your growth as a teacher throughout your professional career.

The topics in *Your First Year of Teaching and Beyond* are the nitty-gritty of any elementary school teacher's daily classroom life. While there is much to know about teaching, learning, and classroom management that is theoretical and research based, advice about the *practical* aspects of setting up a learning environment is best given by practitioners. A list of books and articles related to the topics covered in the chapter for further reading precedes the references at the back of each chapter. You will find a balance of the theoretical and the practical throughout. The feature Notes from the Teacher is scattered through the text. These are personal anecdotes that were solicited for this edition from both beginning and veteran teachers. They tell in succinct format of some trial, tribulation, or triumph of their first year.

This book is designed to address a variety of audiences. It can be incorporated into existing courses or student teaching or intern seminars or it can form the basis for a new course on the practical dimensions of teaching. It is addressed additionally to mentors and mentorees, to principals for sharing with new teachers, and to any novice or any experienced teachers as well who want to take a fresh look at their practice.

The format of the text enables you to interact with the material and reflect on your practice through the use of "reflection boxes," worksheets, and checklists. The Reflection Boxes, with the light bulb logo, appear at the beginning and end of each chapter and are meant to help you interact with the material in a reflective mode. The sentence stems in the first reflection boxes all relate to the material that will be covered in the chapter. It is recommended that you use a blank journal along with this text. Take the time to respond to the sentence stems in your journal before reading. After reading the chapter, use the second reflection box to record in your journal any new ideas or questions you have. The third reflection box will help you personalize this book during your first year of teaching. During the year, take out your journal and compare your previous answers with those that are now based in your own experience. The journal will be a constant reminder of your transformation from student teacher to teacher.

Beginning of Each Chapter

Reflection Box

What I Believe About

    1.

    2.

End of Each Chapter

Reflection Box

In what ways, if any, has the chapter changed my beliefs?

    Questions I Still Have . . .

Reflection Box

What practices actually worked for me in my first year?

Worksheets and checklists are included at the back of the book on perforated pages that you can tear out, copy, and use as you begin teaching. Each worksheet or checklist is referred to at the appropriate place in the text itself and is symbol coded with the logos that appear on page 11. A pencil and paper stand for reflective exercises, a check mark for checklists, a boxed "d" for duplicating forms, and a crayon for sketching. Two worksheets (7.3 and 7.4) that can be duplicated and sent to parents have been translated into Spanish. The worksheets have spaces so that you can add your own criteria or notations where appropriate. If you have not yet secured a position, you may want to begin with Worksheet 1.1, Job Search Checklist.

Worksheet
1.1

In addition, at the end of each chapter there is a short summary paragraph that brings the chapter to a conclusion and ties up loose ends. Here is the first one.

A FINAL FOCUS

Adapt what is here to your very own classroom and grade-level situation and to your very own personal teaching style. Use the resources provided in this text to help you discover what that style is. Use this book to guide you through that first year—beyond which lie the rewards that first motivated your choice of this exciting, challenging profession.

FURTHER READING

Britzman, D. P. (1991). *Practice makes practice*. Albany: State University of New York Press.

Croasmun, J., Hampton, D., & Herrmann, S. (1997). *Teacher attrition: Is time running out?* [On-line]. Available http://www.unc/edu~jck/paper.html

Dollase, R. (1992). *Voices of beginning teachers*. New York: Teachers College Press.

Gold, Y., & Roth, R. (1993). *Teachers managing stress and preventing burnout: The professional health solution*. London: Falmer Press.

Goodlad, J. (1994). *Teachers for our nation's schools*. San Francisco: Jossey-Bass.

Kidder, T. (1990). *Among schoolchildren*. Boston: Houghton Mifflin.

Lieberman, A., & Miller, L. (1992). *Teachers, their world, and their work*. New York: Teachers College Press.

Ryan, K. (Ed.). (1992). *The roller coaster year: Essays by and for beginning teachers*. New York: HarperCollins.

REFERENCES

Advisory Panel for the Comprehensive Review of Teaching Credential Requirements. (1997). *Final report* (SB 1422). Sacramento: California Commission on Teacher Credentialing.

Association of Teacher Educators. (1989). *Assisting the beginning teacher*. Reston, VA: Association of Teacher Educators..

Brock, B., & Grady, M. (1996). *Beginning teacher induction programs* [Online]. Available http://ericae,net/db/riecije/ed399631.htm

California Commission on Teacher Credentialing. (1992). *Success for beginning teachers*. Sacramento: California Department of Education.

Clinton, W. J. (1997, February 4). State of union addresss [Online]. Available http://www.law.uoknor.edu/hist/state97.html

Fineman-Nemser, S. (1996). *The current status of teaching and teacher development in the United States* [Online]. Available http//www.tc.columbia.edu/~teachcomm/BRIEF6.HTM

Freedman, S., Jackson, J., & Boles, K. (1983). Teaching: An imperiled profession. In L. Shulman and G. Sykes (Eds.), *Handbook of teaching and policy* (pp. 261–299). New York: Longman.

Griffin, G. (1985). Teacher induction: Research issues. *Journal of Teacher Education, 36*(1), 42–46.

Huling-Austin, L. (1989). Beginning teacher assistance programs: An overview. In *Assisting the beginning teacher*. Reston, VA: Association of Teacher Educators.

Lidstone, M., & Hollingsworth, S. (1992). A longitudinal study of cognitive change in beginning teachers: Two patterns of learning to teach. *Teacher Education Quarterly 19*(4), 39–57.

Lortie, D. (1975). *School teacher: A sociological study*. Chicago: University of Chicago Press.

Morey, A. (1990). Introduction. In A. Morey and D. S. Murphy (Eds.), *Designing programs for new teachers: The California experience*. San Francisco: Far West Laboratory for Educational Research and Development.

Moskowitz, J., & Stephens, M. (Eds.). (1997). *From students of teaching to teachers of students*. Report of the Pelavin Research Institute, the Education Forum of APEC (Asia-Pacific Economic Cooperation), and the U.S. Department of Education [Online]. Available http://www.ed.gov/pubs/APEC/

Nemser, S. F. (1983). Learning to teach. In L. Shulman and G. Sykes (Eds.), *Handbook of teaching and policy* (pp. 150–170). New York: Longman.

Odell, S. J. (1986). Induction support of new teachers: A functional approach. *Journal of Teacher Education, 37*(1), 26–29.

Ryan, K., Newman, K., Mager, G., Applegate, J., Lasley, T., Flora, R., & Johnston, J. (1980). *Biting the apple: Accounts of first year teachers*. New York: Longman.

Veenman, S. (1984). Perceived problems of beginning teachers. *Review of Educational Research, 54*(2), 143–178.

Yee, S. M. (1990). *Careers in the classroom: When teaching is more than a job*. New York: Teachers College Press.

chapter

2

Curriculum Planning

Reflection Box

What I Believe About

The importance of planning . . .
Long-range planning . . .
Thematic instructional units . . .
Weekly and daily planning . . .
Planning for diversity . . .

School bells ring in September, but if you have not done any curriculum planning for the first day and weeks of school by the time you hear those sounds, you might want to do what one former student of mine suggested—pray.

During student teaching, the curriculum is basically set by your supervising teacher. While you may have some responsibility for designing units of study, an invisible structure has been set up long before you arrive on the scene. The teacher you work with sets out the year's plan, and if you don't ask about it, you may not know how all of the little pieces relate to the plan. You may not, in fact, realize the importance of making all the pieces relate to it.

A Note from the Teacher

Planning is your best friend.

M. PETERSON

THE IMPORTANCE OF PLANNING

Why do you need to plan ahead? In a study of 12 elementary school teachers, McCutcheon (1980) identified both internal and external reasons for planning. The internal reasons included: to feel more confident, to learn the subject matter better, to enable lessons to run more smoothly, and to anticipate problems in hope of avoiding them. The external reasons included meeting expectations of the principal and providing direction for substitutes. Alleviating butterflies might be reason enough for you.

As we noted in Chapter 1, new teachers are first and foremost concerned about the big D—DISCIPLINE (Veenman, 1984). As a new teacher, you may find that your instructional concerns are overshadowed by management concerns. However, if the curriculum is exciting and geared toward the needs, interests, and abilities of the students you will teach, you are more than halfway there.

Of all the responsibilities of a new teacher, none is less practiced during student teaching than curriculum planning. You have probably had ample opportunities to teach, to manage, to discipline, and to evaluate, but if your situation is like most, you designed only a small portion of an already set curriculum. When and if you know your grade level, the period between the completion of your credential program and your first teaching assignment is the time to reflect on what *your* curriculum will be during your first year of teaching. While it is impossible to plan down to the last detail until you have actually come face-to-face with the children, you can use the time between student teaching and the beginning of the school year to sketch out a curriculum and organize it—and to ease some of the panic typically felt as opening day draws near.

A Note from the Teacher

I have been observing, learning, and asking questions, but the one thing I still don't know is what to teach. Where do teachers get their ideas for their units and themes? Do they take them right out of the Framework? Do they just borrow from other teachers? How and when will I be given the key of knowledge?

L. GRAHAM

Curriculum preplanning does not, of course, preclude resting, vacationing, housecleaning, and reacquainting yourself with your family, activities that are vital to teachers who have been in school nonstop. Many of the ideas suggested by practicing teachers are just that—ideas. McCutcheon (1980) found that teachers are engaged in mental planning almost continuously during the day, so why not use the relaxing hours to plan ahead mentally? Thinking about the school curriculum can take place as you float on a raft, lounge in a chair, fish in a pond. It can take place anywhere.

Only you will know how much time to spend planning. I suggest an inverse relationship between experience in the classroom and time spent in preplanning the curriculum:

the more experience, the less time you may choose to devote to preplanning; the less experience in the classroom, the more time you may choose to devote to curriculum preplanning. There is also the panic factor to consider. The more anxious you are about the first days and weeks of school, the more you should preplan. If you are cool as a cucumber about it, the less you need to preplan. But beware! Sometimes a calm precedes or masks a storm, so make sure confidence from competence is producing your calm feeling—and not avoidance or total denial of what may lie ahead come that first day of school.

This chapter focuses on shaping an instructional plan appropriate for your students from the multitude of possibilities the experts have proposed. We will address long- and short-term planning and provide suggestions for organizing your weekly and daily schedule. After all, teachers don't just teach: They teach something in an organized way, using resources and strategies appropriate to the students in their classrooms. In this chapter you will learn what questions to ask about curriculum planning, and you will begin to conceptualize what you must do for the long and short hauls.

LONG-RANGE PLANNING: THE YEAR AT A GLANCE

When I began teaching, I was given—along with a class list, record book, and key to the teachers' rest room—a stack of curriculum materials. Included were various curriculum guides (one each for social studies, science, and language arts). Inside each were the goals, content, and topics to be taught; suggested learning activities for each topic; and a bibliography of print resources that I could turn to—if I ever had time. Math and reading curricula consisted of what the teacher's edition of the texts told me to teach, and art consisted of activities taken from *Instructor* magazine or creatively borrowed from other teachers. Music and physical education were hit-or-miss affairs. Each weekend I brought home curriculum guidebooks and textbook manuals and labored to fit topics into little boxes in a weekly planbook. I hoped I was teaching what the children needed to know. But I always had my doubts!

Elementary teachers today have the same decisions to make about what to teach, how long to teach it, and how much time the kids should be allowed for practice (Clark & Lambert, 1986). Now, as then, they engage in yearly, term, unit, weekly, and daily planning (Yinger, 1980). In the rest of this chapter we will focus on the practical aspects of long- and short-term planning based on the collective wisdom of those who have been there before you.

Getting to Know the Formal Curriculum

The first step in thinking about curriculum planning is to become familiar with the expectations of your district, or what John Goodlad's colleagues Klein, Tye, and Wright (1979) call the *formal* curriculum. This may come in the form of state curriculum frameworks, district curriculum guides, scope and sequence charts, proficiency lists for each grade level, teacher's manuals, and a number of other documents.

How do you get hold of these? The most practical way is to visit the school as soon as you receive your assignment and pick up *all* relevant materials. Some districts even provide a guidebook for new teachers listing all school and district policies. Get copies of all relevant curriculum materials and documents for each curriculum area, including teacher's manuals for all textbooks and computer programs.

Worksheet
2.1

The more familiar you are with the upcoming curriculum, the more comfortable and creative you can be in planning an overview of the year's instruction. If you plan, for example, an individualized math program, make sure the school has materials to support your effort. The givens of curriculum are available, and you need but to ask to have them in your hands.

Use Worksheet 2.1, Curriculum Materials Survey List, to help you ask the right questions. I have found even veteran teachers who are unaware of all the curriculum documents available to them until they seek them out to complete a graduate curriculum class assignment. Be prepared. These materials can be read at the pool, on the beach, by the lake, or on the subway. Remember to survey the computer software and laser disc technology applications available to you. Those of you who will be teaching children whose primary language isn't English need especially to look and plan ahead because of the short supply of good bilingual and ESL (English as a second language) materials and resources.

From Formal to Instructional Curriculum

After looking at this material, you may feel overwhelmed. How are you going to plan lessons in all curriculum areas, given 22 hours or so of instructional time per week? This one question alone provides a substantial challenge to the beginning teacher. In your teacher training program, you may have learned how to develop curriculum using a classical linear, or step-by-step, approach.

One such sequential process was originated by Ralph Tyler (1969), and it still exerts tremendous influence in teacher preparation programs. Briefly, Tyler's curriculum development model identifies the sources of curriculum as learners, contemporary society, and subject matter specialists. Tentative objectives are derived from these sources and then filtered through two screens, one philosophical and one psychological. The first screen helps the curriculum designer identify those objectives that are consistent with the educational philosophy of the school. The second screen assures that the objectives are consistent with developmental and learning theories. Those objectives that survive the filters become the starting points from which the content and then sequenced learning activities are derived. The Tyler rationale includes, as a final step, evaluation to assess the effectiveness of instruction.

Tyler's model is very neat and clean, but considerable research on new-teacher planning behavior suggests that teachers rarely follow the sequential, linear process they learned in the credential program once they are confronted with classroom realities. It turns out that behavioral objectives are not all that central to the actual planning behavior of teachers (Borko & Niles, 1987). Teachers focus instead on content and activities. In particular, elementary teachers specifically rely on textbooks for the content of what to teach and how to teach it (McCutcheon, 1980). In McCutcheon's study, the teachers selected 85 to 95 percent of the reading and math activities from the manuals.

Experienced teachers also circumvent the classical curriculum design model. They tend to consider several curriculum elements at the same time (e.g., pupil interests and abilities, available materials, district expectations, activities, content) (May, 1986). Even preservice students of mine often begin with the topic, generate learning activities, and then go back and write objectives that fit in with the formal curriculum expectations. But objectives are the key to the teaching–learning cycle, since they provide benchmarks and indicators of expected outcomes and help you determine how much learning has taken place. You will be reading more about objectives later in the chapter.

Because we all are unique and may go about planning in diverse ways, the suggestions that follow are not meant to be prescriptive. Allow yourself flexibility to plan in your own unique way, always keeping in mind the givens of the formal curriculum documents. Regardless of your individual planning style, the instruction you ultimately plan needs to facilitate the attainment of knowledge, skills, and attitudes identified by the formal curriculum, by the district, and by you.

The Instructional Curriculum by Subject Area

Begin with a long sheet of butcher paper, a roll of shelf paper, or some computer paper. You will need a lot of room. Set up a matrix like the one in Figure 2.1 on your paper (on a computer you might want to use a database application). As you read through your curriculum documents, jot down the major concepts/topics, skills, and attitudes you are expected to teach for the year. You will begin to see some areas of commonality in all the subject areas. Circle these with a bright-colored marker. This is the start of what I like to call the "killing two or more birds with one stone" approach to curriculum planning. Others call it integrated learning or the thematic approach. But more about that later.

The Instructional Curriculum Month by Month

The next step is to decide on overall monthly plans. The reason to map out your year on a different piece of paper is to check and see that you get it all in. You will need, of course, to pace your instruction according to the children's needs, interests, and abilities, but even a rough sketch of the entire year will be helpful, especially if you think about combining the major skills, topics, and attitudes you discovered into thematic units. Some teachers will want to make a matrix of the months and the curriculum areas and simply distribute the material found in your concepts, skills, and attitudes matrix among the 9 school months (or 12 school months, if you are on a year-round schedule). Others will additionally want to identify a theme for each month and attempt to integrate as many areas of the curriculum as possible. The matrix would be set out as in Figure 2.2.

If you teach all the concepts, skills, and attitudes on your matrix as discrete and unrelated bits, you will never have time to accomplish all your objectives. There is a contin-

	Math	Science	Social Studies	Language Arts	Music	P. E.	Art	Health
Concepts / Topics								
Skills								
Attitudes								

Figure 2.1

Theme	July	Aug.	Sept.	Oct.	Nov.	Dec.	Jan.	Feb.	Mar.	Apr.	May	June
Math												
Science												
Social Studies												
Language Arts												
Music												
P. E.												
Art												
Health												

Figure 2.2

uum of packaging that ranges from teaching each subject area in an assigned time frame each day to totally integrating the curriculum. The middle ground is a compromise position that enables you to teach one unit of instruction, usually in science or social studies, while continuing to teach the subjects in their assigned time slots.

MIDRANGE PLANNING: INSTRUCTIONAL UNITS

Unit-based instruction is an alternative for those of you who want to spend time thinking about curriculum delivery before the first day of school. You can cluster some of these topics and skills into larger chunks of instruction (units) that enable you to cover multiple objectives in several curriculum areas at the same time. Unit planning, while time-consuming and challenging, can save you countless hours later. You will have more fun and your students will experience less curricular fragmentation. Even student teachers, as busy as they are, appreciate the rewards of unit-based instruction.

Once you have some idea of what you must teach, or the curriculum givens, you might consider sketching out a very brief beginning unit in either social studies, science, or literature. Having one beginning unit roughly sketched out will enable you to start the year with confidence. Consider a literature-based unit built around a favorite book you can secure in multiple copies from the book room or favorite student book club. Ultimately, this unit can ease the burden of that first week of school until your roster is set and you have all your teaching texts and materials.

Types of Units

There are at least two types of units, the teaching unit and the resource unit. The teaching unit consists of a set of separate lesson plans all related to one topic and targeted to a specific group of children based on their needs, interests, and abilities. The teaching unit may include lesson plans in many or all curriculum areas. A unit on Mexico, for example,

might include lesson plans for writing a letter to pen pals (language), designing bark paintings (art), learning a Mexican dance (physical education), counting in Spanish (math), and making tacos (math and cooking).

Similarly, a teaching unit on the book *Strega Nona*, a delightful folktale about over-flowing pasta, written by Tomie De Paola (1996) and set in Italy, might include lesson plans for making pasta (cooking), classifying and patterning pasta (math), making a pasta mosaic (art), dramatizing the story (language), and locating and making maps of Italy (social studies).

The resource unit is more general than the teaching unit and can be adapted for any grade level. It is a compendium of ideas for teaching a particular topic through an integrated curriculum. The resource unit consists of a rationale, content outline, set of goals, brief descriptions of learning activities, evaluation, and bibliography. The activities span many curriculum areas, and in order to implement the unit, expanded lesson plans directed to a particular group of children may need to be written.

Designing a Resource or Teaching Unit

The first step in unit design involves finding a topic. There are several sources for good ideas, including, first and foremost, the formal curriculum documents, especially in social studies and science. The new literature-based language arts programs now provide wonderful opportunities for unit building based on literary works. Ask veteran teachers to share any grade-appropriate units. Brainstorm with colleagues about topics and available resources.

Another source for the topic is your own experience. Start with a topic you know and like, and the children will catch your enthusiasm. You may be from a different ethnic or cultural group than many of your students, or you may have spent time living or working or traveling in another culture. You may have a lifelong interest in insects or sea mammals that you want to share. You may have majored in American history and know everything there is to know about the Civil War. It is the best of all possible worlds when your interests mesh with the curriculum expectations for the grade level you are teaching. If they don't, you may need to compromise and create a unit based on your interests to supplement the curriculum.

An excellent source for units are the interests or cultural backgrounds of the children. Early in your first year of teaching, conduct an interest inventory to ascertain what intrinsic motivation there is for various topics in general. In Chapter 7 you will find suggestions for involving parents in culture studies and general curriculum support. Other sources of unit topics include current events, prepared curriculum materials and kits, the textbook, and local community resources (museums, industries, historical landmarks).

When you begin teaching, you will want to involve the children in unit planning. Before you go any further with the topic you ultimately decide on, try it out on your audience to see what they already know, what they want to know, and what their level of interest in the topic is. Glasser (1993) asserts that "quality school" teachers always let students in on the usefulness of the skills and information you will be teaching them, and this principle should guide your search for meaningful material.

Some teachers like to use sentence stems—for example, When I think of Japan . . . or, What I want to know about Japan is. . . . Similarly, you might put up two very large charts and have children brainstorm together: What do they know, and what do they really want to learn about the topic? If you begin the unit by addressing students' initial questions first, you will hook their interest to study the rest.

The next step is to find out about the topic if you are not already familiar enough with it to make your content outline. One of the major benefits of teaching multiple subjects is the opportunity to learn new things as you are conducting your unit research. Many gaps in my own education were filled in as I prepared for teaching fourth, fifth, and sixth graders. Begin with a good encyclopedia or use the interactive CD-ROM encyclopedias available at some school sites or district resource centers. Have your computer mouse browse the Internet and then cruise the information superhighway to amass information on your chosen topic. You will discover Web sites for science, art, and natural history museums, The Library of Congress, The National Archives, The Smithsonian, zoos, observatories, and so on. You can visit the White House, Congress, *National Geographic*, and NASA in your jammies at your computer late into the evening. You can even ask experts on the Web. Use Web guides such as *The Ultimate On-Line Homework Helper* (Salzman & Pondiscio, 1996), designed for kids but very useful for teachers.

Also immerse yourself in the content by visiting libraries and checking out children's books on the topic. This may sound like strange advice, but in the interest of time I found that if I went to texts and nonfictional accounts geared toward children, I would find the material already predigested and written in language that both they and I could readily understand. I remember one such text on the Middle Ages, written at the sixth grade level, that had a table of contents which provided me with a way to organize the unit that, until then, I had been seeking.

The next step should be writing a tentative set of objectives, but since we know that teachers head right for the fun part or the instructional activities, I will come back to the objectives. Sit down with a big piece of butcher paper and think of all the exciting ways you can carry through this unit. Make a web or map of your tentative ideas or simply write them all down and categorize them according to the curriculum areas that seem most dominant. If your topic derives from social studies or science, think back on all the ideas pertaining to language arts and art that might be germane. If your topic derives from literature, think of all the other curriculum areas including language that might pertain.

The unit "My Journey," for example, can integrate many curriculum areas and get things off to a nice start. It can teach the social studies concept of diversity and lead children to understand that we as Americans are both alike and different. A brief sketch of how this unit incorporates several curriculum areas at once after the learning activities have been webbed or classified is shown in Figure 2.3. The "My Journey" unit can be part of a bigger, year-long thematic mega-unit "Journeys: Around the World in 180 School Days" (to be discussed shortly).

Notice that these suggestions are not yet specific for any grade level. At this point this unit probably could be carried out at the first grade or sixth grade level. First graders would measure with string and sixth graders would measure themselves in centimeters, for example. First grade time lines would be pictorial, whereas sixth grade time lines would be researched at home and done on a computer with a program such as *Timeliner*.

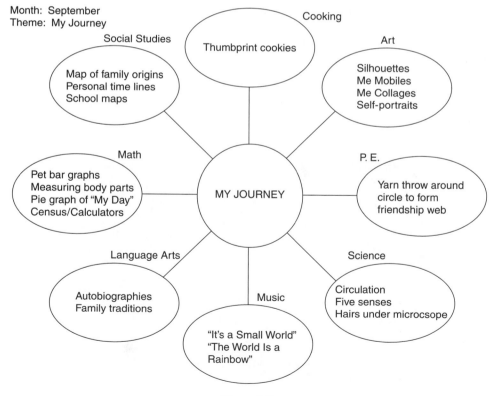

Figure 2.3

"My Day" pie graphs might be approximate and made on paper plates by first graders; sixth graders would be more precise and use knowledge of fractions to complete their graphs. Only when the resource unit is adapted to a particular group of children through specific and complete lesson plans does it become more focused. Use some of the sheltered English techniques when planning your unit activities if you are working with nonnative English speakers who are literate in their primary language. These are discussed in Chapter 6 and include good teaching techniques such as hands-on activities, use of visuals, cooperative learning, and similar projects.

After you have brainstormed the activities to carry through the unit, go back to the list of objectives you outlined for the year. You will notice that many of them fit right in. You have to teach children about graphs anyway, so why not in the context of a self-concept unit? The children need to write, so why not have them write autobiographies? In social studies you are expected, according to the year at a glance, to teach about time lines and construct one, so why not begin the process with personal time lines? Although this is a case of the tail wagging the dog, you will not be the first or the last teacher to design your unit plans this way. Always keep in mind that students learn best when the material is meaningful to them.

Unit-a-Month Club

Some teachers like to alternate social studies and science as the focus for the month. For example, September may be devoted to a social studies integrated unit "My Journey" and a social studies–oriented self-esteem unit, and October may have as its focus "Ocean Journeys," a science-focused unit on the oceans, ocean life, explorers, Pilgrims, ocean transportation, and related topics.

This alternation between a social studies and a science unit focus throughout the year assures that the social studies and science topics will be covered in depth and will be made more interesting through an integrated curriculum approach. You have probably

created units in methods classes. Swap with others so you can begin the year with some units to carry you through at least the first few months. You need to make sure that the units you borrow are consistent with formal curriculum expectations for the grade level and are appropriate to the needs, interests, and abilities of the particular youngsters in your class. Now you can go back to your year-at-a-glance and identify possible focus units or themes for each month.

Curriculum Integration Within Units

The first-year teacher should approach the integration process slowly, with only one or two curriculum areas at first. Starting with your first social studies unit, a unit on self-discovery (or "My Journey"), begin by integrating only art and language arts until you are more comfortable with the process of curriculum integration. As a beginner, unfamiliar with the curriculum for the grade level, you are wise to integrate where possible and to move at your own pace toward making other curriculum connections. You may teach some of your language arts and art and music during social studies, but there are some skills and concepts that defy integration, and you will feel more comfortable easing into integrated teaching slowly.

It is probably best to integrate slowly and naturally, adding one curriculum area at a time, while continuing to teach the basic knowledge and skills at the appointed time in the schedule. A beginning teacher would not expect to teach the entire curriculum in an integrated fashion during the first school year. In fact, it is just as much a burden to force integration of curriculum as it is to teach each curriculum area separately.

Science and math integrate easily, and social studies or science, art, and language arts also go well together. As you can see from Figure 2.4, you need not teach all the curriculum content through integration. Some topics or concepts or skills may simply resist integration into your chosen unit focus. The circles in Figure 2.4 show where the overlap occurs. Other art is conducted during art time and other language arts are taught during language time and so on.

As you feel more proficient, you can add other curriculum areas when they fit until you know the curriculum so well that you decide to integrate all the curriculum areas, as illustrated in Figure 2.5. Note that even when you strive for total curricular integration, as a new teacher you will still sometimes have to teach what doesn't fit.

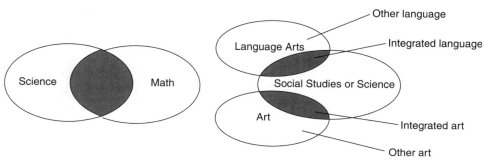

Figure 2.4

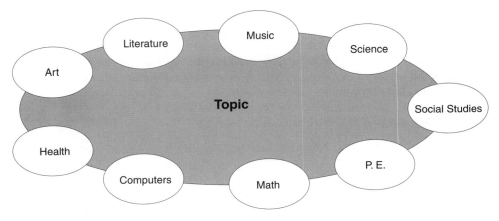

Figure 2.5

Toward a Year-Long Thematic Approach

Some overachievers will want to sketch out the entire year thematically and will follow the advice of Susan Kovalik (1986) and choose one overarching theme for the year and 10 related subthemes, one subtheme per month. A year-long map focusing on "Journeys" may look something like Figure 2.6. As the year progresses, more and more curricular in-

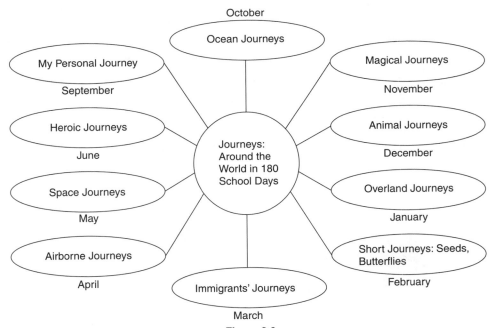

Figure 2.6

Web developed by Mrs. Shirley Clark, third grade teacher at Hillside-University Demonstration School, San Bernardino, CA.

tegration can take place. While this map reflects the traditional school schedule, the year-long map can be adapted to the year-round schedule. You will note here that the first unit is "My Journey," the unit developed in Figure. 2.3.

At this point you may want to sketch out a unit that would be appropriate for the grade level you will be teaching using Worksheet 2.2, Unit Planning. Use the guidelines on Worksheet 2.3, Unit Evaluation Criteria, to both design and then evaluate your own unit.

Worksheet 2.2

Worksheet 2.3

WEEKLY PLANS

After familiarizing yourself with the curriculum and making some global long-range plans, you are now ready to think about and make concrete weekly and daily plans. In some ways it is easier to plan for the short haul when the entire structure, both content and organization, is laid out, even though this process of laying it all out is time-consuming. In the end, however, time spent in the activities described above will save you countless hours on many Sunday nights when you sit down with a blank weekly planbook and have to fill in all those little boxes.

Setting Your Weekly Schedule

When you sit down to write your weekly schedule, you want to have as much information about the parameters of your scheduling decisions as you can. School organization, the master school schedule, and curriculum time allotments and order will all influence the decisions you make about how the week will look. It's better to know at the beginning what the limitations will be, to avoid constant changes in your schedule due to unforeseen events.

The Impact of the School's Organization.   Some aspects of your weekly schedule will be predetermined by the overall organization of the school. Yours may be either a self-contained or a departmentalized program. That is, you may be expected to teach all the subjects over the whole day or students may be rotated among subject-matter specialists, as in a typical middle or junior high school. Mainstreaming is part of many school programs, both for special-needs children and for nonnative speakers or limited-English speakers. This mainstreaming can take many forms. Find out about mainstreaming practices at your school site, and adjust your schedule accordingly.

Other organizational elements may be predetermined as well. For example, some schools use single-age grouping; others use multiage grouping. Having a class of all 7-year-olds will necessitate a different type of curriculum organization than will a multiage group of 7-, 8-, and 9-year-olds. Another decision that will be made for you is whether your children will be homogeneously grouped according to ability levels or heterogeneously grouped, with a wide range of abilities represented. It is important for you to determine the limits of your organizational choices. The best way to do this is to contact the principal or another teacher in the school as soon as your assignment is made. Knowing the givens of school organization will help you exercise control over what can be determined by you and you alone.

Let us assume that your assignment reflects the most common organizational pattern in elementary schools—that is, self-contained, heterogeneously grouped instruction with no cross-class grouping for reading and math. With this information about school organization, you can next determine what the scheduling givens are.

MASTER WEEKLY SCHEDULE					
Time	Monday	Tuesday	Wednesday	Thursday	Friday
9:00		Mainstreaming			Library
10:00		Computer Lab			
11:00		Recess 11:00 – 11:20			
12:00		Band			

Figure 2.7

The Impact of the Master School and District Schedule. Obtain a copy of the district calendar and schedule as soon as possible. Transfer to your own master calendar all holidays, Open House nights, parent conferences, testing dates, inservice days, and any other special school and districtwide events that will affect you and your class. Then when you write up your weekly schedule, you can see if there are days or time slots when you cannot plan on teaching much of anything to anyone.

Next enter on a master weekly schedule the school schedule givens for a typical week. Include the times for recess, lunch, preparation periods, assemblies, library, computer lab, and so forth. Also list the activities that will draw off some of your children, such as speech instruction, band, lunch monitor duty, and resource teacher or counselor visits. You don't want to schedule major new content lessons during these times if doing so can be avoided. Fill in these weekly givens on a schedule like the one in Figure 2.7. Then you can duplicate these masters with key, immutable times already filled in. The blank spaces are yours! You may feel as though the entire week is taken up with special functions, but so it is in a complex elementary school.

The Impact of Time Allotments and Order of Subjects. It is not unusual for states and/or districts to mandate the number of minutes for each school subject. It is also common for schools to recommend an order to the subjects covered during the day. One reason that reading or math may occur schoolwide at a prescribed time is to allow for cross-class grouping of children. You need to find out as soon as you can what your time allotments for each subject area are and if there is any prescribed order to the day. It is common to cover the language arts, reading, and math during the morning hours when children are most alert, but this is not universal by any means.

Writing Your Weekly Plans

District regulations and principal expectations vary when it comes to how much detail you are expected to include in your plans. Some principals collect the plans every week and look through each and every square. Others ask only that the plans be available in a prominent place on your desk. This is important information to gather as soon as you find yourself with a teaching job. You want to get off on the right foot by providing your site administrator with the degree of specificity she or he expects to see in your planbook. If you have done your month-at-a-glance exercise, then it should not be too difficult to divide by four and make up your weekly plans. The most typical format is the weekly schedule or the more detailed weekly format offered on Worksheet 2.4, Weekly Plan. Keep these plans in a loose-leaf notebook.

Worksheet 2.4

Write these plans in pencil. *They will change!* Develop a code for identifying what was adequately covered, what needs to be retaught, and what never got taught because of, say, the special assembly. You also might want to identify those activities that bombed, those that were great fun, and those that needed more time. Use symbols or differently colored check marks as you review the previous week's plan before you begin the following one. Post-it notes or flags are also very popular with teachers. Affix them to your plan-book to help you remember what needs review, what needs total reteaching, what didn't get taught, and so forth. If you create a system that works for you, you will save yourself a great deal of time trying to remember whether you taught an activity or not and how well it went. A temptation you should resist when writing your weekly plan is to teach the entire year's curriculum in a week or a day. Make sure to plan incrementally—that is, in bite-size, easily digestible pieces.

PLANNING FOR DIVERSITY

As your planning becomes more specific, make sure that you are attempting to meet the diverse needs of children in your classroom. Davidman and Davidman (1997) demonstrate how most lessons, activities, and units can be transformed to reflect a multicultural focus. At the point where you are translating your long- and midrange planning into actual classroom instruction, you need to think about how you will modify instruction for special-needs children, for high achievers, or for children who differ in their learning styles. Second language learners or limited-English-proficient students may require modifications in instruction. Those who are literate in their native language will need what is formally called Specially Designed Academic Instruction in English (SDAIE), or, more commonly, sheltered English. Peregoy and Boyle (1996) and Diaz-Rico and Weed (1995) describe many effective sheltering techniques, such as using visuals, concrete objects, and student experiences to support instruction. In Chapter 6 you will find more specific suggestions for modifying instruction to meet individual needs in a diverse classroom. Keep in mind that children generally learn best from hands-on, concrete experiences and that Gardner's (1993) theory of multiple intelligences implies accommodations to the learning styles of your pupils. He has identified seven intelligences that can operate independently of one another: linguistic, logical-mathematical, spatial, musical, bodily-kinesthetic, interpersonal, and intrapersonal. The implications for teaching may be that since children can be intelligent in many modes, instruction might be modified to develop and nurture individualistic, natural proclivities.

DAILY PLANS AND LESSON PLANS

Whether you need to write daily lesson plans or even individual lesson plans as you did or are doing during student teaching depends on how much information you can fit into those little boxes on your weekly plans and how secure you are in your planning and instruction. Certain lessons require more detailed planning than others. Those that need extra planning include art, science experiments, social studies simulations, new physical education (P.E.) games and skills, and any other lessons that introduce a skill or concept unfamiliar to the children. Lesson plans will allay your anxiety as well as provide a substantive instructional guide to a substitute or an administrator who takes over your class in an emergency.

Worksheet 2.5

By all means, use your weekly planbook to sketch in those lessons that are review or routine, such as spelling tests or math drill, or are clearly outlined in the various manuals. But make sure to indicate on your daily plans those lessons that clearly necessitate a more detailed instructional map for you to follow. You can use Worksheet 2.5, Daily Lesson Plan, to sketch out your daily plans, a road map by time for you to follow during the day. Duplicate the basic form and save yourself some writing.

There are even times when you will want to write out your plans in detail. Many a lesson has self-destructed because the procedures weren't clear in the teacher's mind or the teacher hadn't thought through the organizational pattern or hadn't anticipated all the materials that would be needed. The idea is not to duplicate work and have you writing lesson plans ranging from yearly to monthly to weekly to daily to individual into the wee hours of the morning. You will recognize when you need to plan more in detail. Those occasions present themselves as anxious, gnawing feelings that the lesson is too complicated and it may not go well. It's at that moment that you may want to expand the daily lesson plan form (Worksheet 2.5) or write individual lesson plans on forms you are familiar with from your student teaching days. You may want to use the 5E lesson plan (Biological Sciences Curriculum Study, 1997) for discovery lessons. The steps include Engage, Explore, Explain, Elaborate, and Evaluate. Or you might prefer the popular seven-step lesson plan developed by Madeleine Hunter, which prescribes the following stages: Anticipatory Set, Objectives and Purposes, Instructional Input, Modeling, Checking for Understanding, Guided Practice, and Independent Practice. Duplicate whatever forms you plan on using, or mix and match forms as appropriate, with the key headings you need already in place. Then it is just a matter of filling in the blanks. Keep them in a loose-leaf folder.

A FINAL WORD

Your well-thought-out plans will be your security blanket during the first weeks of school and beyond. Your instruction will ultimately result from the dynamic interaction between your plans and the needs, interests, and readiness of your students. Some teachers focus on the curricular content. Others focus on the children. A balance needs to be struck, with the children at the center and the curriculum adapted to them.

Careful planning does not mean that the resulting plans are indelible and rigid. They can and will change! But plan you must. Plans will give you the confidence to step into your classroom as a well-prepared professional ready to make adjustments as you get to know your students. When you feel anxious, open your planbook and take comfort in the undeniable proof written there that you really do know what you are doing.

Reflection Box

In what ways, if any, has the chapter changed my beliefs?

Questions I Still Have . . .

Reflection Box

What practices actually worked for me in my first year?

FURTHER READING

Clark, C. M., & Yinger. R. J. (1987). Teacher planning. In D. C. Berliner & B. V. Rosenshine (Eds.), *Talks to teachers* (pp. 342–368). New York: Random House.

Doll, R. (1995). *Curriculum improvement: Decision making and process* (9th ed.). Boston: Allyn & Bacon.

Kellough, R. D., & Roberts, P. L. (1997). *A resource guide for elementary school teaching: Planning for competence* (4th ed.). New York: Macmillan.

Pasch, M., et al. (1995). *Teaching as decision making: Successful practices for the elementary teacher*. White Plains, NY: Longman.

Posner, G. J., & Rudnitsky, A. N. (1996). *Course design: A guide to curriculum development for teachers* (5th ed.). White Plains, NY: Longman.

REFERENCES

Biological Sciences Curriculum Study (BSCS) (1997). *Science for life and living* (3rd ed.). Dubuque, IA: Kendall-Hunt.

Borko, H., & Niles, J. (1987). Descriptions of teacher planning: Ideas for teachers and researchers. In V. Richardson-Koehler (Ed.), *Educators' handbook: A research perspective* (pp. 167–187). New York: Longman.

Clark, C., & Lambert, M. (1986). The study of teacher thinking: Implications for teacher education. *Journal of Teacher Education*, *37*(5), 27–31.

Davidman, L., & Davidman, P. T. (1997). *Teaching with a multicultural perspective: A practical guide* (2nd ed.). White Plains, NY: Longman.

De Paola, T. (1996). *Strega nona.* New York: Lectorum.

Diaz-Rico, L., & Weed, K. (1995). *The crosscultural, language and academic development handbook.* Boston: Allyn & Bacon.

Gardner, H. (1993). *Multiple intelligences: The theory in practice.* New York: Basic Books.

Glasser, W. (1993). *The quality school teacher.* New York: HarperCollins.

Klein, M. F., Tye, K., & Wright, J. (1979). A study of schooling: Curriculum. *Phi Delta Kappan, 61*(4), 244–248.

Kovalik, S. (1986). *Teachers make a difference.* San Jose, CA: Discovery Press.

McCutcheon, G. (1980). How do elementary school teachers plan? The nature of planning and influences on it. *Elementary School Journal, 81*(1), 4–23.

May, W. (1986). Teaching students how to plan: The dominant model and alternatives. *Journal of Teacher Education, 37*(6), 6–12.

Peregoy, S. F., & Boyle, O. F. (1996). *Reading, writing, & learning in ESL: A resource book for K–8 teachers* (2nd ed.). White Plains, NY: Longman.

Salzman, M., & Pondiscio, R. (1996). The ultimate on-line homework helper. New York: Avon Books.

Tyler, R. (1969). *Basic principles of curriculum and instruction.* Chicago: University of Chicago Press.

Veenman, S. (1984). Perceived problems of beginning teachers. *Review of Educational Research, 54*(2), 143–178.

Yinger, R. (1980). A study of teacher planning. *Elementary School Journal, 80*(3), 107–127.

chapter

3

Materials and Supplies

Reflection Box

What I Believe About

Potential sources of teaching materials and supplies (school, district, institutions, colleagues, parents) . . .
Ordering materials . . .
Technology in the classroom . . .
Sources of free or inexpensive materials . . .

Some things you never learn in methods classes; you learn them only from experience, a bad experience all too often. For example, it takes only one year of being left out when the "goodies" (materials and resources) are distributed among teachers at school to learn that you must be there along with everyone else, if not before the others, to get the supplies you need to teach effectively. In this chapter the experiences of those who preceded you will help you avoid getting passed over and make you an expert at the "school stuff scramble" and the "grab what you can," two strategies your teacher educators may never have taught you.

Classrooms look chock-full of materials and supplies when you are led on the traditional tour of the school during your interview. As you walk around to the resource centers and storage rooms, you can picture yourself in this veritable candy store of materials and supplies, picking and choosing what you need to support your instructional program. Little do you know that at the beginning of the school year, you may arrive to find an empty room with four bare walls, "chock-full" of nothing but tables and chairs and a

---

A Note from the Teacher

On that fateful day in February I got a phone call at 3:30
P.M. from my soon-to-be principal offering me my first job.
They would be creating a new kindergarten class due to
overflow and I would be the teacher—STARTING
TOMORROW!!! I rushed over to the school with eight
hours of waking time before 24 kids would arrive. The
room was bare—no tables, chairs, wall decoration. I
quickly made friends with the other kindergarten teachers—
begged and borrowed chairs, tables, minimal materials and
was ready to go at 8:30 the next morning.

J. CHRISTIAN

---

teacher's desk. Does this sound like a nightmare? Yes, it is, and it can happen to you. It's happened to me, and it's happened to other teachers. But rest assured, as I said before, it usually happens only once. If you learn from the experiences of others, it may not happen to you at all. This chapter will help you gather, order, buy, and use materials wisely.

LOCATING YOUR SOURCES

Some time ago I was touring a soon-to-be opened school with an internationally known primary educator. While the principal guided us through the building, the educator would periodically stop and wistfully look at the refuse—yes, the garbage. In one corner she spotted discarded cartons and commented on what neat art portfolios they would make. In another area she opened the gleaming new cabinets and discovered some other treasures—Masonite boards of various sizes. From a garbage pail she pulled out a large soft-drink cup and a discarded box and proceeded to construct a train. Here she was modeling in person what she preaches in films and symposia—using everyday materials to teach. In her case, as a teacher in less-affluent England, being a pack rat is a matter of teacher survival. In our case, it just makes good sense.

"Junk," you might be saying. "I can see junk piled up in my house or apartment, encroaching on my living space." Yes, you do need to negotiate a closet or a corner of the garage for the needed materials you collect: Although necessity is the mother of invention, the busy teacher in a crunch will either buy what is needed for a project or go without. But what better time than when you have time? The weeks before school starts are a good time for stocking up.

School Resources

In the worst-case scenario, you arrive at your school site before the school year begins and find four bare walls, basic furniture, and no materials. Your first step after breathing deeply for five minutes is to conduct, with the help of either the principal, the resource specialist, the assistant principal, or one of the teachers, an inventory of materials provided by the school. You need to establish the givens and make sure your share of them is reserved. It is advisable to inventory supplies available to you as soon as you are appointed, but the first day of teacher orientation may have to suffice if your notice of appointment is delayed. Instead of asking an open question such as, "What is available?" use Worksheet 3.1, Inventory of School Supplies and Materials, to focus your questions. The worksheet is organized around curriculum areas, and spaces have been left blank so you can add your own needed items. The space for storage location is important. Many experienced graduate students, when asked to survey resources and materials at their respective schools, discovered a treasure trove they never knew existed behind locked doors and cabinets. Make up a key for the storage location column on Worksheet 3.1 (for example, O = School Office, or D = District Resource Center). Learn how to use the equipment safely!

A Note from the Teacher

I was in the teacher's work room and another teacher was using the laminating machine. He gave out a frantic "yelp." The teacher had gotten his tie caught in the laminating machine. Fortunately, a new teacher had enough sense to pull the plug. We had to cut the tie at the knot. Moral of the story: Do not wear anything dangling from your neck while using the laminating machine, and keep a pair of scissors tied to the machine.

A. PETRIE

District Resources

Once you have surveyed what is available at the school and coded where the items can be found, you will find that many No boxes are checked off. You have several options, according to those who have been there before you. The first option is to determine whether your district has a media center, resource center, or curriculum library. These are repositories for materials shared across schools, and it is important to determine the location of this gold mine, whatever name it goes by in your district. When you visit the district resource center, and I suggest an early visit, bring Worksheet 3.1 and check off any materials unavailable at the school-site level that you find at the district level. Under storage location, put a big **D** to remind you later that these materials are available at the district resource center. Make sure to ask about procedures for borrowing materials from the district, length of time they may be kept, and whether they can be renewed.

When you visit the district resource center, you will want to familiarize yourself with the nonprint media resources as well. Ask to see the catalog of films, filmstrips, tapes, videocassettes, videodiscs, computer software, CD-ROM discs, laser discs, photographs, records, cassettes, posters, and other materials. Sometimes these are listed in one catalog, sometimes in several. These references will be very helpful to you later as you plan your beginning instructional units and make decisions about the topics you want to cover. To be perfectly honest, it is acceptable to choose topics on the basis of availability of good instructional materials. If I had the choice between two equally important mandated topics in social studies, for example, I would begin with the one having the most formidable instructional-materials backup system, while I scrounged for materials to support the other. *Carefully screen the materials you select for any gender, racial, ethnic, cultural, or age stereotypes and bias.*

Other Institutional Resources

After you have surveyed the materials at the district level, you may want to consider other, often overlooked, sources of free materials: public and university libraries and local museums. Public libraries are increasingly buying and lending educational games and materials to both parents and teachers. Universities with teacher-education programs often have a vast array of materials available to former students and sometimes to the general public on loan. Special equipment in science or social studies can be borrowed from science and social science departments in local colleges and high schools. Museums lend displays and kits to schools and often have a cadre of docents who bring everything from snakes to Native American artifacts to your classroom.

Colleagues at School

By now the noes on your list should have diminished considerably, but there are still other sources to be considered. Turn to co-workers or the resource specialist at your school. Check with grade-level colleagues to borrow materials on your list when they are needed. In one particular school, posted in the teachers' lunchroom is a list of materials or supplies needed along with the names of the teachers requesting them. A colleague who has what is requested simply signs the appropriate space, and the initiator now knows who to contact (see Figure 3.1). You might want to initiate this system at your school, primarily for your own self-interest, because as a newcomer you will have fewer resources than anyone else. But you won't always be a newcomer, and this system works really well. Items are crossed out as the orders are filled. Use a chalkboard so items can be erased easily.

Materials Needed	#	Date Needed	Requested by	I Can Help
scissors	9	3/22	Sue Jones	Sally L.
globe	1	3/24	Don Gray	Sandy G.
hot plate	2	3/25	Jill T.	Sue Jones Bob R.

Figure 3.1

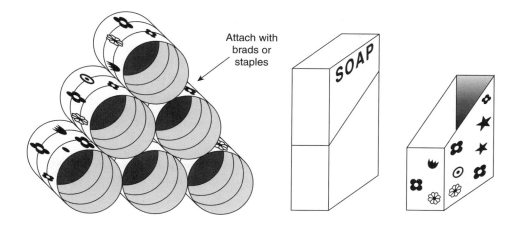

Attach with
brads or
staples

SOAP

Figure 3.2

Parents as Sources

The parents of students in your class are another source of materials and supplies. A simple note home can do wonders, provided you build in choices for parents and don't ask for items that cost money. For example, in your classroom you will need containers—containers of all sorts. Instead of collecting them all yourself, appeal to the parents. Large-size ice cream vats, the type used at multiflavor-type stores, make wonderful cubbies when piled up on one another. Shoe boxes or milk cartons with the front ends cut out suit a similar purpose, as do wine cartons when the cross pieces are left intact. Large-size cereal or soap powder boxes, when cut on the bias, make sturdy file boxes, book holders, and paper caddies (see Figure 3.2). Duplicate (translate as appropriate) your own list of needed containers and send the list home to parents with a polite cover letter. Here are a few suggestions:

Item	Container Needed
paste	film cans
pencils/pens	orange juice/coffee cans
pupil crayons/materials	cigar boxes
math manipulatives or word banks	margarine containers
scissors/paintbrushes/rulers	coffee cans
paint containers	orange juice cans
paint-mixing bowls	margarine containers
file folders, games, copymasters, storage	cardboard boxes, cereal and soap powder boxes
planters	milk containers cut down
cooking bowls	margarine containers, milk containers
math manipulatives: dried beans, buttons	margarine containers
crayons for group use	large margarine containers, berry baskets
assorted materials	styrofoam trays
cubbies	ice cream vats, milk cartons

Your call for materials can be either specific or general. Letters to parents can help you gather needed materials and enable you to save your own resources—or those allotted to you by the school—for materials and supplies more exotic than the ones requested in these letters. See the two brief examples that follow:

Dear Parent or Guardian,

We are setting up a classroom store to help us learn to add and subtract money. Will you please save, wash, and smooth the rough edges of cans of all varieties? Please leave the labels intact. We can also use empty food boxes and plastic containers. Please send the empties to school with your child during the first week in November, and please make sure to stop by toward the end of the week to see us operating our store. We thank you for your help.

Sincerely,
Mrs. Jan Garcia and
Class 3-1
Parkville School

Dear Parent or Guardian,

We are trying to gather a supply of art materials to use all year long. Please look through the list and send to school during the month of September any that you have available.

We thank you in advance for helping us to make art more exciting.

scraps of fabric	old shirts for smocks
yarn	newspapers for papier-mâché
cotton batting	juice cans for paint containers
wallpaper remnants	film cans for paste
bottle caps	margarine containers
wood scraps	coffee cans for brushes
greeting card fronts	wooden spools
shelving remnants	egg cartons
cardboard remnants	brown paper bags
toilet paper rolls	corrugated cardboard

Please pack like items together in a brown paper bag and label the bag as to its contents. This will make sorting materials easier. We thank you for your cooperation and we hope you like the projects we will now be able to make and bring home to you.

Sincerely,
Mr. Mark Horowitz
Class 4-3
Bridgeport School

You can use Worksheet 3.2, Wish List, to generate your own list of supplies and materials to request from parents. You can use it to compose a letter that can go home the first week of school.

By now you have gathered as many supplies as you can. With these sources of materials, you are well on your way to becoming a competitive pack rat. But you may want some specific educational materials that even the best scrounger can't locate.

Worksheet
3.2

ORDERING MATERIALS WISELY

You are now beyond the gathering stage and ready to order what can't be scrounged. How do you find out how much money you have for supplies. What should you order when given the choice?

Policies regarding the ordering of supplies differ greatly from district to district, from school to school. You need to ask your principal, for he or she will be glad to let you know if (1) you are one of those lucky few who are allocated a sum, solely for their own use; (2) your requests, along with all others, go into a large hopper of requisitions that are later ranked by the school principal alone or with the help of a school committee; or (3) the budget this year has been cut to the bone and supplies are parceled out to you as long as they last.

Information of this sort can also be obtained from staff members, the policy manual if one exists, the school secretary, the resource specialist, or the grapevine. Usually, the principal outlines the procedures at the first staff meeting, but since early birds get more of the worms, you might want to get your bids in ahead of time.

If you fall into category (1) or (2) above, you are indeed fortunate and can start thinking about the next question: Given the choice, what should I order? If you fall into category (3), you'll read the advice in the section discussing sources of free or inexpensive materials (p. 41), as you wait for a bigger budget.

Again, your inventory, Worksheet 3.1, is a good place to start. If you subscribe to the philosophy "order big, order for the future," you will want to look at the No column items and subject them to the following criteria:

- Ordered items should help meet individual differences.
- Ordered items should be nonconsumable.
- Ordered items should be sturdy, long lasting, adaptable.

Frequently requested items that meet these three tests of durability include:

pocket charts	computer software
globes, maps, atlas	tapes, CDs, and records
manipulative material	supplementary reading books
handwriting charts	art idea books
number lines	storage and file cabinets
play equipment for kindergarten	bookshelves
science and social studies kits	puzzles, activity centers
videos, CD-ROM discs, laser discs	flannel board and pieces
simulation and educational games	almanac, thesaurus, desk
poetry books	encyclopedia
tapes and cassettes of age-appropriate songs, exercise routines	joke, riddle and brain teaser books

If you gain support from co-workers and approach your administrator with a specified need, a list of the materials that will meet the need, the exact cost of such materials, and a list of colleagues eager to share the materials purchased, you have a better chance of having your request granted.

Some teachers take another tack when considering what to order. These are the "conspicuous consumers" who are either already blessed with a great deal of durable, nonconsumable materials at their schools or don't have even the basic pencil-and-paper supplies we come to expect. Some of the consumable items ordered by this either fortunate or disadvantaged group include:

paper, pencils, markers consumable activity books
copymasters grading book
planbook art supplies
motivational prizes outline maps
award certificates stamps and stickers

Worksheet
3.3

Your own ordering priorities will depend on how well endowed your school is, how much you can gather from other sources, and your own needs. After filling in Worksheet 3.1, the materials inventory, you should have a pretty good idea of what is not available from the school, district, local libraries, high schools, colleges, museums, colleagues, and parents. Begin on Worksheet 3.3, Things I Can't Beg or Borrow, to list the items you would order if you could. These should be items not readily available from other sources. You can always add to your list or remove any items you happen upon. In the second column write a brief justification for each item so that, when you request it from higher-ups, you can build a strong, solid case.

TECHNOLOGY IN THE CLASSROOM

Have you been cruising the information highway? Or are you still a mistrusting, "I don't need all that stuff" technophobe? Or are you in the middle—willing but feeling unprepared to enter the brave new world of technology? You are not alone if you identify with this group. A key finding of a recent Congressional Report (U.S. Congress, 1997) is that schools of education don't do enough to model technology use in their teacher preparation programs, nor do they prepare future teachers well enough to teach with technology across the curriculum.

According to a survey conducted by *Reading Today* (1997), while 93 percent of teachers polled believe that using the Internet in the classroom is a good idea, and more than half believe students should begin to learn to use the Internet before fourth grade, few teachers consider themselves proficient: 28 percent gave themselves an A or B grade, 53 percent gave themselves a C grade, and 19 percent gave themselves an F. But it is never too late to take the first steps toward technoliteracy. If you are already quite the user, read this section to a colleague who needs it.

Don't Look Now But You Are Already There

Life today revolves around our use of various "technotoys": pagers, cell phones, video-cassette recorders (VCRs), automatic teller machines (ATMs), compact disc players, copiers, fax machines, computerized food label scanners, computerized card catalogs, video games, virtual reality games, and on and on. While you encounter new technologies at every turn, you still may resist or feel intimidated by a stroll down that highway in the high-tech sky and/or its lesser earthbound applications in your classroom. Relax. There is

still a great deal you can do on your own to upgrade your knowledge and skills. Increasingly, new teachers will have been required to use computers to complete their own education. The average teacher needs five to seven years to go from technophobe to master, according to a report from the Center for Technology in Education at the Bank Street College of Education (1993). Invariably, in many classrooms, many children have a greater ease/proficiency with computers than their teachers. Together you can all learn about the options that are available to you that didn't even exist when yours truly began teaching.

Why Use Computers?

You have a teacher helper in your room that sits silently, doesn't punch a time clock, and only eats diskettes or CD-ROM discs. It's your computer, and rather than making your harried life more difficult, it can actually ease the burdens of some of the most odious of teacher tasks—record keeping, parent communications, and other time-consuming tasks, such as planning and locating resources to support your curricular objectives and locating activities and resources to meet individual differences, particularly of special-needs students.

Think of your computer as a robot at your beck and call—a tool that serves and doesn't dictate your needs. The first step is to make a list of your computing objectives, assessing what you want to achieve instructionally and organizationally, what you have already, and what additional tools you may need from the vast technology toolbox that exists to serve you (Dockterman, 1993). Your list may include some of the following curricular and personal goals:

Sample Curriculum and Instruction Goals

- Supporting and extending curriculum through motivational software
- Facilitating cooperative learning, socialization, and English language acquisition when one computer is used as a shared tool (Dockterman, 1993; Poole, 1997)
- Hooking your class up with others across the country to share information

- Providing research opportunities using tools such as multimedia encyclopedias, CD-ROMS, videodiscs
- Providing problem-solving opportunities through simulations
- Matching children with "computer pals" around the world on the information superhighway (Internet), by e-mail
- Encouraging the use of information databases
- Facilitating communication skills by enabling student participation in forums for kids such as Kidsphere, Hilites, Kidlink, and Ednet (Wilson, 1995) (See resources at the end of the chapter.)
- Promoting writing and desktop publishing
- Reinforcing specific skills

Personal Teacher Time-Savers

- Managing portfolios
- Finding lesson plans and thematic units hot off the Web
- Researching content for your own plans on the Web
- Generating tests
- Making presentations for your students or inservices
- Communicating more effectively with parents
- Locating and/or constructing curriculum-related games, crosswords, word searches, worksheets
- Grading and record keeping
- Providing personal productivity for the teacher (communications)

Getting Started

The teacher reading this may have already given up because some of the terms themselves are daunting and unfamiliar. You are not the only one. Most of us have learned what we have learned through effort, trial and error, inservices, or colleagues, not through some magic, innate technological advantage. If this is an area foreign to you, start with a scavenger hunt for all available technology in your school/district and, more importantly, your classroom (Garfield & McDonough, 1996). Do you have access to a computer, a modem, a CD-ROM drive, a television, camcorder, digital camera, laser disc player, scanner, LCD (liquid crystal display, which enables you to project computer images on a screen for all to see), or the Internet? Check out the resources that make the preceding hardware come alive—like software programs of all sorts, including interactive books, skills programs, word processing, graphics and art programs, databases, spreadsheets, hypermedia programs, and so on. If you are unfamiliar with any of these terms, consult a kid's glossary of computer terms, which will make it really simple, like the one I used at the back of *Managing Technology in the Classroom* (Hayes, 1997).

Also, commit some time to a teacher utility program so you can see immediate benefits. *Teachers Tool Kit* (Hi Tech of Santa Cruz, CA), for example, enables you to design word searches, word scrambles, and multiple-choice tests. *Grade Busters* (Jay Klein Products), is an example of an easy-to-use database for record keeping and grading. A program such as *The Print Shop Deluxe* (EdMark) or *Kid Pix* (Broderbund) can help you design fliers, invitations, bulletin board banners, and awards. Suggested software for beginning computer users who have money to spend can be found in a variety of educational catalogs.

Inform yourself step by step as the need arises. When I needed to communicate with colleagues from home, I learned how to set up my e-mail and read messages at home any time, day or night. Saving time and energy can be a terrific source of motivation for learning new things. Try some of these suggestions as they appeal to your learning style: Ask for help from teachers or any "tekkies" in your school; plan to take a course or attend any workshops or inservices offered; engage the children in helping you learn; or join a computer-users group and swap public-domain software. Computer Using Educators (CUE), P.O. Box 2087, Menlo Park, CA 94026, can point you to a local group. Also, general teacher magazines often include ideas for using your computer effectively, and specialized computer magazines, such as *Leading & Learning with Technology* and *Electronic Learning,* supply lesson plans and teaching strategies, even on managing the one-computer classroom. The addresses for these resources are listed at the end of the chapter.

Finally, take every opportunity to play around on the computer yourself. There are many resource directories of Web sites specifically geared to teachers (Helms, 1997; R. Sharp et al., 1997; V. Sharp, et al., 1996) who want to integrate technology. Many of the Web sites have prepackaged, time-saving lesson plans that you can adapt. If this doesn't get you on the Internet, nothing will!

The One-Computer Classroom

The main question teachers have about computers in the classroom, once they have some basic knowledge of their operation and applications, is, "How do I manage computer-assisted instruction with 30 children and only one computer, or maybe two or three, if I am very lucky?"

In the primary grades, teachers use the computer as one of many learning centers to which children rotate. The program is demonstrated to everyone in the class using a connector to a VCR or to an overhead projection device (LCD panel). Then the children rotate to the center in groups of two to work on the activities. Aides and parent volunteers can help you manage computer-assisted instruction in the lower grades. Cross-age tutors from the upper grades can be invited in to help the younger students, especially when you are using word processing programs such as *The Bank Street Writer* (Scholastic).

In the upper grades, these same techniques can be used. The teacher, using a VCR connector or overhead projector, can conduct whole-group lessons with word processing programs, simulations, or educational games. Children take turns suggesting the next sentence, editing documents, or volunteering answers, while the whole class watches the screen. Or children can work in groups at the computer during center time or on a rotating schedule that provides equal time and access. In the upper grades, often two or three children can work together on a simulation or educational game such as *The Oregon Trail,* published by MECC. These sessions are structured as cooperative learning sessions with rules, the task specified, and group interdependence assured through the assignment of specific roles. McDonald (1989) suggests that the *checker* seeks everyone's input, the *keyboarder* inputs the data, and the *recorder* summarizes the steps and results on paper. These roles shift each time.

Other teachers arrange a rotation schedule for the computer(s) in their classroom and appoint a monitor, a class "tekkie," whose job is to see that the rotation schedule is followed and that each child on the list gets his or her allotted computer time. Start slowly with peer tutoring or matching a computer-using student with a novice. Focus on a curriculum area you like and select one program to support instruction in that area. Teach this program, after you learn it yourself, to a few students, who can then teach it to others. Then you can work on learning other programs or on using several technologies all at once to carry through a unit of instruction. The publication by Teacher Created Materials, *Managing Technology in the Classroom* (Hayes, 1997), and Garfield and McDonough's *Creating a Technologically Literate Classroom* (1996) have many samples of technology-supported units.

Ask yourself these questions when you are assessing software:

- Does the program support and expand the educational goals you have set?
- Is the program attention grabbing as well as instructionally sound?
- Are activities developmentally appropriate?
- Does the program have open-ended opportunities so that children can use it again and again?
- Are there several levels of increasing difficulty?
- Is the program child friendly and easy to use?
- Does the program give immediate feedback in a positive way?
- Can the program be run without sound so the computer does not beep, clink, and squawk while you are working with the rest of the class?

There are excellent catalogs of educational software. Apple (1-800-800-2775) offers one-year subscriptions to Apple Education Resource CD. This CD–ROM disc provides a complete listing of Apple-compatible software, tips, and support services. Once you move into the techno lane, you may become so hooked that the children have to tear you away from the screen.

GOING THE EXTRA MILE FOR MATERIALS

By now you may know more about resources and materials in your school or district than you care to. However, one question remains: What are some outside sources of free and inexpensive materials? If you are satisfied with what you have scrounged so far, you may want to skip this section. But if you aspire to become a true pack rat, a connoisseur of the school supply world outside the district, and an accomplished bargain hunter of instructional resources—stay tuned. If you are like most beginning teachers, your salary precludes excessive spending, so let's start with freebies and move into sources of inexpensive materials later.

Freebie Guides

First and foremost are books that, through their titles, appeal to parsimony. Although these guides are far from free themselves, they do contain a wealth of materials for teachers that more than makes up for the initial investment. You might suggest ordering one of each title for the school professional library or resource room. This would be a sensible way of sharing the free wealth contained in the books. Educators Progress Service, Inc., 214 Center Street, Randolph, WI 53956, publishes the following books and other equally useful titles and updates them annually:

Educators Index of Free Materials (to look for a specific topic)
Elementary Teachers Guide to Free Curriculum Materials
Educators Guide to Free Filmstrips and Slides
Educators Guide to Free Films
Educators Guide to Free Videotapes
Educators Guide to Free Science Materials
Educators Guide to Free Guidance Materials
Educators Guide to Free Social Studies Materials
Educators Guide to Free Health, Physical Education, and Recreation Materials

Instructor magazine, 800-544-2917, publishes a monthly column called "Best Bets," which includes freebies. Other teacher magazines have similar features.

In addition, you may want to purchase some of the paperbacks listed at the end of this chapter for your own library, given the relative low cost. The only disadvantages to using these excellent sources are the time lapse between letter of inquiry and receipt of materials and the possibility that some materials are out of stock or no longer available. If you plan ahead, you will have a better chance of obtaining the freebie you want, when you want it.

Another way to ease your time crunch is to have the youngsters in your class do the work for you. They can practice business letter form, handwriting, grammar, and spelling by selecting a needed item and writing for it as your representative. They can also write for innumerable items listed in their own freebie guide, *Free Free Stuff for Kids* (1998), available from Meadowbrook Press, 18318 Minnetonka Boulevard, Deephaven, MN 55391.

Free Books

Free books for your classroom can be slowly amassed by encouraging your children to subscribe to pupil book clubs, if district policy allows this. Usually, given a certain quantity ordered, the teacher can select a specified number of titles free. Although this seems like a small reward, the books do pile up, and they are free and current. You can join teachers' books clubs advertised in the various teacher magazines and pick up some freebies for your own professional library. Less-current titles can be obtained from public libraries, which often cull their collections to make room for new titles. Inexpensive trade books can be found at swap meets, garage sales, and used-book stores.

Cutting Corners

Some teachers recommend *The Teacher's Pet* (1983) and the *Primary Teacher's Pet* (1984) by Linda Schwartz as a time-saver. These resources contain reproducible materials for teaching: awards, borders, contracts, learning activities, schedules, form letters, bulletin board ideas, games, name tags, invitations, notes to parents, progress charts, and so on. They are published by the Learning Works, P.O. Box 6187, Santa Barbara, CA 93160.

The Local Community

If you are searching for a real bounty of assorted free supplies and materials, look to all the various commercial establishments in and around your neighborhood. Here are just a few examples of what a superb scrounger can discover:

rug companies	sample books for art projects
	remnants for sitting
	foam for stuffing projects
	carpet tubing
wallpaper stores	sample books for art projects
	remnants to cover books children have written
supermarkets	cardboard cartons and boxes
	Styrofoam trays
	plastic berry baskets
	seasonal displays
	old magazines
lumberyard	scrap wood
	dowels for puppets
	wood curls for hamster cage
notions store	buttons, sequins, glitter, yarn, tape, trimmings, needles, thread
shoemaker	scraps of leather, laces
ice cream stores	3-gallon containers for cubbies
cleaners	wire hangers, plastic bags for clay projects
copy/print shops	paper of all colors, shapes
tile companies	scraps of mosaic tile for art projects, hot plates
garages/auto repair	wheels, tires, assorted junk for construction

telephone company   colored wire, telephones on loan
florists   wire, Styrofoam blocks, tissue paper
travel agencies   travel posters, brochures

A Note from the Teacher

I purchased 2 white shower boards at a home improvement
store and they cut them up for free into 12 smaller pieces
that are highly prized by the students for recording their
group work using the dry erase markers. These "cheap
version," dry-erase boards are highly motivating and the
students love to use them.

I. MARTIN

The first time you ask you will be embarrassed. The second time you will be ill at
ease. By the third inquiry, you will be a pro, reinforced by the positive responses you
most probably will receive. Check through your local community directory and telephone
Yellow Pages. Identify some potential sources. Use Worksheet 3.4, Scrounging Directory, to begin your own foraging list. It will help you keep track of your sources when materials need to be replenished.

The community can also be a source of free, nonconsumable resources, services, and
field trips. One assignment that I feel yields a wealth of information in methods class asks
student teachers to seek out unusual and free services or field trips in the immediate
neighborhood. This is the ultimate in scrounging, and the results are always astonishing.
Here are a few examples of unlikely, free field trips that can be arranged through local
business establishments in my own area:

Worksheet
3.4

fast-food restaurant   tour of the operation
a florist   children are taught to make a corsage
tortilla factory   students sample and see how tortillas are made
county courthouse   tour, including courtroom; visit to a trial in progress
dairy   tour of milking facility
newspaper   tour of newspaper facility
radio station   tour
public library   tour and story hour
post office   tour of facility
medical center   tour in which children have blood pressure taken
                               and have a finger cast applied; a slide show about
                               hospital procedures is included

yardage store   tour, including discussion of different fabrics
bakery   tour
grocery chain   tour; children receive butcher's hats
recycling plant   tour
beauty college   tour

veterinary clinic	tour (4th–6th grades)
Western Union office	tour and explanation of telegram delivery
City Hall	tour, including City Council in session when possible
bank	tour of operations
stables	tour and presentation on care of horses
pizzeria	tour and demonstration of pizza-making process
burger chain	children make their own hamburgers
police station	tour, often including fingerprinting
fire department	tour
sheriff's helicopter	tour and demonstration

These off-the-beaten-path field trips often require no buses, no money, and no bother. Student teachers who gathered the information found merchants willing and able to set up tours where none had been operated before. It's good for business, excellent public relations, and, most of all, stimulating for both the tour guides and the tourists. Explore the free field-trip options in your own immediate area. I purposely included only generic names, not actual names, in my list because the same services may not be available from a different branch of the same international or national chain in your area.

Worksheet 3.5

Use Worksheet 3.5, Local Field Trip Directory, to start your own listing of free, nearby field-trip adventures. Begin with your friends or neighbors. Is one neighbor an optometrist? Ask if you can tour the office with your class. Does another work in a local hospital? Arrange a visit. Does another work in a bank? Get behind the scenes. Use your influence liberally. Friends and relatives will be very understanding, as will local professionals and businesspeople. A thank-you card or gift from the class will be much appreciated by those who offer their services and time as tour guides. What better way is there for incorporating career education into your curriculum? Share these sources with your colleagues. Get a schoolwide directory going.

Teacher Stores

Finally, we come to outside sources of inexpensive materials for those of you who have saved so much money by following the suggestions in this chapter that you want to be a bit extravagant and feel comfortable doing so!

Many teachers spend money at a local teachers' supply store. You can probably find out from a colleague the name of the supply store frequented by most teachers in your area. These stores are to teachers what candy stores are to kids. You can buy everything from entire bulletin board displays to scratch-and-sniff stickers, from whole kits of materials to award certificates, from records and tapes to colored chalk. Use your funds sparingly here and make sure that items you are purchasing cannot be obtained free with a little ingenuity. Most often they can be!

Bargains and Discounts

Other sources of inexpensive materials are the various discount stores in your neighborhood. These are the bottom-line stores, the bargain hunter's paradise, the ultimate in cost cutting. Here trade books for children may cost $0.59, as opposed to $3.50. Art supplies may be bought at a fraction of the regular cost. Generic brands of food for cooking experiences can be found for a fraction of the cost of a retail supermarket. Remember to shop for school supplies as you shop for large items for yourself. Look for the least expensive items that will hold up with constant use.

A Note from the Teacher

Go to the thrift store. Buy clothing: big shirts for painting, costume jewelry, dramatic costumes for readings. Buy any electronic gadget kids can take apart. Buy puppets. I got some as low as $0.17. Create a classroom veterinary office with secondhand and washed stuffed animals. Buy vases and cheap plastic flowers for a classroom florist shop.

K. CIABATTINI

Buy plastic glasses (the sillier the better) and remove the lenses. Pass the basket of glasses and tell them to "put on their reading glasses."

J. CHRISTIAN

Garage sales, swap meets, bazaars, and the exhibit halls at conferences are a final source of inexpensive materials. Buy what you need, buy what you anticipate needing, but remember that *free* is possible, preferable, and more gratifying, having been more challenging to obtain. Organize your materials in large, colorful, and well-marked boxes so you can keep the clutter to a minimum at home and at school.

A FINAL FREEBIE OF ASSURANCE

Don't be too concerned about not having everything you want during those first days and weeks of school. You will gather materials slowly, and pretty soon you will be competitive with the other pack rats at your school. And remember that in ancient Greece, Socrates did pretty well without a fully stocked classroom—in fact, without a classroom at all!

Reflection Box

In what ways, if any, has the chapter changed my beliefs?

Questions I Still Have . . .

Reflection Box

What practices actually worked for me in my first year?

FURTHER READING

Freebies Publishing. (1998). *Freebies for teachers*. Carpenteria, CA: Author.

Lockard, J., Abrams, P., & Many, W. (1997). *Microcomputers for twenty-first century educators* (4th ed.). Glenview, IL: Scott, Foresman.

Loring, P. (Compiler), & Staff of the Learning Exchange. (1986). *Free and inexpensive teaching tools to make and use*. Available from Good Apple (1-800-321-3106).

McClure, N., & Rhodes, J. (1987). *Free & inexpensive arts & crafts to make and use*. Available from Good Apple (1-800-321-3106).

Morlan, J., & Espinosa, L. (1989). *Preparation of inexpensive teaching materials* (3rd ed.). Available from Fearon Teacher Aids (1-800-321-3106).

National Council for the Social Studies. (1995). Technology and Social Studies (special issue). *Social Studies and the Young Learner, 7*(3).

Newell, C. (1994). *Forms for all reasons*. Greensboro, NC: The Education Center, *The Mailbox* magazine.

Oehring, S. (1993). The one-computer classroom. *Instructor* (July–August), 84–87.

Osborn, S. (1993). *Free (& almost free) things for teachers*. Available from the Berkley Putnam Group, 200 Madison Avenue, New York, NY 10016.

Salzman, M., & Pondiscio, R. (1996). *The ultimate on-line homework helper*. New York: Avon Books.

Simonson, M. R., & Thompson, A. (1996). *Educational computing foundations* (2nd ed.). New York: Macmillan.

REFERENCES

Center for Technology in Education. (1993). *Telecommunications and teachers*. New York: Bank Street College of Education.

Dockterman, D. (1993). *Great teaching in the one-computer classroom*. Cambridge, MA: Tom Snyder Productions.

Garfield, G., & McDonough, S. (1996). *Creating a technologically literate classroom*. Westminster, CA: Teacher Created Materials.

Hayes, D. (1997). *Managing technology in the classroom.* Huntington Beach, CA: Teacher Created Materials.

Helms, R. (1997). Exemplary World Wide Web resources. *Social Studies and the Young Learner, 9*(3), 7–8.

McDonald, P. (1989). *Cooperation at the computer.* Des Plaines, IL: Looking Glass Learning Products.

Poole, B. J. (1997). *Education for the information age: Teaching in a computerized classroom* (2nd ed.). New York: McGraw Hill.

Reading Today & Sun Microsystems. Teachers favor Internet use in classrooms (a poll). *Reading Today, 14*(4), 29.

Sharp, R., et al. (1997). *The best math and science Web sites for teachers.* Eugene, OR: International Society for Technology in Education.

Sharp, V., et al. (1996). *The best Web sites for teachers.* Eugene, OR: International Society for Technology in Education.

United States Congress, Office of Technology Assessment. (1995). *Teachers and technology: Making the connection.* OTA-EHR-616. Washington, DC: U.S. Government Printing Office.

Wilson, J. (1995). Media corner. *Social Studies and the Young Learner, 7*(3), 24–26.

COMMERCIAL INTERNET ACCESS

America Online	800-827-6364
AppleLink	508-947-8181
Classroom Prodigy	800-776-3449
CompuServe	800-848-8990
National Geographic Kids Network	800-368-2728
Scholastic Network	800-246-2986

COMPUTER PERIODICALS

Electronic Learning	Scholastic, Inc. P.O. Box 5397 Boulder, CO 80322-3797
Technology and Learning	330 Progress Road Dayton, OH 45449
Learning and Leading with Technology	International Society for Technology in Education 1787 Agate Street Eugene, OR 97403
Tech Trends	Association for Educational Communications and Technology 1025 Vermont Avenue N.W. Washington, DC 20005-3516

Instructor	**TEACHER MAGAZINES** Scholastic, Inc. P.O. Box 53895 Boulder, CO 80323-3895
Mailbox	P.O. Box 29485 Greensboro, NC 27499-0736
Teaching PreK–8	P.O. Box 54805 Boulder, CO 80323-4805

4

Classroom Organization and Management

Reflection Box

What I Believe About

Designing my classroom environment (furniture grouping, accessories, bulletin boards, etc.)

Establishing classroom climate . . .

Establishing routines and procedures (exits, entrances, materials use, bathroom, wastebasket, water, etc.)

Using monitors . . .

Now that you have gathered the materials and supplies described in the preceding chapter and have a house or an apartment cluttered with your booty, it's time to call the classroom interior decorator—you along with the children! Setting up your classroom, arranging the furniture, and decorating the space are key challenges at the start of the school year. That richly decorated space you were shown during your first tour now has bare walls and furniture arranged helter-skelter. Pretend it's moving day at your own house and confront the work involved with the same underlying motivation—to create an organized, efficient, attractive home away from home for you and your students.

The physical environment is one aspect of organization; however, the more important aspect is the management system you devise to make the total environment support your instructional program. So in this chapter you can reflect on and actually plan procedures and routines to ensure the smooth and efficient functioning of your delightfully decorated and artfully arranged classroom environment.

ROOM ENVIRONMENT

Some of you reading this will remember bolted-down wooden desks arranged in neat rows, all facing the front, and ink wells that were filled each afternoon from a common ink can. On command, children dipped a wooden-shafted pen into the ink, wiped it with a rag, wrote a few letters, blotted with a blotter, and began the cycle anew. What ceremony and ritual—gone forever in most parts of the country. The room had an alphabet above the chalkboard, a cleanly pressed flag, a world map, and a bulletin board or two. Overall, it was a bleak and depressing place to learn.

The modern-day classroom still has the American flag as a constant, but now the room reflects the personality and instructional style of the teacher and takes into account the needs (intellectual, emotional, and social) of children. Hannah (1984) reports that children, when asked about their ideal classroom, prefer to sit up high (lofts) or low (floor); they like pretty, bright colors; and they value comfort and privacy. Their preferences need to be considered in light of the teacher's overriding responsibility for creating an environment that reflects and supports his or her educational goals and teaching style. Hopkins (1993) suggests creating the total classroom design with the students during the first days and weeks of school. He recommends pushing all the furniture to one side and starting from scratch, asking children to make a list of priorities or criteria with you and then arranging the furniture to meet those needs. This technique may be a bit much for the beginning teacher, but keep it in mind and allow the students some input into the room design.

A Note from the Teacher

I changed my desk arrangement six times in the first three weeks of school. I was pretty satisfied with the sixth arrangement, so when the kids came in for recess, I had them all stand while I made final adjustments to my latest decorating scheme. This is the exact moment my principal comes in for her first unannounced observation.

C. McDowell

Arranging the Furniture

You will still find the desks arranged in rows or all the tables oriented toward the front of the room in some schools, but this is not necessarily the norm. Seating arrangements vary from classroom to classroom. A first step is to look at various arrangements in classrooms around the school to see the alternatives available. Ask your colleagues which arrangements seem to work best for them. Collect as many ideas as you can. Find out how many children are on your class list and see which configurations accommodate that number

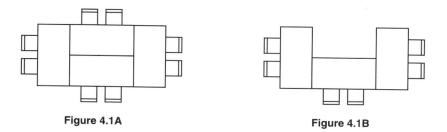

Figure 4.1A   Figure 4.1B

best. But ultimately, *your seating arrangement should be determined by how you want to conduct business in your classroom.* The way seats are arranged tells the visitor about your instructional program—yes, even if the room is devoid of children.

Row upon row of seats will convey the message that group work is not primary and that children work independently and look literally and figuratively to the teacher at the front. Tables composed of desks clustered together (Figure 4.1A) provide a more social environment for children, promote cooperative learning, and facilitate projects needing space, such as cooking, art, or science experiments. Clustering also allows for grouping in math and reading and enables children to change their seats when necessary.

This cluster arrangement can be slightly modified (Figure 4.1B) to form a mini-horseshoe configuration. In this arrangement, children are given more space, and interaction among them may be cut down. More children are oriented toward the front of the room, and the teacher has access to all students at once when she or he is standing in the open area.

The horseshoe configuration can be used on a larger scale as the design for the total seating pattern (Figure 4.1C). While the large center space is open for class meetings or drama, the majority of children are perpendicular to the chalkboard and group work is discouraged.

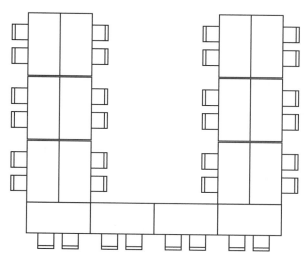

Figure 4.1C

These three basic building blocks—the individual desk, the cluster, and the mini-horseshoe—can be arranged in any number of ways, or the three elements can be combined in the same classroom.

A Computer Work Station

Where will you locate your media/computer center? Dockterman (1993) and Hayes (1997) offer actual floor plans for different configurations and purposes. Make sure, however, you organize this area so that you have access to it for your own work and that you can use it for presentations as well as for cooperative learning groups and individual projects. Other considerations include making sure that cables are wrapped neatly and are out of the way of tripping feet, that the computer is near outlets, telephone connections, and other peripheral equipment, that there is bulletin board space nearby to post assignments and display work. Make sure there is room to post your computer rotation schedule and to neatly store all the software you will be using. In the best-case scenario, Hayes (1997) suggests that an extra table be located nearby for computer cooperative group meetings.

Worksheet
4.1

Before you go any further, use Worksheet 4.1, Sketch of Ideal Classroom Environment, or you can diagram your ideal classroom arrangement to scale. The dimensions of classrooms vary, but in California a typical classroom measures approximately 30 feet by 30 feet. If you don't know the dimensions of your room, take a guess or use these figures as an exercise. Remember to consider your teaching style and instructional belief system. Is peer interaction important? Is art a central activity? Do you encourage independent work or cooperative learning? Do you want all children facing the front? Is there a dust-free, well-lit, quiet, and glare-free space for your computer? Is there room enough for class meetings, or can furniture be quickly moved to form a circle? Are there areas near the sink for art and cooking? These are only a sampling of questions you need to ask yourself before your design idea is set in stone.

Now look at your plan and consider these additional questions:

	Yes	No
Vision. Can all pupils see the chalkboard without doing yoga contortions?	☐	☐
Monitoring. Can the teacher keep an eye on the total classroom environment from key locations (chalkboard, desk, reading area)?	☐	☐
Traffic Control. Are there wide traffic lanes so children and you can move swiftly and easily from one part of the room to another, especially in an emergency?	☐	☐
Obstacles. Is your room free from obstacles such as bookshelves to be tripped over, a wastebasket near the door to be stumbled over, pupil desks too near the exit? Are storage areas blocked by pupil desks?	☐	☐
Messy/Clean and Noisy/Quiet. Are all potentially messy areas such as a cooking or art center near the sink? Are the quiet areas clustered together away from potentially noisier areas? For example, are the library corner and listening center far enough from the games and reading groups?	☐	☐

	Yes	No
Flexibility. Can desks be moved easily if the mood to square dance strikes you or you want to practice the play but the auditorium is being used? Can desk clusters be converted to centers easily, or does this involve a call to a moving company?	☐	☐
Suitability. Finally, is your arrangement conducive to the kind of instruction you believe in? Are you leaving space for total-group as well as small-group and individual activities?	☐	☐

Now revise your sketch if you need to on Worksheet 4.1.

Because furniture and seating arrangements should derive from and not direct the instructional program, try to build flexibility into your seating arrangement. Move furniture around when the instructional program requires a different configuration. Let the program determine the arrangement and not vice versa. If furniture remains stationary too long, it may just revolt and nail itself to the floor.

A Note from the Teacher

This year due to class size reduction there is good news and bad. The good news is that I have a job and the bad news is that I share my classroom space with another teacher and her class for most of the year. I also change classrooms every three months in our multitrack school. This necessitates sharing with three different teachers during the year. My room sharing has been made easier by coordinating quiet times with my roommate.

N. WILLIAMS

Classroom Accessories

Desks and chairs, although functional, are not very comfortable. You can jazz up your classroom with the addition of bean-bag chairs, carpets or carpet remnants, a small sofa, and, perhaps, a discarded lamp or two. Reading lamps rest the eyes from the fluorescent lights and can calm children. These items are particularly useful in a library corner separated from the rest of the room. After all, how many of you read while seated in a straight-back chair with feet flat on the floor? These items can easily be obtained from thrift stores, garage sales, or parents. Add a few live plants and a minimal-care pet such as a turtle, a hamster, or some mice. Children love live things, and the care of the plants and animals can be assigned to a monitor.

Arrange for some private, get-away-from-it-all spaces. A refrigerator carton can become a hideaway after some windows and a door are cut into it and the entire thing is painted. For older children, bring in an umbrella-type folding tent. Or use a table covered with an overhanging cloth. A quiet, secluded space should be allocated to the classroom library. If your principal permits, build yourself a loft for reading. If you can't or don't know how, you might bring in an old mattress and cover it with a pretty floral sheet and use it for a reading area. One resourceful teacher I know uses an old-fashioned bathtub filled with pillows for a special reading space. Bring in a small inflatable pool or rubber dinghy for the same purpose.

These added touches create a unique, stimulating environment in place of a cold, sterile one. Sketch alternative floor plans on graph paper or use a computer graphics program if you have one. Then put on your oldest clothes and try out the various arrangements at school, sampling every seat to assure visibility. Keep your room arrangement dynamic. At the outset, you can arrange your desks in rows for maximum control and then you can relax and create a more open environment as the school year progresses.

Bulletin Boards

The importance of planning a visually attractive and instructionally sound room environment cannot be overemphasized. You and your students spend approximately 30 hours each week in the classroom, and an aesthetically pleasing environment can do much to stimulate the senses and teach at the same time. The physical environment is the first thing children and observers notice about a classroom, and you want yours to deliver the message that exciting and sound instruction is going on there.

When children enter on the first day of school, the room environment tells them a great deal about you and what their year will be like. Before you utter the first word on that first day of school, you will have delivered your message nonverbally to children through your attention to the walls of your classroom. Careful lettering will tell them you are precise and want them to take pride in their work. Bright colors will tell them you have a vibrant and exciting program planned. Bulletin boards that focus interest on students, a Star of the Week board, and a Good Work board tell them they are important. A Helpers Chart tells them they will share in the responsibilities for their classroom with you. In primary grades the calendar and weather chart will let children know you provide the security of routines they are used to. A subject-matter bulletin board clues them into the mysteries that will be unraveled as the year progresses. A word wall makes them more independent as they master the basics of literacy.

Labels on all the objects in the classroom will let the first graders feel confident that they will learn to read these markers soon. Labels on all objects will be useful for second language learners. The American flag, cleaned and pressed, with the Pledge of Allegiance carefully lettered, lets youngsters know you place importance on the flag as a symbol of our country. The medium of bulletin boards, to summarize, delivers very powerful nonverbal messages to children. Thinking about your bulletin boards or actually designing and constructing some of them before school starts will help you avoid the tendency to throw up anything at the last minute just to cover the walls.

Some teachers purchase or order from catalogs a great deal of prepackaged material, including bulletin board borders; others use available materials to draw or construct their own, freehand. A good method for those of us who "aren't creative" is to project coloring book images or cartoon characters onto the bulletin board background using an opaque projector and simply trace the image in bold marker. It's certainly a less expensive solution than buying a multitude of materials that will stay up only a few short weeks. Mounting pictures on black paper creates contrast on bright bulletin boards and gives depth to your creations. Die-cut presses that are available in districts turn out borders and bulletin board letters with no fuss and no bother. Morlan and Espinosa (1989) offer many timesaving and laborsaving ideas for bulletin board preparation. In addition, there are many bulletin board idea books available to you. Some are listed at the end of this chapter. Looking at the four walls is the only respite children have from their daily work. Create warm, bright spaces that instruct and motivate. Teachers caution you not to overstimulate the senses. Strike a balance between excitement and quiet, restful places.

Teachers report that these bulletin board ideas are pretty standard:

- a calendar
- weather chart
- students' Excellent Work board
- rules
- current topics in science, social studies, etc.
- helpers' (or monitors') chart
- handwriting chart
- Pledge of Allegiance
- word wall

Another common theme is a board listing all children's birthdays by month. This reminds everyone that a special occasion is nearing and the proper preparations can be made for celebrating. In the primary grades, a similar bulletin board marks the loss of each tooth. A large cutout tooth for each month lists the name and date. Children enjoy marking these important milestones in their lives. A Star of the Week board, with one student highlighted each week, can be found in many classrooms. The child decorates the board with photos, hobbies, work, or whatever he or she chooses.

For the first day of school a welcome-back bulletin board is also suggested. One teacher draws a huge popcorn popper and little kernels with pupils' names under the banner "Look Who's Popping Up in Our Class." Others use an all-star approach and ask each child to bring a photo from home to paste in the center of large cutout stars. Another pictures a large tree and leaves falling from it either with pupils' names or photos with the banner "Fall into School." The easiest way to get the photos is to take them yourself with a Polaroid-type camera on the first day. Plan for grouping two or three children together and leave space so you can cut out individual faces if you choose.

Another delightful idea is to ask each child (and you) to bring in a baby picture, which is then posted on a bulletin board with number identification only. A contest can be held to see who has correctly identified the most classmates and the teacher after two weeks. Other ideas include drawing self-portraits or making silhouettes, described in Chapter 9, which suggests activities for the first day of school. A bulletin board introducing the teacher is also suggested in Chapter 9. You might include photos, samples of your hobbies, a favorite poem, or other information about you.

Many teachers use initial bulletin boards to stress the importance of reading. Book jackets make an effective display. Others use the bookworm idea and encourage children to read a book and add a segment to the worm.

Another suggested theme is current events at the school, local, national, and international levels. "Nose for News" or "News Roundup" or "News Hound" banners can evoke charming, simple drawings or cutouts done by you using an opaque projector.

Instructional bulletin boards are typical as well. They either introduce some concept or provide an overview or preview of some content area. Primary teachers use color, shape, or alphabet bulletin boards, while in the middle or upper grades the first social studies or science unit might be highlighted. An overview of the entire year might be attractively depicted under a headline, "Solve the Mystery of What We'll Learn in Third Grade," complete with Sherlock Holmes and his ever-present magnifying glass. In the intermediate grades, children, working in cooperative groups, can assume responsibility for designing, gathering materials for, and arranging bulletin boards on specific content-related topics. This is a less-work-for-teacher and more-learning-for-children activity—the best kind!

More than one teacher solves bulletin board worries by dividing the largest wall in the classroom into equal sections, one for each child. This can be done with colorful yarn. In the rectangles each child displays his or her best work, a photo, a favorite item from home, an art project, or a creative writing assignment. The display can be changed according to a schedule or when the child decides on displaying some other aspect of his or her life at home or at school. Whatever your initial bulletin boards, make sure they are neatly lettered, thoughtfully arranged, have attractive, bright-colored backgrounds, and can be read from all parts of the room. Finally, consider using the space overhead for displaying student work. Wires strung across the room enable you to hang student artwork with paper clips above. Use Worksheet 4.2, Initial Bulletin Board Ideas, to develop more bulletin board concepts.

Worksheet 4.2

Emotional Climate

Now that you have decorated the physical space of your classroom, it's time to look to the emotional space requirements and to contemplate establishing as warm an environment psychologically as you have physically. The tone you set for your class is often referred to as "climate." No matter where you live, try to establish a climate more like Southern California and less like Chicago in February. The most attractive, well-designed room will lose its attraction if an icy, frozen, and rigid climate prevails.

Establishing a warm climate comes naturally to most elementary school teachers. Conveying a positive attitude toward children and thus enhancing their self-concepts may alleviate many behavior problems before they begin. After all, children crave attention. If they get it from you for their positive behavior, they are less likely to act out to elicit a response.

Some of the simple teacher behaviors associated with positive climate are:

- smiling when appropriate
- moving around the classroom in physical proximity to all children
- having an open body posture, as opposed to a closed one (hands folded in front or seated behind desk)
- listening attentively to what children say
- telling appropriate personal stories about yourself or your experiences
- saying something complimentary to each child each day
- conducting classroom meetings in a circle to give the class a sense of belonging and cohesiveness
- using cooperative learning strategies to create a sense of belonging
- allowing students choices—as simple as which opening exercise song to sing or which game to play during physical education
- calling each child by name

- including self-concept activities as part of your everyday program
- encouraging active participation
- giving immediate feedback

ROUTINES AND PROCEDURES

Those of us who are creatures of habit adhere to certain routines and procedures throughout the day. When the alarm goes off, it sets in motion for each of us a unique and regimented set of procedures for meeting the day. Almost with eyes closed we perform the daily rituals, day in and day out, in the same order without fail. When we are thrown off guard by a faulty alarm clock, the ensuing panic is partly a result of not having time to go through our morning routines. If we lose a half hour, some of our daily rituals have to go. Either the cat doesn't get its customary attention, or we can't have fresh-brewed coffee; we can't read the morning headlines, or we can't complete our aerobic exercises. In short, the day gets off to a bad start.

In a positive sense, these routines, as stylized as they are, serve a vital function. Because they are habitual and can be performed automatically, we set our minds free for more creative and critical thinking activities. While we mechanically perform our routines in the morning with one part of our brain, the remainder is free to plan the day's activities, consider problems, and anticipate whatever challenges face us.

Routines in the classroom serve the same functions. They enable the teacher and the class to function smoothly and provide the safety and security needed by all. The more stability in the classroom, the less likely it is that disruptions will occur. If certain activities or procedures are learned and practiced in rote fashion, the time saved and effort spared can be used for more stimulating instructional activities and events. Routines will create order, and when the basic operation of the classroom is under control, you and the students will feel less stressed.

Making order out of chaos in a complex elementary school classroom is a challenge. Just when you thought there was a system or procedure for just about every aspect of classroom life, a situation pops up that necessitates development of new procedures or routines. While we are enculturated to a flag salute and patriotic song to start the day, there are many other aspects of classroom life that could use some routinization. These I have grouped into four major categories. You will undoubtedly need other routines, according to your unique situation, but if you haven't considered the following, confusion may result. In fact, when kids act confused or unsure of what to do or how to do it, it's a good sign that you have to think through yet another routine or procedure.

Materials and Equipment

The first thing to establish with children is what belongs to you, to them, and to both of you. The teacher's desk and file cabinet or special supply shelf should be off-limits to the children unless they have your permission. Similarly, their cubbies, desks, and coat hook are off-limits to you. Shared paper supplies should be pointed out to children, and you need to be clear about how these supplies are to be distributed. Will children be allowed, for example, to get whatever papers they need when they need them, will monitors give paper out, or will you pass the paper out yourself to individuals or to monitors?

While these seem like basic questions, if you don't anticipate procedures for materials distribution, confusion could result. Conversely, collection of finished work should be routinized. Will monitors collect papers, or will you collect them? Will you have a central collection tray that individuals can use when they finish their work? How will children get pencils, crayons, scissors, and paste? Will these items be on the desks or at a central location? Will children be allowed to come up at will to get what they need, or will supplies be distributed by you or by a monitor?

Worksheet
4.3

Use Worksheet 4.3, Materials Location and Distribution, to help you make some decisions about how materials will be placed and distributed. The worksheet has space at the bottom for you to generalize some procedures that can be communicated later to your class.

Entrances and Exits

Entering the Room.   The way in which students enter the room sets the tone for how the day will go. Meeting children at the door helps you establish your presence and allows you to greet each child individually. This is the perfect time for saying something positive to each child. It may simply be a "Good morning" (in child's native language as appropriate) or "I like your new haircut" or "That's a pretty dress." While school rules may be more relaxed, you might want to consider having children form lines outside the classroom prior to entering, if only at the beginning of the year. Lines diminish pushing and shoving and discourage barreling into the room; lines also help to make a smooth transition from play outside to work in the classroom. These same procedures can be followed during any entrance into the room, whether from recess, physical education, or another part of the building. Children can be shown how to line up (not by gender), and this expectation is most easily imprinted when it applies to all situations involving entrances into the room.

Establish a procedure for what children do when they enter the room (e.g., go to seats, quietly clear desks, and wait for instructions). Try turning off all lights when you leave the room and establish the turning on of the lights as a signal that the next activity is about to begin. Or, better yet, have an activity on the desks or on the board for children to do as soon as they enter the room in the morning or after breaks. Some teachers have students write in their journals first thing in the morning and read their books first thing after lunch. These alternatives give you a few minutes to collect your thoughts, especially in the morning and after lunch, when clerical tasks command your attention.

A Note from the Teacher

During my first month of teaching in my first year, the school at which I taught had a lap-running fund-raiser. As our P.E. activity that day we went out to practice running. I decided to take the classroom wall clock out with us so the kids could see how long it took. When we returned to the classroom, I noticed a stony silence coming from the other classrooms. Apparently, the clock had stopped and it wasn't until another teacher noticed my kids that I realized that my entire class had missed their buses to go home.

H. THOMPSON

Leaving the Room.   Teachers dismiss either by table, the quietest table leading the pack, or en masse. I strongly recommend the former, because the latter leads to noise, pushing, shoving, and general mayhem. Combining the group dismissal with the line is another alternative. By table, students line up for P.E., recess, lunch, library, assembly, or final dismissal. Or you can dismiss by some attribute—children wearing stripes or red or tennis shoes or a sweater, for instance. This is not only a good way to have children line up for dismissal, it also provides a nonthreatening way to teach basic concepts to limited-English-proficient children.

Again, transitions are unstable times in a classroom, and the more structure you give to the situation, the more likely it is that safety and low noise level will prevail, especially when the exit from the room is required for simulated emergencies like fire drills or earthquake drills (in my part of the country). If you have a well-established procedure for exit, you can rest more assured in times of real emergency that everyone will get out safely and quickly and can hear your directions. Make sure the children know the signals and frequently practice the procedures used in your school for these emergency situations. Even if your school does not require it, it is best to have a copy of the class roster accessible so you can grab it in an emergency and count heads immediately. When moving around the school with your class, walk in the middle, not at the front. If you lead the line, the children in the back will have a party. If you bring up the rear, the children in the front may get away from you. Give clear directions about stopping points along the way.

Bathroom and Water Fountain.   Typically, recesses, both morning and afternoon, are the specified times for bathroom breaks. Realistically, however, nature does not adhere to such schedules, and it becomes necessary to establish procedures for bathroom breaks during those in-between times. Most teachers use a pass system—one pass for boys, another for girls. Only two children at a time (one boy, one girl) are allowed out of the room. Some teachers use clothespins as a pass, others Mickey and Minnie Mouse dolls; still others fashion large passes out of wooden blocks. Others suggest that since the pass often ends up on the floor of the restroom, you should consider around-the-neck passes. Whatever your pass system, make sure the room number is on the pass, that there are only two of them, and that children understand these procedures:

- They should not leave during instructional time or when directions are being given.
- They must wait until a pass is available.
- They must keep all restrooms neat and tidy for others.
- They must leave and return without disturbing others.

It is best to remind kindergarten parents to make sure boys know how to undo their belts or, better yet, encourage parents to buy elastic waist pants. In kindergarten, look for signs of imminent bathroom need. By the time these busy folks in kindergarten raise their hands, it is sometimes too late. Keep spare clothes for such emergencies.

Water fountains are a slightly different story. Some are in the room, others outside. Bathroom breaks are more strategically necessary than water breaks, especially if water is available at recess. When fountains are in the room, you may choose to allow children to drink as they require liquid nourishment. Since there is a direct connection between drinking and bathroom requests, you may be simply adding to your own management problems if you provide access to water all day, even within the room. A compromise would involve water lineup after transitions into the room for those who need it. On very hot days, in very hot classrooms, you can always suspend the rules or allow water bottles at desks.

Movement Within the Room

Children are like jacks-in-the-box. They pop up out of their seats, and superstrength glue is probably the only remedy. Teachers, after all, have freedom of movement around the classroom, and children, especially the energetic ones, also need opportunities to stretch and amble. This need can be satisfied by periodic exercise routines that you structure. There are several excellent recordings (like Disney's *Mousercize*) with controlled exercise routines. When you provide the opportunity for exercise, fewer kids are likely to make their own individual opportunities, which can disrupt and cause delays. In the upper grades, after establishing a signal for returning to work, schedule periodic five-minute minibreaks to enable children to socialize.

To Sharpener and Wastebasket.   You can't eliminate totally the need to get rid of dirty tissues, to sharpen broken pencils, or to get materials, library books, or games for free-time activities. So you need to establish yet another set of procedures for movement within the room. The extreme position some teachers hold is that all broken pencils and wastebasket material must be held until specified times, usually early morning and after lunch. Realistically, however, pencils don't break on schedule, and if you are sensible, your students will be too. Consider allowing them to sharpen pencils at any time you are not giving directions or providing direct instruction; but stipulate that only one person at a time is allowed at the sharpener. Or have a supply of pencils at each table in a coffee can. One table leader is responsible for sharpening them at the start of the day. During the day, children can exchange their broken pencils for sharpened ones and thus avoid using the sharpener. As for the wastebasket, assign a monitor to pass the basket during transition times or use an ice cream vat–type container under each table cluster and have the children use the vat when necessary as a wastebasket without leaving their seats at all!

To Groups.   If your classroom is typical, at least part of your day will be spent in cooperative learning or small-group instruction. To ease transitions from groups to seat work to activity, you will need to make two charts, one listing the names of all members of each group and another that signals what activity each group is engaged in. A wheel arrangement works very well in this case. When you have established your schedule, set up a procedure for switching efficiently and quietly. Some teachers use a timer, others a bell, and others simply announce that it's time for a change. You will want to post rules for working in cooperative groups. Consider these:

- Help each other.
- Share and take turns.
- Praise each other.
- Talk quietly.
- Evaluate how the group worked.

Another procedure you might establish structures how students, when they are left to their own devices because you are busy with a small group, can get help when they need it. Alternatives are a monitor of the day, cross-age tutors, volunteer parents, or a directive to do what they can do, skip the hard parts, and wait until you are free to help. One teacher wears a sign that says, "Please see me later" when she is involved in small-group instruction and wants to discourage interruptions. While this may sound extreme, you are actually establishing independence and making it more likely that students will either solve the problem themselves, learn to rely on peers for instruction, or discover the virtue of patience. There is nothing more frustrating than children tugging at your sleeve when you are involved in a lively discussion during a small-group session. If you explain clearly what the children are expected to do, encourage procedural questions, ask one student to repeat the directions, write all assignments clearly on the board, identify alternative sources of help, and provide something meaningful for children to do when their work is completed, you can really enjoy and profitably use the time you spend in small-group instruction.

Instructional Routines

By now you are well on your way to becoming a logistics expert. You will need to establish just a few more instructional routines to govern beginning and ending the day, noise control, help seeking, free time, and computer rotation.

Beginning the Day.   The day normally begins in the same way and often includes the following rituals, sometimes in a different order:

- collection of money, permission slips
- attendance, pupil count
- flag salute
- patriotic song
- announcements and review of the day's schedule, which should be on the chalkboard
- birthday celebration, tooth fairy update, etc.
- sharing, current events, show and tell, or a classroom meeting in a circle
- calendar, weather

Noise Control.   To abate noise pollution, some teachers differentiate between whispering, talking, and silence. These distinctions are useful to make because total silence is hard to maintain during an entire day. Try it yourself sometime! Using a homemade cardboard traffic light can help control the noise level—green signifying talking, yellow for whispering, and red for silence. Although it sounds silly, children at the beginning of the school year need to practice differentiating between whispering and talking. You can make a game of this. Teachers usually have a signal for total silence, like lights off, a bell, or a hand signal, and allow whispering at all other times. Make public beforehand the acceptable noise level for any one activity and be realistic about how much silence can be expected in any one classroom. If you teach children to whisper, you will have a quiet classroom—not a silent classroom, but a quiet one. One teacher puts a doll in a basket and announces that the baby is sleeping. Another cautions children not to awaken the rabbit. Still another cautions that the canary is getting nervous.

Hand Raising.   To raise hands or not to raise hands is always the question, especially during a dynamic discussion, debate, or creative activity. My advice is to have a hand-raising rule with an option to suspend the rule when the activity dictates. Called-out responses or questions frustrate beginning teachers. Be consistent about hand raising and avoid questions that elicit choral responses. Preface your questions with the "Raise your hand and tell us . . ." phrase. Always compliment and encourage children who remember to raise hands, especially at the beginning of the year. You may prefer to use a system for calling on children that assures equity. Teachers write the names of students on ice cream sticks and place these in a coffee can. Ice cream sticks are chosen on a random basis and removed from the can until the can is empty (everyone has had a turn). The can is then re-filled with the ice cream sticks and so on. Another teacher uses a deck of cards and writes a child's name on each. The cards are used the same way as are the ice cream sticks, but they are more compact and more age-appropriate for intermediate grades.

Getting Help.   Waiting time becomes causing-a-disruption time when children need your attention because they are stuck and you are busy with another child or with a group. Preventive measures include making sure your directions are clear and understood before children are directed to independent work and providing some options for them when they run into trouble, such as telling them to:

- skip the parts they can't do
- use reference materials
- whisper to a friend for help

These alternatives can be posted on a bulletin board for easy reference. When children need feedback and you are unavailable, two systems seem to work better than raising hands. The first involves what I call the *bakery method*. Prepare a duplicate set of numbers on cards. When children need help, they take a number from a hook and go on to something else while they wait. You simply call out the numbers in order or put the duplicate numbers up on a hook one at a time. Children then come up to your desk when they see or hear their number. This works very well and provides a first-come, first-served, fair method of getting help.

Since a raised hand can get very tired, an alternative method is to give each child a red and green cup. When help is needed, the green cup is placed in the red one and when all is fine, the colors are reversed. Another variation on this theme is a "Help Wanted" sign attached to a pencil holder made from a milk carton, a brad, and cardboard strips (see Figure 4.2). The raised sign substitutes for a raised arm.

Or give each child a red and a green cube or block (Legos work well) and instruct the children to display cubes with green on top if all is well or red on top if help is needed. You can see at a glance who needs assistance. If too many need help, it's a good indicator that either you need to reteach that segment or the work is too difficult for the children.

Free Time.   Waiting time occurs not only when children are stuck but also when they are finished with their assignments. If children are finishing too quickly, it may be evidence that the work is too easy or insufficient in volume. Establish a routine for what chil-

Figure 4.2

dren do when they finish work, and post this on a bulletin board as well. Some suggestions include:

- Read a book.
- Play a game quietly.
- Take a puzzle and work it out.
- Work on some other unfinished project.
- Make up a crossword puzzle or acrostic.
- Work at the computer.
- Play with class pets, clean cages, and feed.
- Help others with their work or with learning English.
- Listen to a story using headphones.
- Tidy up your desk.
- Review your portfolio.

Computer Rotation. If you have only one computer in your room, you will need to devise a routine to allow equity in access. Oehring (1993), a classroom teacher, suggests cut-out apples with children's names on them arranged in a pocket chart; the appropriate apple is turned over when a student completes his or her work. Another suggestion is a clothespin chart divided down the middle into *waiting* and *completed* sections. When the children go to the computer in order, they move their name clothespin from waiting to completed. Or simply have a class list posted and have children check off their turns. You will also need to decide if and how you will time children. A kitchen timer works well, as does having the day divided into segments, assigning children in turn to segments based on their access chart.

End of the Day.   Tying up the loose ends at the end of the day is important so that your students have a sense of closure before they go home and so that they can begin the next day fresh. Use the last 15 minutes for a quick review of the day's activities with children, discussing what they learned or enjoyed most that day. Provide at this time a preview of the next day. Use this interval for clearing off desks, cleaning out desks, tidying up the room, and making sure that all papers and notices that need to go home are distributed. Finally, use the procedures for cleanup dictated by the school. Placing chairs on tables is common practice. Add a special, individualized, and positive comment to as many children as time allows as you dismiss them. This will send them home floating and eager to return the next day.

It may seem to you, after reading the preceding section, that you should have pursued a management or tactical operations degree instead of a teaching credential. Teachers report that they learned these routines by trial and error, common sense, or observation of other teachers, especially during student teaching. One reported "stumbling into what worked best." The children assisted one new teacher by recounting how they did things last year. While a few teachers recommend establishing procedures as they come up, other veterans offer specific advice to the beginning teacher:

- Begin on the first day to establish the procedures that will be in use the whole year.
- Be very specific as to how you want things done.
- Have the children practice each procedure until they get it right.
- Liberally compliment students when they follow procedures.
- Reteach the routines and quickly deal with deviations from established procedures (for example, "I hear a good answer, but I can't call on anyone who doesn't raise his or her hand").
- Give rational reasons for each routine as it is introduced.
- Don't introduce all routines the first day, just the ones relevant for that day. For example, movement to and from centers need not be discussed immediately; however, bathroom routines are a priority the first day.

- Be prepared to add new routines as the need arises, and be prepared to change or delete procedures that simply don't work for you or are no longer needed.

Use Worksheet 4.4, Classroom Routines Planning Forms, to plan your initial set of routines. You can add others in the extra spaces as needed.

Monitors in the Classroom

Good managers know how to delegate authority, and the teacher who wants to delegate can use monitors to manage a great many of the routines of classroom life. Besides reducing your own role as manager, you are enabling children through the monitor or helper system you set up to assume responsibility, gain independence, enhance self-concept, and practice leadership skills.

Types of Monitors. While some teachers have no monitors and some enlist random workers, especially those children who have completed their work, most employ a cadre of monitors as follows:

> messenger/office runner
> P.E. monitor to pass out and collect equipment
> cleanup director
> paper passer
> board eraser
> pet feeder
> plant waterer
> door monitor
> lunch count taker
> leader of flag salute
> calendar updater
> library assistant
> row leaders/table monitors/class officers

Many of your routines can be handled through delegation of authority. While you may not need all the monitors listed above, the opportunity is there for half the students to be involved in running the classroom at any one time. Use this list when deciding on monitors. Blank spaces have been left for you to add your own special jobs. Make sure that your nonnative speakers or second language learners participate fully in monitorial duties. This will help them feel a part of the social fabric of the classroom and help them gain a sense of belonging and acceptance that Peregoy and Boyle (1993) remind us is vital to their self-esteem. Embrace this motto as well: *Less work for teacher and more independence and responsibility for children.*

Assigning Monitors. Most teachers rotate jobs on a weekly or semimonthly basis, with the changing of the guard usually occurring on Monday. Children should sample each job throughout the course of the year; alternative methods of assignment follow:

Volunteering. Students volunteer for positions, but this method may discourage shy children from participating.

Worksheet
4.4

Lottery. Each child's name is on an ice cream stick in a can or on a card in a fishbowl. As names are chosen, the child gets to choose the job he or she would like to do. Once the names have been drawn, they are removed from the lottery until all children have had a turn.

Class List. The names are taken in order from a class list displayed on the bulletin board. Clothespins with the job titles are attached to the chart next to the name of the person who chooses it.

Reward. Some teachers attach monitorial positions to good behavior. This system discriminates against the poorly behaved student who may need the chance to exercise some responsibility to change his or her behavior and never gets the opportunity under this system.

Predetermined Schedule. The teacher each week selects children for each job and makes sure everyone has an opportunity. While this may assure the "right person for the job," it takes the choice of position out of the children's hands.

Elections. Most teachers hold elections for class officers or leaders, some in very sophisticated ways, simulating the election process in our democracy, including nominations, campaigns, and secret-ballot elections.

Worksheet
4.5

Application. Some teachers simulate the entire job-hunting process. This is a good time to teach youngsters how to fill out a simplified application, write a cover letter, and even make up a résumé. A student committee can interview each prospective job applicant and select the most experienced and qualified for each job.

Use Worksheet 4.5, Classroom Monitors, to check off the kinds of assistants you plan to use. At the bottom of the worksheet, devise a system for choosing monitors.

A FINAL ENCOURAGEMENT

Many books have been written about the organizational aspect of classroom life, and you will probably want to read some more and talk with experienced teachers about how they juggle routines and monitors and how they create a stimulating classroom environment. While the tasks described in this chapter seem a bit overwhelming at first, and you may feel a need for a vacation two weeks into the school year, the time and effort you expend at the beginning will allow you freedom to enjoy and exercise your primary function— instruction. With all the skills you develop in the beginning weeks of the school year and with all the time you save as a result, you can even moonlight as an interior decorator or efficiency expert during the rest of the school year!

Reflection Box

In what ways, if any, has the chapter changed my beliefs?

Questions I Still Have . . .

Reflection Box

What practices actually worked for me in my first year?

FURTHER READING

Cangelosi, J. S. (1996). *Classroom management strategies: Gaining and maintaining students' co-operation* (3rd ed.). White Plains, NY: Longman.

Charles, C. M., & Senter, G. (1995). *Elementary classroom management* (2nd ed.). White Plains, NY: Longman.

Evertson, C., Emmer, E., Clements, B., & Worsham, M. (1997). *Classroom management for elementary teachers* (3rd ed.). Needham Heights, MA: Allyn & Bacon.

Flores, A. (1983). *Instant bulletin boards: Month by month classroom graphics.* Carthage, IL: Fearon Teacher Aids.

Grewe, G., & Glover, S. (1994). *The classroom management survival kit: Bulletin boards, student activities, and teacher ideas to help you motivate, educate, and collaborate.* Carthage, IL: Good Apple.

Harrison, A., & Spuler, F. (1983). *Hot tips for teachers: A collection of classroom management ideas.* Belmont, CA: Fearon Teacher Aids.

Novelli, J. (1990). Design a classroom that works. *Instructor, 100*(1), 24–27.

Prizzi, E., & Hoffman, J. (1981). *Teaching off the wall: Interactive bulletin boards that teach with you.* Carthage, IL: Fearon Teacher Aids.

Spitzman, R. (1989). *Bulletin boards plus.* Carthage, IL: Good Apple.

REFERENCES

Dockterman, D. (1993). *Great teaching in the one computer classroom.* Cambridge, MA: Tom Snyder Productions.

Garfield, G., & McDonough, S. (1996). *Creating a technologically literate classroom.* Westminster, CA: Teacher Created Materials.

Hannah, G. (1984). Jazzing up your classroom. *Learning, 13*(1), 68–71.

Hayes, D. (1997). *Managing technology in the classroom.* Huntington Beach, CA: Teacher Created Materials.

Hopkins, M. (1993). Rethinking class design. *Instructor* (July–August), 44–48.

Morlan, J., & Espinosa, L. (1989). *Preparation of inexpensive teaching materials* (3rd ed.). Carthage, IL: Fearon Teacher Aids.

Oehring, S. (1993). The one-computer classroom. *Instructor* (July–August), 84–87.

Peregoy, S. F., & Boyle, O. F. (1996). *Reading, writing and learning in ESL: A resource book for K–8 teachers.* White Plains, NY: Longman.

chapter

5

Positive Discipline in the Classroom

Reflection Box

What I Believe About

The importance of discipline . . .
Culturally sensitive discipline . . .
Criteria for evaluating my discipline plan . . .
Preventive discipline . . .
Establishing classroom rules . . .
Underlying causes of misbehavior . . .
Asking for parent cooperation . . .
Positive discipline methods . . .

The word *discipline* strikes more fear into the hearts of teachers than it does into the hearts of misbehaving students. The overriding anxiety of beginning teachers is focused on control of the classroom, and for that reason this chapter is long and detailed. Even though you may have heard much of what is said here in other courses, you may need to refocus on the subject when you contemplate your first day in the classroom.

Even experienced teachers are concerned about discipline. Why? One explanation is that today's children come to school with different experiences in their book bags and go home to very different family configurations than they did years ago. Drugs, gangs, violent neighborhoods, homelessness, hunger, abuse, and neglect are just some of the social ills you will see reflected in the behavior of some of your students. Single-parent and dual-income families may have less time and energy for their children, and even wealthy families often relegate child rearing to someone else. Schools by default have taken on more of the responsibility for meeting children's needs in all developmental areas, including self-control and self-esteem. C. M. Charles (1996) suggests additional reasons for the persistence of discipline problems: Children have been raised more permissively; some parents increasingly take the child's side against the school; and some teachers and administrators have been worn down by the discipline struggle.

Discipline has never received as much attention as it has in the past few years. When I began teaching, there was only one golden rule: *Do not smile until Christmas.* All the rest was left up to the individual. Now books on discipline proliferate, as do workshops, seminars, and inservices. Along with the fitness craze, the health food fad, and the dressing-for-success seminars come the discipline disciples, each with a no-fail system for keeping kids in order. Teachers flock to these workshops, waiting for the definitive word. If the various exercise emporiums and health spas offered discipline classes along with life cycle and aerobics classes, memberships would soar and profits would triple.

Discipline is an aspect of human behavior, and as such, it derives from a complex interaction between the individual and the environment. It is the latter that must be established before the other facets of discipline can be explored. In this chapter the focus is on prevention of discipline problems through an organized plan for learning and a well-managed environment. Specific techniques for dealing with minor infractions will be discussed along with strategies for dealing with serious behavior problems in positive, reasonable, respectful, and dignified ways.

WHY DISCIPLINE?

Developing a rationale for your discipline plan is the first step toward an effective system. It's simply not enough to adopt someone else's system, although this appears to be the easiest approach. The recipes abound, but they simply may not meet your tastes. No one system of discipline will suit you perfectly, and no one system will work for all children in your classroom. This is one aspect of classroom life that must be custom-fit, both to your needs and to the needs of your students. Take a few minutes to think about some reasons for discipline and then compare your answers to those that follow.

- *Safety.* Children need to feel physically safe and secure and free from threat and intimidation both in the classroom and outside on the playground. School may be the safest place in their lives. Children also need to feel emotionally safe and secure. When an atmosphere of mutual respect and consideration prevails in the classroom, children will more likely risk being open and honest and true to themselves. These safety needs are the most basic human concerns after the physiological needs of survival (Maslow, 1987), and a safe physical and emotional environment free from harm can be achieved only when discipline prevails.
- *Limits.* Children need to have limits and learn what is appropriate and inappropriate behavior. This is the other side of the safety issue. To ensure an environment that is safe for everyone, each one of us must limit our individual freedoms and must temper individual rights for the good and welfare of all. In a democratic so-

ciety we all live by a code of law that is created by us through our representatives and that, ideally, is enforced equally and consistently.

- *Acceptance.* According to Maslow (1987), acceptance needs come after survival needs and safety needs are met. Children need and desire the approval and love of others. When they are behaving in a socially acceptable manner, they will feel good about themselves and feel they are behaving in ways that bring them acceptance from others and a sense of belonging in the classroom.
- *Self-Esteem.* Self-esteem needs follow closely those of acceptance (Maslow, 1987). Children who can control their behavior will gain a sense of mastery and will feel competent and respected by their classroom community. Feeling competent in one area of life can help shore up poor self-esteem in other areas.
- *Learning.* Self-actualizing needs emerge after all others are met (Maslow, 1987). A classroom teacher who wants to encourage these needs in students must try to create an environment that helps children develop their gifts, talents, and abilities. Children have both the need to reach their potential and the right to an orderly classroom environment free from distractions, interruptions, and behavioral disruptions that interfere with their learning.
- *Responsibility.* Children need to learn that for every action there is a logical and sometimes equal reaction. Taking responsibility for one's actions is a cornerstone of democratic society. Any consequences should be related to the offense and must respect the dignity of the child. (A complete discussion of logical consequences follows later in the chapter.)
- *Democratic Training.* John Dewey (1980) advocated schools that would be mini-communities, training grounds for citizenship. In a workable discipline system, the foundations of democratic society should pertain: one person, one vote; the rule of law; self-responsibility; the rule of the majority, with respect for minority views; consequences for actions against the greater good; individual freedoms balanced against the common good; and respect for all, regardless of viewpoint.

YOUR PHILOSOPHY

Children, then, have some basic needs that are met through a discipline system, including physical and emotional safety needs, acceptance and belonging needs, and self-esteem and self-actualizing needs. Discipline also teaches children about the democratic processes and the tension that exists among individual rights, the rights of the majority, and respect for minority opinions. What your ultimate system will be depends very much on your own belief system about children and discipline. This chapter has been written with a philosophy in mind, which will become more apparent as you read further. I have sifted and winnowed through all the competing philosophies, the research studies, and the experiences of many teachers to formulate my own philosophy. You will be doing the same.

All of our actions are derived from our belief systems. If we believe that children are little gremlins who must be controlled, then control them we will, at all costs. If we believe that children must express themselves without constraint, then express themselves they will, by throwing blocks or paint or pencils, as we sit and marvel at their creativity. Take some time to complete Worksheet 5.1, Discipline Clarification Activity. Rank-order

Worksheet 5.1

these positions vis-à-vis discipline from 1 to 8, with 1 being the position most like your own. This will help you conceptualize your own starting position regarding discipline. You may want to reach consensus with others if you are doing this activity in class.

These positions reflect a continuum of discipline strategies from the laissez-faire to the strict authoritarian. In between one finds the counseling approach, the democratic approach, the logical consequences approach, and the behavior modification approach. It was probably hard for you to rank these statements, as most people are eclectic in their beliefs and practice walking the thin line between laissez-faire and total authoritarianism. Do your best balancing act.

The emphasis on eclecticism and value-based discipline and real suggestions from real teachers makes this discussion of discipline different from others you may have read. The various discipline models or systems are elaborated in other books, and are just briefly mentioned in this chapter. You will find a list of suggested readings at the end of the chapter for more information. The purpose here is to help you articulate a humane, positive, reasonable, and respectful system of discipline based on what you can extract from the information provided by teachers who have been through all the discipline fads and models and have synthesized what is meaningful and achievable. Teachers combine elements of many approaches. What follows is a smorgasbord for you to sample; remember, however, to check and recheck the tidbits you choose against your beliefs about children, your value system, your rationale for discipline, and your own philosophy of discipline. As you read, you might also consider that, whatever plan you ultimately design, it should be checked against the criteria discussed below and listed on Worksheet 5.2, Discipline System Criteria.

Worksheet 5.2

Your overall discipline system should be, first and foremost, reasonable, respectful, dignified, and sensitive to cultural norms. If we accept Maslow's (1987) assertion that we all require a sense of significance, belonging, acceptance, security, and safety, then discipline plans cannot undermine children's intrinsic needs. Children new to this country, whose primary language is different, have even greater safety and security needs that must be considered. Any plan that is unfair or unreasonable, or that humiliates or demeans children in any way, will simply backfire. Put yourself in your students' place. Would you find the discipline system reasonable, respectful, and dignified? Dreikurs, Grunwald, and Pepper (1982) tell us that misbehavior is symptomatic, a message from a discouraged child who feels that he or she doesn't belong and is insignificant. Any system we choose should not add to the discouragement that the child already feels. It should, instead, encourage and satisfy the child's basic human needs.

Especially as a new teacher, you should develop a discipline plan that will ultimately be consistent with the overall school plan. Find out first if there are schoolwide rules that your class is expected to follow. These are usually pretty general, and you will probably have an easy time living with them. If the school has adopted any one system of discipline that simply goes against your grain, it is imperative that you discuss the issue with the principal as soon as possible and see if there is any wiggle room for you. The best time to do this is at your interview, before you are hired. You will be very unhappy if you are expected to follow a plan that is counter to your own belief system about children and contrary to your general value system.

Your discipline system should also be appropriate for the age group and flexible enough to take individual differences into account. Although young children may respond to happy faces as rewards, sixth graders would justifiably feel patronized. Watch out for whole systems of discipline that are so rigid that you have no flexibility in dealing with hyperactive children who are unable to sit still or be silent, or for systems that have stringent penalties that require, for example, that you call parents, when you know that certain parents are capable of overreaction or potential abuse. Make sure that your plan takes into account that culture influences children's reaction to being disciplined. In Latino cultures, for instance, lowered eyes are a sign of respect, and, therefore, the teacher who asks for direct eye contact is discounting individual differences and being culturally insensitive.

Your ultimate discipline plan should be time-efficient, easy to administer, and stress-free. You don't want to implement a plan that is ultimately more burdensome to you than the discipline problems themselves. Will you spend more time administering your plan than teaching children? Will your plan turn you into a police officer or a secretary keeping track of points or a candy machine dispensing food rewards? Will your system create in you positive feelings, or will it add anxiety to your already stressful life? Will your system make you feel like the professional educator you have been trained to be?

Can your plan be easily communicated to the children and their parents without a 10-page manual of directions? Is it easily translatable to a child's primary language for parents? Is it a system that a substitute can understand should the need arise? Can you articulate it simply and easily to your principal when asked? If it's too complicated to write down in one paragraph in a letter to parents, it's probably too complicated for you to manage without hiring an Assistant Teacher in Charge of Discipline, a Secretary in Charge of Tracking Points, and a Treasurer in Charge of Dispensing Rewards.

PREVENTING DISCIPLINE PROBLEMS

Much of what has preceded this chapter has set the stage for what follows. If you accept the premise that children respond and react to the situation at hand, then the more you control the variables of instruction, including the physical arrangement of the classroom, the less likely it is that you will have to control the children. I am not proposing that good teaching and organized, efficient classroom management will solve or prevent all discipline problems. I am suggesting that as long as these variables are under your control, it's best to start with a look at the context in which problems arise.

The Physical Environment

It is 105 degrees outside as I sit in an air-conditioned office that has been cleaned and organized to help me concentrate. Likewise, starting out in a comfortable classroom environment may increase the likelihood that children will attend to their learning tasks with minimum distraction and disruption. Pay attention to these parameters:

- a well-ventilated room
- glare-free lighting
- colorful and informative bulletin boards
- a clean and orderly room with clear organization

- private spaces for children to get away from it all
- visibility from all areas of the room for you and the pupils
- compatible seatmates
- teaching style conducive to your furniture arrangement

Meeting Individual Differences

Some underlying causes of behavior disruptions are related to instruction and include the inability to do the work, sheer boredom, lack of challenging assignments, and expectations that are too high. These can be countered by your recognition that each child is an individual and deserves to have his or her learning needs met as much as is humanly possible. Unmet needs lead to trouble—that is, attention-getting behavior that undermines your classroom control.

Differentiated Assignments.   Make sure each child can succeed at the tasks you assign. This may necessitate rewriting some assignments, tape-recording assignments, or providing more challenging work for the advanced learner. Plan for extension and enrichment activities as well.

Grouping.   Individual needs can also be met by grouping, when appropriate, according to specific needs, abilities, and interests. Cooperative learning groups promote social skills as children engage in tasks that foster positive interdependence and problem solving. Other ad hoc groups can be formed on the basis of a specific skill need, a common interest (rock collecting or dinosaurs), common reading materials (children who all are reading detective stories or animal books), a project (a class play or a newspaper).

Choices and Decisions.   Children's individual differences may also be met by providing choices whenever possible: in creative writing topics, in art assignments, in P.E. games, and in seating. Choice empowers children and thus may inhibit them from exercising power in unacceptable ways.

Realistic Expectations.   One of the ways to determine if your expectations are too high or too low is to put yourself in your students' place. Try sitting in one spot yourself for five and one-half hours, totally still and quiet. I've tried, and it's quite difficult. Realize perhaps that giving 50 examples of a particular skill is tedious or that the literature selection is boring. Make revisions whenever you have the sense that you wouldn't be able to complete the assignment if you were in the students' shoes.

Capitalizing on Interests.   Finding out what motivates each child and gearing instruction around common interests will accomplish two goals. First, you will capture attention more easily; and, second, you will convey the message that you care about individuals. Developing rapport with children is easy if you are honest, sincere, and genuine with them. Conduct an interest inventory. Using current fads as themes in your instruction may just be the spark to keep students involved and out of trouble.

Planning

Your planning, both long range and short term, if thorough and well formulated, will help you cut down on potential disruptions.

Plan for Success.   If your planning allows for every child to succeed, you are maximizing your chances for effective discipline. It is far better to underestimate your children's abilities during the first few days than it is to go over their heads. Err on the side of easy before you have actual diagnostic data. The worst thing that can happen is that they will feel successful!

Worthwhile and Meaningful Activities.   If children feel the work is worthwhile and meaningful, they are less likely to question your authority and rebel through negative behavior. Motivate individual lessons and let children know the purpose or objective of the lesson. Use a variety of media and technology in your instruction and vary your teaching strategies. Plan a balance among individual work, cooperative learning in groups, and teacher-directed instruction, to create variety and to maintain involvement and interest. Glasser (1993) sets forth six criteria for quality schoolwork. These are:

- a warm, supportive classroom environment;
- useful work;
- students are asked to exert their best effort;
- students evaluate their own work and improve it;
- quality work feels good;
- and is never destructive.

Orderly Procedures.   The clarity of your directions and the availability of all teaching resources will allow the smoother operation of all activities within the classroom. Make sure you have gone through the lesson in your mind as well as written it on paper so you can anticipate any skipped steps or procedures that potentially might sandbag your lesson. Make sure materials are at the ready. If you have to go back to a closet to get the scissors, you will interrupt the flow and undermine your lesson.

Sponges.   Cutting down on lag time can be accomplished by overplanning and the use of "sponge" activities. You can always cut down on activities, but it's hard to think on your feet if you have an extra few minutes after you complete a lesson. If you don't have something to keep students actively involved, they may create their own diversions, ones you may not approve. Some ideas for sponges are listed below, but the sponges should relate to the curriculum:

- Name farm animals.
- Name community helpers.
- List one county for each letter of the alphabet.
- Name things that fly.
- Name things that run on electricity.
- Name green vegetables.
- Name things with wheels.

- Name things that come in pairs.
- Name something found in King Tut's tomb.
- Name things you need to peel before eating.

Having a general list of things to do after children complete their work will also help. These activities must be rewarding in some way. Making more work the reward for early completion soon will lose its appeal, and children, wise to your scheme, will slow down and even avoid finishing in the allotted time. Keep a basket/box of children's books on each table grouping and rotate the book baskets as needed. This gives the children something to do at all times without leaving their seats.

Instruction

During instructional time, you can cut down on potential disruptions by adhering to principles of good teaching. Although good instruction cannot guarantee good discipline at all times, you can reduce potential problems by considering the possibility that a strong link exists between the two. Many of the following principles of good instruction, which correlate with effective classroom management, were first identified by Jacob Kounin (1970) in his seminal book, *Discipline and Group Management in Classrooms*. The terms in *italics* are his.

Focus Attention/Group Alerting.   Before beginning any lesson, make sure the children are looking at you and you have everyone's undivided attention. If you begin while children are talking or inattentive, the situation can only get worse. Clear desks will alleviate the probability that children will find something to play with during teacher-directed lessons. *Group alerting* is a key element in well-managed classrooms. Keeping the group alerted involves encouraging individual and unison responses and not calling on someone before you ask the questions; otherwise, the other students will tune out. It means keeping everyone on his or her toes. Calling on students randomly with name sticks is one way of keeping them on their toes.

Pacing.   Make sure that lessons proceed at a steady clip. If you allow yourself to be distracted or slowed down, the delays will enable minor disruptions to erupt like mini-wildfires. Be careful of *overdwelling* and *fragmentation*. A teacher engaging in overdwelling is spending too much time on directions, on irrelevant details, or on the physical props of the lesson. A teacher engaged in fragmentation divides the lesson into too many unnecessary steps or procedures or has each child do something individually when a group or the entire class could do it more efficiently all at once.

Monitoring Attention.   Kounin (1970) invented the term *withitness* to describe teachers who have eyes in the backs of their heads. They seem to know what's going to happen and who the culprit will be, and they move in quickly to nip the misbehavior in the bud. Observe and be alert during all presentations. Maintain eye contact with each child and move around the room. Pretend you are a bat hovering over the room with everyone under your wing. Children are less likely to act out when they feel they are in direct contact with you.

Stimulate Attention.   Avoid boredom by showing enthusiasm yourself, by enabling the children to feel they are making progress or getting somewhere as a result of all their effort, and by including variety. Vary the lesson formats, the group size, the media and materials; and to keep everyone involved, ask stimulating and sometimes unpredictable questions. Use "every pupil response" techniques whenever possible, as these allow everyone to be involved in responding at the same time. They enable you to diagnose on the spot who understands the lesson and who doesn't, saving you hours of grading written work. Some ways of engaging the whole group are:

- Say it aloud.
- Use a finger signal (thumbs up or down, for exampie).
- Display responses on individual sets of flash cards.
- Select students' names from a bundle of ice cream sticks or a deck of cards that have been individualized with their names and then randomized.
- Display responses on individual chalkboards or laminated cardboards or white boards.

Overlappingness.   Kounin's (1970) term *overlappingness* is a key to effective classroom management and simply refers to the ability to handle two or more things at the same time. An example would be walking over to a student who is tapping his or her pencil while still conducting the lesson, or checking a paper while working with a small math group and not missing a beat.

Smooth Transitions.   Avoid *dangles, flip-flops, thrusts,* and *truncations.* While these sound like terms used in aerobic dancing, here are the definitions: *dangles* and *flip-flops* occur when the teacher leaves one activity dangling or hanging, goes on to another, and returns once again to the initial activity. *Thrusts* occur when a teacher barrels into an activity without attention to pupil readiness. *Truncations* occur when a teacher aborts an activity and never returns to it.

Closure.   Terminate lessons that have gone on too long. Know when children have reached their saturation point, and attempt to bring closure to the lesson before that time. Always leave students asking for more.

Checking for Understanding.   Before dismissing a group after a teacher-directed activity, make sure your students know what to do next. This can be accomplished by asking one child to summarize the lesson's content and directions for seat work or follow-up. Always ask if anyone has any questions about what to do next. This will prevent the sudden rash of questions that develop when you are happily engaged and settled in with the next group. When kids persist, just nonverbally motion to them to get to work. They are often testing to see if you mean it.

Organization

A well-organized classroom is not, to paraphrase a current slogan, the sign of a sick mind but rather a signal to children that all is safe and secure. Disruptions are less likely to occur in such a well-prepared environment.

Procedures and Routines.   Everything you wanted to know (and probably more than you ever wanted to know) about routines and procedures has already been covered in the previous chapter. An efficiently run classroom will cut down on disruptions and delays, which are the precursors of some discipline problems. Most important are transitions, exits, and entrances. The smoothness with which these are orchestrated has a direct bearing on the behavior of pupils. The more adept you become as efficiency expert, classroom traffic controller, systems analyst, and employment agent for monitors, the less effort you will have to expend on discipline.

Signals.   Most teachers use some sort of signal when they want the students' attention. This signal is explained on the first day of class, and its use is reinforced from that day forth. You might consider asking children to answer your signal with one of their own. For example, when your hand goes up, they need to raise their hands too. When you clap out a pattern, they respond with the same pattern. Some of the most common signals are lights off, a chord on the piano, a bell, a note on the xylophone, a red light up on the traffic signal, two fingers or a hand raised, a finger to the lips, a message on the chalkboard, and so on.

Materials.   A common cause of disturbance is the slow or unequal distribution of materials and supplies. Countless arguments occur over paste, scissors, and other items. Although sharing is a virtue to strive for, making sure you have enough supplies to go around is a preventive measure. Keep a basket supplies on each table grouping. Chapter 4 describes various material distribution procedures.

Worksheet
5.3

Use Worksheet 5.3, Setting the Stage for Discipline Checklist, to help you determine whether your stage is set to prevent discipline problems. Any No column responses should start you thinking about how your variables of instruction can be restructured and reshaped to discourage behavioral disturbances.

OFF TO A GOOD START

The first day of school is not too early to discuss with children a rationale for discipline and to set down with children the rules and regulations they are to follow for the entire year. Sanford, Emmer, and Clements (1983) stress the importance of having rules and procedures clearly communicated and monitored closely at the beginning of the year.

In this section you will have the opportunity to reflect on how to introduce a needs-based and democratic discipline system to students. Some steps you may want to consider include discussing the importance of discipline, establishing classroom rules, establishing logical consequences for infractions, institutionalizing the class meeting as a problem-solving forum, and informing parents about the rules and consequences.

The Importance of Discipline

To bring home the importance of rules to my fourth through sixth graders, at least in my more radical days, I neither made rules nor extracted any from my class during the first week of school. I sat back as disruption became chaos and bit my tongue more than once during that week. On Friday afternoon I called a classroom meeting (not sure that the children would even come to the circle). When they did, we discussed the problems that had arisen during the previous week. These included noise, inconsiderate behavior, a messy room, assorted arguments, and general confusion. The children themselves suggested the need for some classroom rules and boiled all the suggestions down to two: *Respect each others' rights,* and *Clean up the room.*

While I would not suggest this approach to all but the most experienced and coura-geous among you, you can use the scenario as a guided fantasy to accomplish the same end. Questions such as the following will get you started:

1. Why do we have rules at all?
2. What would happen if we had no rules?
3. What makes a good rule?
4. What rules do you think are necessary for our room?

Children should ultimately come to understand the concepts of costs and benefits. While rules and laws help us remain safe and secure, we also have to give up something in return. This something is most often freedom to do what we want when we want to. Children should be helped to understand that classroom rules are a specific application of these basic concepts of law. Time spent in discussing the need for rules is time well spent. You are laying a foundation for life in a democratic society where rules, legislated by rep-resentatives for the good of all, may sometimes impinge on the total freedom of some, if not all, of the members of society to do whatever they please.

Establishing Classroom Rules

Experienced teachers report setting rules on the first day of school. Common practices include:

- eliciting rules from the students;
- ranking the rules with the children and selecting a maximum of five;
- stating the rules positively; and
- telling the children that as school progresses they can add or delete rules.

Good rules tend to be needed, fair, applied equally and consistently, enforceable, reasonable, and respectful. Good rules are sensitive to cultural norms and understandable to nonnative speakers.

The most common rules in classrooms are listed below. If you find that your students do not come up with a rule for your pet peeve, simply cue them into thinking along those lines.

- Respect rights and property of others.
- Follow directions.
- Work quietly in the classroom.
- Be a good listener.
- Raise hands to speak or leave seat.
- Be kind and courteous.

These rules were mentioned time and time again by experienced teachers. In fact, the first rule covers a lot of ground and was one of the two rules in my classroom. The other was to clean up after yourself. One teacher posts the following as the sole guiding princi-ple: *When I am responsible, I will have a good day. When I am irresponsible, I will pay the consequences.* When children are given the opportunity to learn what makes a good rule, to discuss why rules are needed, to make up a limited set of good rules, and to moni-tor their enforcement, they are more likely to follow them.

> ## A Note from the Teacher
>
> Class Constitution (Grade 1)
>
> We promise to be peace builders and follow all classroom rules. We will always pay attention and listen to our teacher and each other. We will be safe and respect each other.
>
> M. PETERSON

Rules (and translations for nonnative speakers) should be posted in a prominent place in the room. Some teachers really go all out and call this list the Classroom Constitution. A good creative writing experience for older children is to write a fancy preamble. All children can then sign and date the rules to reinforce ownership of these self-imposed limits.

The Classroom Meeting

In a democratically run classroom, children can share not only in rule making but also in the process of monitoring and enforcing the rules. William Glasser (1975, 1986) believes that children can control themselves and will choose the appropriate behavior if those behaviors satisfy their basic needs for survival, love, power, fun, and freedom. It is the teacher's role to assist children to make positive choices by setting up a learning environment in which teaching strategies (e.g., cooperative learning) and noncoercive management strategies satisfy children's basic needs. One vehicle Glasser proposes for this decision making is the classroom meeting.

Entire class or individual problems are appropriate for a class meeting, and they can be introduced by any student or by the teacher. During the meeting, everyone sits in a tight circle and the problem is exposed and solutions are discussed with everyone participating. The discussion is directed toward solutions, not punishment or faultfinding. The teacher facilitates the discussion, although it is the students' role (not the teacher's) to make the value judgments about the behavior. In simple terms, the children weigh the costs and benefits of continuing the behavior against the costs and benefits of desisting. Then they brainstorm and debate the effectiveness of various proposed ways of redressing the wrong or solving the problem. After a solution is agreed upon, the children are expected to commit to it or sign a paper saying they are unwilling to commit to it. It is the very act of learning how to solve problems that is empowering, not any one particular solution. The class meeting has been simplified by Jane Nelsen (1996).

Consistency

Veteran teachers agree that once the rules are elicited, consolidated, voted on, and posted, they should be strictly enforced the first day and in the weeks that follow until they are set in the minds and hearts of the children. You should generally follow through on rule enforcement by:

- encouraging children's efforts to follow the rules;
- demonstrating *withitness*;

- reminding, privately and immediately, those who forget;
- conveying your commitment to rule-bound behavior through your own actions, voice, and nonverbal behavior; and
- bringing rule-enforcement issues to the class meeting.

Communicating Rules to Parents

On the first day most teachers send a note home to parents (in translation, if needed) explaining the classroom rules, or they have the children rewrite the rules for their parents to sign. While this might not be feasible on the first day given all you have planned, don't delay very long. Parents need to know the ground rules so they can help you. Should infractions occur, parents will have been forewarned about rules and will more likely accept the news that their child has broken one or two of them. A typical letter follows:

Dear Parent or Guardian,

Thank you for sharing your child with me this school year. I will do my best to help your child reach his or her full potential. In order to have a safe, secure, happy place to learn, we have written these classroom rules:

I know the children will work hard to follow the rules they developed. At school, I will encourage them in their efforts at self-control. If I need your help at home, I will be in touch with you by phone or note.

I you have any questions or wish to speak with me, I can be reached at the school (phone number) between 8:00 and 8:30 A.M. and during recesses (10:00–10:15 or 2:15–2:30). If these times are inconvenient for you, please leave a message and I'll return your call as soon as possible. I am looking forward to working with you and your child during the coming school year.

Sincerely,
Mrs. Leticia Jones
Class 4B
Public School #94

My child and I have read this letter and we will support the rules regarding behavior as best we can.

Signature _____

Child's signature _____

Comments or Conference Request:

Should it become necessary, phone parents about any serious infractions. You can gauge their reaction on the phone and direct them to positive strategies for working the problem through with you and the child. Notes are far more impersonal, and you need to be careful about provoking an unreasonable overreaction.

Communication with parents regarding discipline should not be confined to instances where children are remiss. Rather, make liberal use of certificates of effort and achievement (translated if necessary) for self-control (Figure 5.1). These awards can go home weekly, and parents will appreciate the positive feedback. Catch a child trying to be on his

BEHAVIOR AWARD

_____

has been awarded this certificate

for effort in self-control in the classroom.

Figure 5.1

or her best behavior, award a behavior certificate, and you'll get more mileage out of it from parents and students alike than you will from all the detention notices in the world.

LOOKING FOR CAUSES

The orientation of this chapter has been prevention of discipline problems through careful arrangement of the physical environment, attention to the variables of instruction, collaborative rule making, and classroom meetings.

Another way to prevent discipline problems is by looking for underlying causes and dealing with them before they break out in more serious, attention-seeking symptoms. As I noted earlier, Dreikurs and others (1982) tell us that all behavior is related to goals we are seeking. The primary goals we all seek are _to belong and to feel significant_. A misbehaving child is a discouraged child who, when thwarted from seeking these primary goals, substitutes four mistaken goals: attention, power, revenge, and assumed inadequacy.

The teacher, according to Dreikurs and colleagues, must be a detective and find the mistaken goal, so that children's behavior can be redirected—primarily through encouragement, mutual respect, and understanding—to return to the original goals. The teacher has three clues to go on. The first, the _recognition reflex_, is a child's smile that gives it away when you seek and get permission from the child to guess why he or she is behaving this way: "Could it be that . . .?" The second clue is your visceral reaction to the misbehavior. The third clue is what the child does when told to cease and desist.

Attention

An attention-seeking child irritates or annoys us, and when the child is told to stop, he or she ceases and then resumes or substitutes another attention-getting behavior. Remedies include spending special time with the child, redirecting the behavior, ignoring the behavior, imposing a consequence that is related, respectful, and reasonable, and presenting choices to the child (Nelsen, 1996). A now-retired kindergarten teacher was often heard to tell her block-throwing students, "Make a better choice," and they did. Other terminology is, "Make a different choice," or "Make a choice: either (expected behavior) _____ or (logical consequence) _____ ."

Power

A power-seeking child threatens us and, when told to stop, may passively resist or defy you. Remedies include withdrawing from the situation, cooling off first, problem solving with the child, redirecting the child's power needs, focusing on what you will do instead of what you will make the child do, and scheduling special time with the child (Nelsen, 1996).

Revenge

A revenge-seeking child makes us feel hurt and, when asked to stop, is destructive or hurtful. Remedies include allowing a cooling-off period, engaging in problem solving with the child, giving encouragement, and scheduling special time with the child (Nelsen, 1996).

Assumed Inadequacy

Not surprisingly, a child whose goal is assumed inadequacy makes us feel inadequate, and the child remains passive when confronted. Remedies include making success incremental, training the child in what to do, using encouragement, not giving up, and arranging for special time with the child (Nelsen, 1996).

Nelsen (1996) presents a very clear and concise discussion of the work of Dreikurs and of Glasser. You may want to read more about them either in Nelsen's interpreted version or in the original works listed in the references at the end of the chapter.

This is but one framework for understanding children's underlying motivation to misbehave. You need not accept it fully; in general, however, you will do well to try to see things from the child's point of view. Ask yourself, "Why is the student doing this?" Make some good guesses. Instead of just meting out punishment, which works only in the short haul and builds up long-term resentment in children, stop and think about probable causes or motives. Your hypotheses may be incorrect some of the time, but there is a possibility that some of your theories may be tested out and even proven. You gain much more by canceling out a negative with a positive solution than by doubling the negativity by assessing an immediate penalty.

TWO VIEWS OF CHANGING BEHAVIOR

A prominent psychiatrist and expert on discipline remarked in a speech that if Pavlov had experimented with cats instead of dogs, his behavior reinforcement theories would have been long forgotten. But Pavlov didn't, and behavior modification techniques are much in vogue in schools today. Positive reinforcement and penalties are imposed by teachers to modify behavior extrinsically.

There is an alternative view of effecting change in children's behavior that capital-izes, instead, on children's intrinsic motivation to belong and to feel significant. This view relies on encouragement and logical consequences to effect change. The two viewpoints will be compared and contrasted in this section.

Rewards and Penalties

In most behavior modification systems, after the rules are handed down (or, in some in-stances, established with the children) and then practiced, an intricate system of rewards and penalties is initiated. Canter's work in *assertive discipline* (1980, 1989) is an example of a system based on rewards and penalties. Some of the positive rewards that teachers use for appropriate behavior are shown in the following lists:

Individual	**Whole Class**
certificates	popcorn parties
special activities	field trip
stickers, small gifts	extra P.E. time
food	ice cream party
homework exemption	special cooking activity
verbal praise	verbal praise
Honor Roll	free time

A Note from the Teacher

My emotionally disturbed children find it difficult to be positive toward others in the room (euphemism). I have a soup can decorated with a colorful sleeve for each of them. There are ten kids in the room and at the end of each day, each gets nine tokens to distribute in the cans of those students who have been nice to them or with whom they have gotten along during the day. We tally the tokens at the end of the week, and the Top five MVPs (most valued people) get to use the limited number of study carrels for the following week. Within weeks of starting this, they were able to see the glimmerings of quid pro quo and what goes around, comes around.

D. Gillman

Rewards can be earned individually, in groups, or as a whole class. Designing a record-keeping system is fairly easy; maintaining it is difficult. Teachers make a chart of students' names and use stars or move pushpins or color in the spaces when children earn points. If the record keeping is done by groups at a table, the entire table is listed and points accrue when all the children at the table are doing the right thing. Some teachers run the system by total class and add marbles or popcorn kernels to a jar when everyone is behaving appropriately. A full jar means a popcorn party or special treat. Some teachers announce the number of points or marbles to be earned before each activity begins.

As you can see, this procedure takes time, and you must be consistent and fair in using the system if you choose it. Children will clamor for points and keep you on your toes if you forget. Beware of the management problems! Also, beware of making your children reward junkies who behave only because of the material rewards they will receive. *If discipline is ultimately self-control, you may be acting counterproductively by relying too much on extrinsic motivation. The management of these systems may cause more disruption in your class than the behaviors they were designed to correct in the first place.*

On the flip side of the rewards system are the various penalties that teachers assess for infractions of the rules. When this happens, depending on the system, children gather negative checks, on the board or on a teacher's clipboard, that translate into increasingly more negative consequences. These may include staying in for recess, staying after school, going to the principal, carrying a note home, or missing favorite activities. I recently compiled a list of the more unusual penalties first-year teachers use, and some of the most medieval punishments follow anonymously:

A Note from the Teacher

I keep a cell phone on my desk and have the misbehaving kid call home on the spot.

I add or take away the letters that spell QUIET. If they are all erased, the class gets no free time.

I make the "bad kids" sit in the middle of the circle.

I make everyone put their heads down.

Although punishment may stop the behavior immediately, Nelsen (1996) cautions that over the long term, punishment results in the four Rs: *revenge, resentment, rebellion,* and *retreat.* You may win the battle but lose the war if you base your strategy on punishment. One teacher has changed the omnipresent pocket chart of increasingly negative color-coded tickets to a color progression that stands for positive consequences. She flips the card when the child or group is doing the "right thing." The first color stands for good, flips to great, then to terrific, and last to excellent. Special rewards are given to those who reach excellent. This turnaround of ever-increasing negatives to ever-increasing positives has had a profound effect on the climate of the classroom.

Encouragement and Logical Consequences

Encouragement is offered by Dreikurs and others (1982) as an alternative to praise. While praise is showered upon those who succeed, those who have not yet succeeded need encouragement. Encouraging the small steps on the way to success is as important as completion of the whole task. If a misbehaving child is a discouraged child, as Dreikurs and colleagues assert, then the teacher's goal is not to give false praise that the child knows is not deserved but rather to help each child achieve small victories by encouraging and praising in a positive direction. Teachers need to provide all children, and especially the discouraged ones, with opportunities to experience success. Ways of encouraging children suggested by Dreikurs and veteran teachers include recognizing effort, pointing out useful contributions, sharing with children the improvements you see, finding special jobs that the child can succeed in, having the child share a special interest or talent with the class, asking the child to assist others who need help, displaying the child's work, and showing the child in every way that you believe in him or her. Reimer (1967) offers a list of encouraging words, which include:

> Keep trying. Don't give up.
> You have improved in . . .
> Let's try it together.
> You do a good job of . . .
> You can help me by . . .
> I'm sure you can straighten this out.

A Note from the Teacher

What students really yearn for is some extra attention from the teacher, either academic or personal. I make "private deals" with them, like the opportunity to be a monitor or to spend lunch with the teacher, to assist me with yard duty or be my special teaching assistant. These "disruptive" students often become my greatest success stories.

T. HONG

Just as encouragement is an alternative to praise, logical consequences (Dreikurs, 1992) are an alternative to punishment. While punishment is applied by an outsider, in the logical consequences approach the child experiences the natural or logical consequences of his or her own behavior. What further distinguishes logical consequences from penalties or punishment, according to Nelsen (1996), are the three Rs. Logical consequences are always *related* to the offense, *reasonable*, and *respectful*. A child who writes on the desk cleans it up during recess; a child who fights on the playground sits on the bench for a day or two; a child who spills the paint mops it up. Children are usually given the choice between stopping the misbehavior and accepting the logical consequence. Logical consequences are never humiliating, and they teach children about responsibility and the relationship between actions and consequences. Remember to use the phrase "make a better choice" before you try anything else.

COUNTERACTING MISDEMEANORS

Less is really more in dealing with minor infractions in the classroom. Although you may simply want to react at once, it's best to take a breath, examine any possible causes, and then intervene in the least obtrusive way possible. I caution "least obtrusive" because some reactions to infractions may be more disruptive to the learning process than the original sin. Be sure that students understand their choice of improper behavior, because language, cultural, and socioeconomic differences may create misunderstandings. What follows are some laid-back measures that experienced teachers use to nip minor infractions in the bud.

Overlooking Minor Incidents

If every single infraction received your attention, you would never get any teaching accomplished. Use your judgment, and don't make mountains out of mole hills. We all forget ourselves from time to time, and a margin of error should be allowed. Henkes (1996) has the right idea when Lily the rodent brings an attention-getting purple purse to school in his book, *Lily's Purple Plastic Purse.* Yes, the teacher, Mr. Slinger, takes it away, but he returns it with a note: "Today was a difficult day. Tomorrow will be better."

Nonverbal and Low-Key Interventions

If you want to continue the flow of classroom interaction, practice *overlappingness* and deal with minor infractions nonverbally, if possible, without missing a beat. Some of the more effective low-key techniques that teachers use follow.

The Look.   Establishing eye contact with the offender and staring until the behavior diminishes works for some teachers. Jones (1992) advocates this practice, along with other nonverbal interventions. Remember that cultural norms may disallow the child from looking directly back at you.

Physical Proximity.   Walking toward the offender will usually stop the behavior (Jones, 1992). You may need to move closer to the child and stand nearby. The increasing invasion of the child's space will usually cause him or her to desist. A hand on the desk as you pass is also effective, if moving to the edge of the desk hasn't achieved the desired outcome. You may want to learn more about nonverbal limit setting by reading the work of Jones (1992).

Signals.   Signals can be established ahead of time with individuals. A finger to your cheek tells John you see what he is doing and want him to stop. This helps John save face, because the preestablished signal is private. Signals that work in general are a shake of the head, the raising of the eyebrows, a quick arc of the finger.

Enlisting Cooperation.   When you notice someone starting to act out, you can check the misbehavior by enlisting the child's aid for some small task relevant to the lesson. You might ask the culprit to erase the board or to be an assistant in handing out materials.

Whatever the job, both you and the offender will know why he or she has been chosen, and you still won't miss a beat in your instruction.

Questioning.   Often, by posing a question to the child who has just started to act out, you can halt the behavior before it causes disruption by redirecting his or her attention to the task. Make sure it is a question that can be answered easily, as your goal is not to embarrass the child but to channel his or her attention in a productive way. If you feel the child cannot answer the question, have him or her select someone whose hand is raised to supply the answer.

The Encouraging Moment.   If you catch the offender doing something right or trying to do the right thing among all the "wrong" things, you are better off waiting for that moment to take your chance to turn a child in the direction of success. Strike when the iron is hot and encourage the child. Having gotten your attention, the offender may cease and desist.

"See Me" Cards.   You can duplicate cards that you can unobtrusively place on a child's desk that say something equivalent to "See me" (Figure 5.2). You may also have a place for students to write in why they think they received the card and what a better choice would have been.

Delayed Reaction.   Rather than interrupt the flow of instruction, if the preceding techniques don't work for you, simply and firmly tell the child in question that you want to speak to him or her at the end of the lesson. This invitation to a private conference, only one sentence in length, may in fact cause the child to shape up, negating the need for a long conference. The delayed reaction also gives you a chance to cool off and consider an appropriate response. Nelsen (1996) suggests that this cooling off is most important when you are angry or frustrated and are likely to exacerbate the situation by responding in kind to the child's discouraged behavior. When the infraction involves two students, tell them to write their names on the class meeting agenda and let them cool off as well.

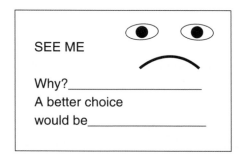

Figure 5.2

DANGEROUS AND DISRUPTIVE BEHAVIORS

These suggestions and techniques have no money-back guarantee that all misbehaviors can be handled without sacrificing instructional time. There will be times (it is hoped not too many) when the misbehavior steps over the line from misdemeanor to classroom felony. These behaviors include fighting, name calling, stealing, destruction of property, constant defiance, refusal to work, and profane language. These serious acts need to be treated differently from the rule-breaking behaviors or the manifestations of mistaken or misdirected goals.

> ### *A Note from the Teacher*
>
> He was cussing and swearing. I tried to ignore the behavior. He pushed me out of the chair and then hit me with it. The student was suspended for three days. During his "vacation" I needed to figure out a way to at least gain some respect. I decided to tell him that I loved him every time he said something nasty. It worked and before long that student was able to converse and ask me for help with his homework.
>
> L. BENNETT

There are no tried-and-true recipes for dealing with these behaviors either, but certain general principles obtain. Except when children are in danger, it is best to deal with serious infractions when you are calmer and better able to act in a rational manner. Keep detailed records (anecdotal) of the child's behavior, with dates, descriptions of behavior, and your response. This is a time to look for causes and seek assistance. Detailed anecdotal records will be helpful when discussing the problem and seeking solutions with school personnel or with parents. It's best to devise some long-range plans or strategies by enlisting the aid of your principal, school or district psychologist or counselor, student study team, special-education resource teacher, and the child's parents. Other, more experienced teachers can help as well, especially those who have encountered the child in earlier grades.

When you suspect that a child will persist in the inappropriate behavior, ask for help early on. By using resource persons available to you at the school or district level, you are demonstrating that you are resourceful, not incapable! After speaking with the principal and the school or district counselor, enlist the aid of the child's parents or guardians. Make your first contacts by phone, and, if you need to, initiate a conference. Use an interpreter on the phone as needed, and make sure one is available during the conference. The parent should already have a great deal of information from your prior contacts. During the conference:

- Make the parent comfortable. Say something positive about the child.
- Describe the inappropriate behavior, using anecdotal data. Watch for overreactions by the parents and head them off.

- Stress to the parent that the child is capable of behaving and has many positive attributes despite his or her negative behavior.
- Elicit data from parents about the child's attitude toward school, the child's behavior at home, how inappropriate behavior is dealt with at home, and what the parents see as possible causes of misbehavior at school.
- Devise a plan together that is grounded in encouragement and logical consequences and does not run counter to cultural norms.
- Follow up and inform parents about the child's progress.

RESPONSES TO AVOID

The hardest part of dealing with discipline problems of the more serious kind is repressing some of the very human responses that serious offenses provoke. If there is ever a time to put on your angel's wings and sit under a halo, it's when a serious offense occurs in your classroom. A calm, cool manner on the part of the teacher will not only disarm the offender but will also soothe the other students, who may be as upset as you are. What follows are various responses to avoid. They have been suggested by experienced teachers who know that it is impossible to avoid all of them. But they try!

> ### A Note from the Teacher
>
> One student continued to misbehave during a lesson so I sent him to the back of the room to stand for a time-out. Unfortunately, the fire extinguisher was at the back of the room and the student, seeking revenge, proceeded to spray the room. I immediately escorted the class out of the sand and dust cloud so we could breathe. Needless to say, that was the last time I ever used time out.
>
> D. CLARK

- *Holding a Grudge.* When the behavior has been dealt with, try to wipe the slate clean and forgive and forget. Begin each day anew. As one teacher phrased it, "Never let the sun go down on your anger."
- *Taking It Personally.* Separate yourself from the situation and realize that the behavior is symptomatic of some disturbance within the child and doesn't necessarily reflect his or her attitude toward you. This may require that you schedule frequent pep talks with yourself.
- *Everyone Suffers.* It simply isn't fair to apply consequences to the entire class, such as no recess or no art project, because a few of your charges are misbehaving. Discriminate between the offenders and the nonoffenders and go on with business as usual.

- *Ejection from the Room/Time Out.* It is illegal in many districts to place children outside the room unsupervised. Were it not, it is still not a good solution. Children will simply fool around in the halls or on the playground. You can be sure they won't stay where you put them. Avoid sending them to another classroom or to the principal except in rare instances. Not only does this burden the other teachers and the principal, but if you exercise this option too frequently, your actions may send a message to your class and to your administrator that you cannot deal with misbehavior. Try to tough it out and deal with problems in your own classroom.
- *Physical Contact.* Although you may be driven to distraction, never grab, pinch, or hit children. They will magnify some of the slightest restraining techniques, and you need to protect yourself. Also, you don't want to model a physical response to the rest of the class, as you are hoping to extinguish this kind of behavior in them.
- *Humiliation.* Included in this category of don'ts are using sarcasm, nagging the child, having the child wear a dunce hat or sit in a corner, or imposing other public embarrassments. Children need to save face, and if you can talk with the child privately, you are denying him or her an audience for further defiance or face-saving entrenchment of the negative behavior.
- *More Work.* Writing sentences 25 times or more or doing extra work may not change the behavior. Rather, it may negatively associate work, which should be intrinsically pleasurable, with punishment.
- *Threats You Can't/Won't Carry Out.* You will lose your credibility if you back down, so avoid this by thinking carefully about consequences before you announce them. Try withdrawing from the situation and establishing a cooling-off period. Find a way out for both of you to win if you are in a stand-off situation. Simply saying, "I am choosing to let that go this time, John, although I expect that you will not be fighting on the playground again" allows you both an easy out, and you are still in control of the situation by making the choice. Or have the child choose between desisting and the logical consequence that pertains.

A FINAL DON'T

Try to relax in regard to discipline and adopt the attitude, "I did the best that I knew how in that situation." If you make an error in judgment, you have the opportunity to recoup your losses the next day. Children are very forgiving and flexible. If you've been too lax, then tighten the discipline the next day. If you've been too harsh, then lighten up. Remember that until a few years ago, teachers had few written guidelines for dealing with discipline problems.

Try not to become obsessed with classroom discipline matters. Doyle (1985) cautions that although discipline is essential, it is not the only component of effective instruction. In fact, if you are too focused on discipline and too concerned about control, you may not risk some of the more active learning and inquiry activities that aren't easy to manage. If you play it safe and opt for a quiet classroom as your highest value, you may be tempted to go the worksheet or lecture route, and education of the child will suffer as a result. This is the biggest *don't* of all.

Worksheet 5.4

Now it is your turn to synthesize all you have read and articulate your own comprehensive plan for discipline. On Worksheet 5.4, Discipline Letter to Parents, make a first attempt at conceptualizing your own system, based on your beliefs about children and your philosophy of discipline. Then use Worksheet 5.2 to apply the criteria for discipline systems to your own discipline plan. You will have time to refine your views over the years.

Trust yourself and your intuition. Your experience, the experiences of colleagues, and the children themselves will help you figure out what works and doesn't work for you.

Reflection Box

In what ways, if any, has the chapter changed my beliefs about discipline?

Questions I Still Have . . .

Reflection Box

What practices actually worked for me in my first year?

FURTHER READING

Burden, P. R. (1995). *Classroom management and discipline: Methods to facilitate cooperation and instruction.* White Plains, NY: Longman.

Canter, L., & Canter, M. (1996). *Succeeding with difficult students: New strategies for reaching your most challenging students.* Santa Monica, CA: Lee Canter & Associates.

Canter, L., & Canter, M. (1996). *Assertive discipline: Positive behavior management for today's classroom.* Santa Monica, CA: Lee Canter & Associates.

Charles, C. M., & Senter, G. (1995). *Elementary classroom management* (2nd ed.). White Plains, NY: Longman.

Curwin, R. L., & Mendler, A. (1988). *Discipline with dignity.* Alexandria, VA: Association for Supervision and Curriculum Development.

Dreikurs, R. (1992). *Discipline without tears* (reprint ed.). New York: Hawthorn Books

Evertson, C. M., Emmer, E. T., Clements, B. S., Sanford, J. P., & Worsham, M. E. (1997). *Classroom management for elementary teachers* (4th ed.). Boston: Allyn & Bacon.

Ginott, H. (1997). *Teacher and child* (reprint ed.). New York: Macmillan.

Glasser, W. (1992). *The quality school: Managing students without coercion* (2nd ed., expanded). New York: HarperCollins.

Kameenui, E. J., & Darch, C. (1995). *Instructional classroom management: A proactive approach to behavior management*. White Plains, NY: Longman.

REFERENCES

Canter, L. (1989). Assertive discipline: More than names on the board and marbles in the jar. *Phi Delta Kappan, 71*(1), 57–61.

Canter, L, & Canter, M. (1980). *Assertive discipline: A take charge approach for today's educator*. Los Angeles: Lee Canter & Associates.

Charles, C. M. (1996). *Building classroom discipline: From models to practice* (6th ed.). White Plains, NY: Longman.

Dewey, J. (1980). *The school and society* (paperback ed.). Carbondale: Southern Illinois University Press.

Doyle, W. (1985). Recent research on classroom management: Implications for teacher preparation. *Journal of Teacher Education, 36*(3), 31–35.

Dreikurs, R., Grunwald, B., & Pepper, F. (1982). *Maintaining sanity in the classroom: Classroom management techniques* (2nd ed.). New York: HarperCollins.

Glasser, W. (1993). *The quality school teacher*. New York: HarperCollins.

Glasser, W. (1986). *Control theory in the classroom*. New York: HarperCollins.

Glasser, W. (1975). *Schools without failure* (paperback ed.). New York: HarperCollins.

Henkes, K. (1996). *Lily's purple plastic purse*. New York: Greenwillow.

Jones, F. (1992). *Positive classroom discipline*. New York: McGraw-Hill.

Kounin, J. (1970). *Discipline and group management in classrooms*. New York: Holt, Rinehart and Winston.

Maslow, A. (1987). *Motivation and personality* (3rd ed.). New York: HarperCollins.

Nelsen, J. (1996). *Positive discipline*. New York: Ballantine Books.

Reimer, C. (1967). Some words of encouragement. In V. Soltz, *Study group leader's manual* (pp. 67–69). Chicago: Alfred Adler Institute.

Sanford, J. P., Emmer, E. T., & Clements, B. S. (1983). Improving classroom management. *Educational Leadership, 40*(7), 56–60.

chapter

6

Diversity and Authentic Assessment

Reflection Box

What I Believe About

    Authentic vs. traditional assessment . . .
    Portfolio assessment . . .
    Authentic diagnosis . . .
    Grouping and cooperative learning . . .
    Adapting instruction for children with special needs . . .
    Teaching second language learners . . .

Now that you've arranged your room, decided on routines, gathered materials, and thought long and hard about discipline, you are ready for the one and only money-back guarantee in this book: *You will have a perfectly successful year if all of your children are cloned from one individual of your choosing.* I can make this offer knowing that sometime in the future, readers of *Your First Year of Teaching and Beyond* might collect on this guarantee, but I feel confident at the moment.

On that first day of school, the individual differences in your class will jump out at you. Gender and physical differences are only the tip of the iceberg. Beneath the surface are children from different socioeconomic strata; children who come from various family configurations; children with special needs, differing interests, and abilities; children with different cultural backgrounds, different languages, different learning styles, and different attitudes toward school. The permutations are endless.

95

In our public demonstration school of 850 children, 10 percent of the population are African Americans, 44 percent Latinos, 4 percent other, including Native Americans, Pacific Islanders, and Asians, and 42 percent are Anglos. Five hundred sixty children are free-lunch recipients, and 290 students are recipients of Aid for Families with Dependent Children (AFDC). Of the students, 36 are identified as gifted, 193 are language minority students, and 120 have an individual education plan (IEP). There is one team-taught total inclusion class—that is, a class of severely disabled children spends the *entire* day integrated into a first grade class, doing *everything* the "regular" first graders do. The special educator and the regular teacher team teach all day long. And a special day class of children with learning disabilities is mainstreamed into a "regular" fourth grade class for part of the day. Some children are homeless or living in group homes, some are on probation. Add to this an average class size of 27.5 in kindergarten, 20 in first and second grades, and 32 in grades 3–6. While the figures in your school may differ, increasingly you will find that diverse classrooms are the rule rather than the exception. You can look at this new population as a daunting challenge or as an opportunity to stretch your skills and abilities in new directions while celebrating the multitude of unique individuals relying on you to guide and assess their progress fairly and on the basis of effective diagnosis of their needs.

Barnes (1985) reports that teachers approach student evaluation (a process that leads to a judgment about quality or merit) with trepidation. They find this particular aspect of teaching difficult because they don't want to hurt students' feelings, they don't feel they know enough about assessment techniques, and they don't know how to factor student effort, as opposed to actual performance, into the grading equation. If *evaluation* is the judgment, then *assessment* can be defined as those measures or indicators the evaluation is based on. Realistically, assessment is an inherent part of teaching. New practices and procedures of *authentic assessment* can go a long way toward helping you focus on assessment as an integral part of the teaching-learning cycle.

This chapter addresses how to diagnose needs and assess progress authentically as well as how to cycle the information back into the instructional process to meet the needs of your diverse students.

A Note from the Teacher

If you are taking over a class midyear, review previous grading practices and assessments before entering grades on report cards. I took over for a teacher two days before report cards were due, so I recorded her grades and her grades alone. Parents started calling the teacher who preceded me to complain about me and the grades I had given their kids. She neglected to own up to her own grades and blamed me for being incompetent. Thankfully, the administration backed me and followed up with all concerned parents.

C. JONES

AUTHENTIC ASSESSMENT AND PORTFOLIOS

Authentic assessments focus on the process and continuum of learning, not just on the outcomes, and they take into consideration many more facets or dimensions of a student's progress than just standardized tests, which measure isolated, discrete skills and assume equal starting points. Authentic assessments are based more on performances—on demonstrations of knowledge, skills, and attitudes. The feedback from authentic assessments helps teachers modify or adapt the instructional process to better meet the needs of the students. Authentic assessments are made by those closest to the process—the teacher, the student, and, often, the parents. The assessments are conducted in the context of what normally transpires in the classroom rather than on exams created by outsiders.

What follows are descriptions of authentic assessment measures that are increasingly being used by teachers for diagnosis and formative evaluation along with required standardized measures. Standardized measures are in the midst of a revolution as well. In California, for example, standardized, objective tests are being redesigned to emphasize performances, experiments, structured investigations, and more open-ended questions and essays.

Portfolio assessment is the term that describes an organizational and management system for collecting evidence to monitor student progress. As defined by Vavrus (1990), a portfolio is a "systematic and organized collection of evidence used by the teacher and student to monitor growth of the student's knowledge, skills, and attitudes in a specific subject area." Items for the portfolio are selected by the teacher, the students, parents, classmates, and even administrators. Portfolios include not only these samples (audio, visual, and print) but also commentary by selectors as they periodically review the contents and assess progress in light of predetermined goals. This reflective aspect empowers children to make decisions and to evaluate their own progress based on established criteria.

Portfolios are shared with parents at conference time and serve as your data when completing report cards along with the more objective measures. Portfolios can be passed on to the next teacher in addition to other records or given to the child to take home at the end of the year. It is tangible evidence of how far the student has progressed. The portfolio is an ongoing diagnostic tool as well.

Viechnicki and colleagues (1993) found that portfolio assessment had a far more positive impact on teachers than the researchers anticipated. Participants in the study of 36 primary teachers reported that their classrooms became more child-centered. Teachers integrated the curriculum, used more cooperative learning and inquiry approaches, strengthened their organizational skills, and became more willing to share portfolio information with colleagues and parents. Teachers reported that they were able to see potential in children that otherwise might have been overlooked They felt motivated and inspired by the fresh outlook portfolio assessment afforded. Students benefited from the emphasis on cooperative learning, interest-focused groups, opportunities to discuss their products with peers and teachers, and the freer atmosphere that enabled them to engage in hands-on activities.

Teachers are beginning to write about their experiences using portfolios. Read all you can about managing portfolios, talk to colleagues, and attend all inservices or seminars on this hot new topic. Some practical resources on portfolio assessment are listed at the end of the chapter. In these references you will find very practical advice about portfolio management. Here are a few key timesaving ideas:

- Manning and Manning (1994) suggest taking time each day to examine a few portfolios with the students so the work doesn't get overwhelming. In this way you can be on a two-week cycle of review.
- You might want to collect everything from one or two children each day. You can sort through the work and decide together what will be included. In this way you have a two-week or monthly cycle of collection, and according to Manning and Manning (1994), this approach will enable you to collect and conference at the same time with these one or two children.
- Use Post-it notes for anecdotal records that you can quickly jot down and add to the folder, attached to a larger reflection sheet for your expanded commentary.
- Artesani (1994) recommends a video portfolio for every student. The class can be videotaped doing oral reports, plays, puppet shows, and other activities. Then copies of the tapes can be edited for the students to keep as part of their individual portfolios.
- Computers can help you organize your writing portfolio if each child uses his or her own disc. The drafts, edited versions, and final products, along with reviews by peers, teacher, and even parents, can all be included on the same disc in the same folder, and easily printed out.
- Parker (1996) suggests that each child have "traffic light" color-coded file folders for organizing their writing portfolios: green for rough drafts, yellow for editing and teacher conferences, and red for final drafts.

The mechanics of portfolio assessment have been simplified by many writers (Batzle, 1992; De Fina, 1996), and a list of references is at the end of the chapter. However, your district guidelines are the first place to look, as many districts set up their own formats and provide inservice instruction for teachers. Some of the authentic assessments and diagnostic measures listed below can in fact become part of the student portfolio.

AUTHENTIC DIAGNOSIS: INTERESTS AND ATTITUDES

The children themselves can provide you with a wealth of information not obtainable elsewhere and give you a baseline for building on the diversity in your classroom. There are a variety of techniques from which you can choose.

Interviews and Inventories

Some teachers take time during the first week to interview each student. While this is very time-consuming, the face-to-face exchange allows you to ask follow-up questions and individualize the questions to suit the child. You might prepare ahead of time a list of questions from which you draw as appropriate. Some sample questions follow; however, you might want to devise your own on Worksheet 6.1, Interview and Interest Inventory, before you read further.

Worksheet 6.1

- What language or languages are spoken in your home?
- What is your favorite family tradition?
- What do you like to do after school?
- What kinds of books do you like to read?
- What would be the best birthday present?
- What are your favorite television programs? How much time do you spend watching television each day?
- What are your favorite possessions?
- What subjects do you like best in school?
- What are your least favorite subjects?
- What sports interest you? Do you play on any teams?
- What faraway place would you like to visit?
- Do you have a pet? Tell me about it (them).
- What question would you like to ask me about the coming year?
- Describe yourself in three words.
- Tell me one thing you are very good at.
- What new thing would you like to learn to do?
- What do you want to be when you grow up?

Questions can be written out, copied, and distributed to the children, who fill in the answers themselves or who interview a classmate and then fill in the answers. While this saves a great deal of teacher time, it does not allow the teacher to follow up and give children individual attention. An alternative is to give children a long list of choices such as the following and have them use appropriate symbols to mark the ones they are good at and those they want to get better at, or the ones they like versus those they don't like at all.

reading aloud	going to the library
reading silently	singing
writing stories, poems	dancing
speaking in front of the class	video games
math problems	riding a bicycle
art projects	cooking
science experiments	drawing
board games	computer work
puzzles	listening to music
P.E. games	team sports

Use Worksheet 6.2, Pupil Self-Evaluation, to design a student-completed evaluation measure for the appropriate grade level. You can use pictures for primary children.

Attitude inventories are filled out by children and usually involve a scaled response from high to low. You might use numbers for your scale or even a progression of faces

Worksheet 6.2

from happy to sad. Some sample questions follow. Use Worksheet 6.3, Attitude Inventory, to construct your own student attitude measure for the appropriate grade level.

Worksheet
6.3

How do you feel about reading in a group?
How do you feel when someone reads to you?
How do you feel about coming to school each day?
How do you feel about math?
How do you feel about science?
How do you feel about social studies?
How do you feel about art?
How do you feel about listening to music?
How do you feel about going out for recess?
How do you feel about watching television?
How do you feel about speaking in front of the class?
How do you feel about being a class monitor?
How do you feel about writing stories?
How do you feel about working in cooperative groups?
How do you feel about working on computers?

Autobiographies

Older children can write autobiographies as an early assignment. These will be quite revealing and may answer questions you never even thought to ask.

AUTHENTIC DIAGNOSIS: INSTRUCTION

In order to diagnose individual differences related to instruction, you have to know what your students are expected to learn during the school year. Chapter 2 described the process of establishing instructional goals and planning the curriculum. After you've gleaned some idea of what it is you need to teach during the coming year, find out from others what diagnostic tools are currently available in the school. Gather information about diagnostic testing resources and procedures at staff and inservice meetings, from colleagues (principal, resource teachers, school psychologist, teachers at your grade level), and from teacher's manuals, which often include relevant diagnostic tests and directions for their administration and interpretation. It would be a shameful waste of your time if, for example, you designed math diagnostic tests only to discover, at the opening of the school year, a whole resource room full of graded math placement tests keyed to the texts in use in the school!

Diagnosis of needs, abilities, interests, and attitudes should be a primary activity, starting on the first day of school and continuing during the first weeks. You'll need to make early determinations, through broad diagnosis, for grouping purposes or for totally individualizing the instructional program for particular children.

In addition to your broad diagnosis, you'll want to make finer and finer distinctions among children's interests and abilities as the year progresses to ensure that you are really meeting their educational, social, and emotional needs. Your diagnosis should be ongoing, and keeping very accurate records will enable you to concentrate on specific curriculum areas that need more individualization. The general or broad diagnosis you plan for the beginning of school should be "underwhelming" for you. You'll want to use existing records, where possible, and some diagnostic measures that are easy to administer and score, short and relevant to the educational objectives, nonthreatening to the student, and administered in a group rather than individually in order to save time.

While you may not use all the following data-gathering methods for each child, these methods suggested by experienced teachers give you a variety of choices when attempting to diagnose strengths and weaknesses and respond to individual differences in your classroom. Diagnostic assessments can be added to the student portfolios as well.

Teacher-Made Assessment/Diagnostic Tests

Once you have decided on your curriculum, you can make up your own easy-to-score diagnostic tests for basic skills and concepts to determine the appropriate starting level for instruction or to assess progress. Speak to other teachers on your grade level. They may have diagnostic and review tests on file that are appropriate for your class as well.

Conferences with Other Teachers

Sometimes teachers relieve their frustrations by discussing individual students in front of a whole group of colleagues. It's not the best policy, but it happens. Don't overreact and clam up totally about children who baffle or frustrate you. Instead, seek out the child's previous year's teacher and present your concerns and questions. You may find that (1) your perceptions are confirmed, and/or (2) the teacher saves you from reinventing the wheel by sharing how he or she was able to reach the child last year. Be prepared for a third possibility—that you get no greater insight from this individual. Then seek out the appropriate resource person at the school, whether the special-education resource teacher, the principal, or the school psychologist.

Conferences with Parents

Parents can provide you with a great deal of information that will be helpful in assessing children's strengths and pinpointing weaknesses. You don't have to wait until formal parent conference times. If you need data that parents can best provide, call them and let them know that you need their help in providing the best possible learning situation for their child. One kindergarten teacher interviews each child's parent(s) during the first few weeks of school using a nonthreatening set of questions that elicit information about the child's strengths and weaknesses, interests, fears, food preferences, childhood traumas, developmental milestones, health problems, and other concerns. Arrange for an interpreter if you need one. These extra efforts on the part of the teacher result in greater parental cooperation and support and provide the teacher with a wealth of insightful information not otherwise available.

The Cumulative Record

The cumulative record provides continuous and succinct documentation of the child's educational experiences in elementary school through high school. It is used extensively by teachers and other school personnel, since it follows a child from grade to grade and is an easy reference for many aspects of the child's growth and development, academic performance, and behavior in school. Information usually found in a cumulative record includes identifying data (photographs in some districts); family and home data; records of social, emotional, and academic experiences by year; health records; test data; interests, abilities, attitudes; and a listing of all schools attended.

Teachers disagree about whether or not to look at cumulative records before they have made their own judgments about a child. Those against doing so are afraid they will prejudge and perhaps prejudice themselves against a student. In addition, the argument goes, the child may have changed over the summer, or previous teachers may have had different expectations than your own. On the plus side, looking at cumulative records early in the school year will enable you to detect any physical, social, emotional, or academic problems and plan for them. Forewarned is forearmed, this argument goes, and the information you gather about individuals will give you a preview of the group as a whole and facilitate your planning. There are even teachers at the extreme who first look at the cumulative records at the end of the year when they fill them out themselves.

Decide for yourself whether to examine your students' records ahead of time or wait until you've made your own analysis based on other data sources. Not to look at all leaves open the possibility that you are missing something important that may not be revealed through other means.

Profiles or Proficiency Records

In some school districts continuums or proficiency profiles (lists of expected outcomes) direct the instructional program, especially in math, language, and reading. Even before school starts, examining these profiles will give you some idea of which children in your current class mastered the prerequisite skills last year. Although you can't ignore the vacation "forgetting" factor, at least if a child mastered the material last year, there's a chance that, after some review, he or she will quickly "get it" again. If many children lack the same skill, you'll begin to form natural groupings. If all are missing a skill, you can begin to think of some large-group review lessons. These proficiency lists and checklists can also become a permanent part of the student portfolio.

Use Worksheet 6.4, Portfolio Contents, to check off those items that would be appropriate to collect in children's portfolios. As you learn more about the portfolio process, you can list additional items that might be appropriate for the level you teach.

If you use some of the data-gathering techniques mentioned above, you will have a fairly well rounded, general picture of each child. But still you may not know where he or she stands in relation to the three Rs. You can obtain this information using common diagnostic instruments such as the Informal Reading Inventory, teacher-made math diagnostic tests, a writing sample, and, for younger children, a drawing or scribbling sample. You need not be a certified educational psychologist to use these instruments or data-gathering techniques. They are not clinical evaluation tools but, rather, the methods classroom teachers actually use, given the numbers of children and the time constraints.

Worksheet
6.4

Teachers report that they do some preassessment or diagnostic testing using these instruments and techniques beginning on the first day and continuing on during the first few weeks of school.

That is not to say that more sophisticated measures should never be used, but that they should be administered by a trained reading, math, or learning disabilities specialist following your own broad diagnosis and after you have gone through the appropriate referral process.

Reading Level

Teaching reading presents a special difficulty for elementary teachers because student reading ability varies so widely in any one classroom. Some of the techniques you can use to compile a reading profile have already been mentioned. These include interviews with the child, observation, an attitude inventory (with a focus on attitude toward various aspects of reading), an interest inventory (with questions geared to determine reading interests), profiles or competency checklists, and standardized scores for reading in the cumulative record card. Other sources of data include those presented below.

Textbook Diagnostic Tests.   Several publishers include very comprehensive directions and test materials for assessing how proficiently children read. Check your teacher's manuals to see if survey tests, placement tests, or checklist materials are included.

Last Year's Book Title(s)/Reading Level.   Information regarding the book(s) completed along with the approximate grade-level equivalent is often passed from teacher to teacher in some formal reading record, as part of the cumulative record, or as part of the student portfolio. Note that the trend toward individual titles and literary readers may necessitate looking instead at student-generated lists of book titles read last year.

Cloze Tests.   Cloze tests require children to use context clues to fill in blank spaces in text material. They can be administered quickly and to more than one child at a time in the upper grades. They are quite reliable in matching the child to the reading material, and they are quite simple to construct.

1. Select passages of about 250 words in length, one from each level of reading difficulty or reader you might anticipate as appropriate.
2. Keep the first and last sentence intact and then delete every fifth word, making sure that the space you leave when retyping gives no clue to word length. There should be at least 50 blanks in all.
3. Run these off as copies, and beginning with the lowest level, ask children to fill in the missing words. The exact words must be supplied.
4. Keep administering passages at progressively more advanced reading levels until the child can supply about 40 to 60 percent of the exact words. A child who can do this has reached his or her instructional level. Below 40 percent is the frustration level and the rest of the material in that basal reader would probably be too difficult. Generally, 60 percent and above is the child's independent reading level.

Informal Reading Inventory.   The informal reading inventory (IRI) is an individual test and, therefore, it is more time-consuming to administer. However, it provides a reliability check for the cloze test. Detailed instructions and materials for using the test are provided as part of most reading series. Basic instructions follow for constructing your own informal reading inventory.

1. Select passages of approximately 100 to 200 words from readers at a variety of levels (two passages from each level). One will be used for oral reading, the other for silent reading.
2. Develop at least four comprehension questions for each of the passages, making sure to include questions at both the factual and the inferential level.
3. Retype the passages and arrange them sequentially in transparent sleeves in a looseleaf notebook and have your own copies of the passages duplicated. Write the questions on index cards, one card for each passage.
4. Develop a marking sheet that enables you to list the child's name and record his or her scores in both word recognition and comprehension.
5. When administering the test, establish rapport with the child. Start with a passage at least two levels below the child's probable instructional level. Have the child read the first passage of the level you choose orally and then ask him or her the four questions. Next, have the child read the second passage silently and then ask him or her the four questions. When the child is reading orally, count the number of significant miscues (omissions, mispronunciations, insertions, or substitutions). Mark these on your own copies of the passages. You may also want to note less significant repetitions and hesitations.
6. If four questions are asked, score the IRI as follows :

	Word Recognition	*Comprehension*
Independent reading	99 percent	90 percent
Instructional level	95 percent	75 percent
Frustration level	Below 90 percent	Below 50 percent

7. Keep administering successively more difficult sets of passages until the child has reached the instructional level.
8. Directions for administering the IRI will vary slightly. Consult any basic text in elementary reading methods for a more detailed description of the informal reading inventory and the more specific analytical tool, the running record, which enables teachers to diagnose specific miscues.

Trial and Error.   This technique is loosely based on the IRI and presumes that if a child can answer about 75 percent of questions posed about the text and can decode using a variety of cuing systems, then the child can probably read that particular book. The child may be asked to read from two or three levels of texts and then is placed for a trial run in the text he or she appears to read and comprehend best. Since these decisions are tentative, it's probably best, in the event of a close call, to place the child in the easier text and then move him or her up if further evidence and observation warrant it.

Ongoing Assessment in Reading.   You can learn a great deal by observing children and talking with them about their reading interests. Despite all your efforts to determine the appropriate level of instruction, you will need to use your observational skills to monitor each child in reading and to determine when changes need to be made. Listening to each child read aloud to you from time to time is a good idea. Carefully monitoring participation and responses during reading-related activities is also effective. Discussions with small groups or with individuals about current reading interests will give you additional information. Asking children to keep records of library books read will be a further account of their motivation to read on their own.

Prepare to be flexible and relaxed about your reading diagnostic procedures because your own experience and intuition will quickly let you know if a child is reading at his or her instructional level, way above it, or way below it.

Math Diagnosis

Several of the techniques for assessing reading are comparable for mathematics. These include use of proficiency lists or competency profiles, use of standardized test scores from the cumulative record card, use of book level from the previous year, diagnostic instruments included with the math series, and teacher-made diagnostic tests.

In some ways, teacher-made diagnostic tests are easier to construct for mathematics. For each concept and skill area to be tested, you simply need to make up copies with progressively more difficult examples relating to the skill or concept. With some detective work, you can probably find these already made up as review tests or practice sheets in math workbooks. Again, so you don't have to reinvent the wheel, ask your colleagues if they have math diagnostic tests to share with you. The advantage to these teacher-made diagnostic tests or ones found in the math series is that they can be administered on successive days to all the children at once. Children can exchange papers and mark them on the spot before you check them to find and record error patterns.

English Language Proficiency

In order to assess second language ability, Diaz-Rico and Weed (1995) suggest observation, use of an interpreter, and interviews with previous teachers and parents as good alternatives to standardized English proficiency and placement tests and scales. Since this topic is so important, sources of additional information are included at the end of the chapter.

Written Language Skills

A writing sample is the easiest way to assess a variety of written language skills all at once. While you want to avoid "What I Did on My (Summer) Vacation" as a topic, children can write a story for you early on so you can assess grammar, punctuation, spelling, handwriting, usage, and, above all, thinking skills. By carefully noting errors common to a number of students, you'll have your first language lessons planned in no time.

AUTHENTIC ASSESSMENT: SOCIAL AND EMOTIONAL GROWTH

Student interaction in the classroom and on the playground enables you to spot any potential social, emotional, or behavioral problems. Keep anecdotal records on children you suspect may need support in these affective areas. While you need not immediately call in a counselor, psychologist, or special educator, you want to be watchful and professional about beginning a trail of observational data that may be useful later when you meet with parents, counselors, and others.

CYCLING ASSESSMENT INFORMATION INTO INSTRUCTION

Once you have gathered information about children's competencies and needs, you will have to decide how to handle the individual differences that come to light. You will probably discover, for any particular curriculum area, that there are instructional needs common to everyone, instructional needs common to some, and instructional needs common to only a few. Here is a simple rule of thumb: If everyone needs it, teach it to everyone at the same time in whole-class instruction. If some need it, establish ongoing and ad hoc instructional groups. If only a few need it, individualize instruction.

Grouping in Reading

A wide range of individual differences will be evident in reading. The children will not sort themselves out neatly into three equally divided guided reading groups. You will have to make some hard decisions, in light of your diagnostic results, about the number of groups you can handle at any one time. Current practice suggests that instead of basing your groupings solely on reading achievement, you form ad hoc groups as well on the basis of interests and specific skill needs. Keep your groups flexible and take into account, when making your group placement decisions, not only your diagnostic results but also all the information you have regarding that child's needs and interests.

The trend in some of the literature-based reading series is toward one level of book for the entire class, regardless of the range of reading ability, so that all children will be exposed to the same literary content. If your reading series prescribes the same text for everyone and you find children unable to read it, use techniques that are suggested in the manuals. A few methods of meeting individual needs include having students listen to the story on tape or as the teacher reads it; using choral reading; having children read to and question one another in pairs; encouraging echoic reading, in which children repeat what is read by the teacher; and working in small-group teacher-directed sessions.

Grouping in Math

You will run into the same problem of wide range in math ability. While many teachers conduct whole-class instruction in math, they accept the fact that not everyone will "get it." Because there tends to be only one math text per grade level, you do not have the option of placing a child in a "lower" book unless you want him or her to repeat exactly last year's work. It may work to your advantage to be very flexible in math groupings and combine and recombine groups according to the topic. For example, if you are teaching adding unlike fractions, diagnose the children according to all the subskills involved. You might need to introduce the topic and then conduct three small ad hoc groups: adding like fractions, finding lowest common denominators, and adding unlike fractions. While the whole class can be introduced to the topic at the same time, you can conduct these mini-groups to make sure that children who do not have prerequisite skills can build on what they know and learn any new skills required for the task at hand.

Cooperative Learning Groups

Cooperative learning groups are heterogeneous groupings of children who work together to complete tasks while learning social skills that foster cooperation. Dishon and O'Leary (1984) cite five principles underlying cooperative learning:

- Cooperative groups promote distributed leadership, meaning that each member of the group is an active participant.
- Cooperative groups are heterogeneous with regard to ability, social class, gender, ethnicity, and so forth. In other words, cooperative learning groups reflect the real world.
- Cooperative groups foster interdependence among the members through the sharing of materials, group accountability, or individual contributions to one final product.
- Children practice social skills (saying "please" and "thank you," using names, making eye contact) in cooperative groups.
- In cooperative learning groups children are encouraged to solve their problems without teacher intervention.

Teachers who use this strategy begin with groups of three or four students. Some of the tasks students can work on in cooperative groups are preparing research reports, with each member an expert on a part of the topic; editing stories; creating a crossword puzzle; deciphering a word search; making a collage; playing matching games; conducting experiments; brainstorming; making a chart or graph; and solving a puzzle. In fact, many class-room activities lend themselves to cooperative learning. Cooperative learning is one of the strategies that can facilitate learning in a multicultural classroom (Coelho, 1994) and can help second language learners (Johns & Espinoza, 1992). In the cooperative group they can learn from one another while participating in ways that address their strengths. The value of the strategy for addressing diversity of all kinds cannot be overemphasized. Vermette (1998), in reviewing the research on cooperative learning, cites among others the following outcomes:

- increased gender tolerance and friendship
- increased understanding of children with disabilities
- increased self-esteem
- increased problem solving and academic achievement
- increased comfort with computer technology

Specific techniques for combining cooperative learning strategies and technology are found in sources cited in Chapter 3 (Hayes, 1997; McDonald, 1989).

ADAPTING INSTRUCTION FOR STUDENTS WITH SPECIAL NEEDS

While totally individualized instruction has fallen from teacher favor because of the sheer amount of work involved, some children in your class will need some individualized attention because they have specialized needs. Extreme individual differences may point to a need for further testing. If you suspect that a child is either gifted or learning disabled, notify your principal, who will outline to you the legal requirements for arranging more intensive testing by the school psychologist, nurse, or special-education resource teacher.

Although you may already be overwhelmed by the number of children in your class-room who fall within the norm, direct your attention to those who need your extra effort. Here are some simple suggestions for children who may require differentiated assignments because they are at the extreme ends of your classroom continuum. Seek out your resource teacher for suggestions that can be tailored to the child you have in mind.

The Low Achiever

Think back to something that was difficult for you to learn. For me it was skiing. While all of my fellow beginners soon graduated to the next level and the next class, I repeated the A level class four times. Each time I go skiing, I start from scratch. But I am determined, and I will ski. It may take more time, and I may not be an Olympian, but ski I will. You will have students in your class who need extra support in one or a few areas. Here are a few adaptations you can make to help those who need that extra support:

- Allow time for plenty of practice.
- Conduct student-teacher conferences.
- Break assignments into smaller, manageable parts.
- Use peer tutors.

- Underline important directions and key words.
- Give shorter assignments, and allow more time for completion.
- Tape-record stories; use other media.
- Give immediate feedback and lots of encouragement.
- Use large type in worksheets.
- Keep directions simple; write them out; give them orally.
- Provide many opportunities for success.
- Provide low-reading-level, high-interest reading material geared to the child's interests.
- Use visuals and manipulative materials when available.
- Use cooperative learning strategies.
- Recognize that children have different learning styles and demonstrate their intelligence in diverse ways. Gardner (1993) describes seven intelligences (linguistic, musical, logical-mathematical, spatial, kinesthetic, interpersonal, and intrapersonal).
- Watch for fatigue and boredom.

Higher-Achieving Students

It is also probable that you will have students in your class who excel in one or more areas, especially if you subscribe to the theory of multiple intelligences. For these students, more of the same is not acceptable. You will want to consider adaptations for these students as well:

- Encourage the reading of library books and, perhaps, totally individualize the reading and/or math program.
- Encourage individual research, construction, or science projects geared to the students' abilities and interests, for extra credit.
- Provide opportunities to sit in on special-unit activities in other classes.
- Introduce new and challenging materials, games, puzzles, and brain teasers.
- Have individual conferences with the student to guide her or his progress.
- Encourage creative responses to stories (e.g., writing to the author, creating a play script from the story, devising a puppet show).

THE SECOND LANGUAGE LEARNER

El que sabe dos lenguas, vale por dos.
(He who knows two languages, is worth double.)

Increasingly, you will find in your classroom children with limited English proficiency (LEP). They are also currently referred to as language minority students or second language learners. Teachers who themselves have had the experience of learning a foreign language and also have an understanding of students' cultural backgrounds are better equipped to sustain high academic performance on the part of language minority students (Diaz-Rico & Weed, 1995).

A Note from the Teacher

I began in the bilingual program thinking that it was just another one of those "government programs." As luck would have it, my first grade class was almost evenly divided—half had been in the program and half had not. I found that those who had been in the program previously were more advanced than those who hadn't. The disparity between the two groups was so noticeable that I was sold on the value of bilingual programs in our district. If there was some way that people who are opposed to bilingual education could experience what I have, they would have a different perspective on the value of the program.

V. ZUPANCICH

While many of these children may be enrolled in bilingual classes taught by bilingual teachers, others will be in regular classes due to the shortage of bilingual teachers or because the district philosophy promotes either English immersion or sheltered English classes. Sheltered English, also referred to as specially designed academic instruction in English (SDAIE), presents grade-level-appropriate content in English (Peregoy & Boyle, 1996) using special techniques. In these latter two programs (immersion and SDAIE), the language of instruction is English. The regular teacher, often untrained in effective practices for working with language minority children, has to be prepared to teach the language minority children in the regular classroom. Johns and Espinoza (1992) point out that the teachers are better prepared to facilitate the language development of second language learners than they realize, because teachers often have an intuitive knowledge of the language learning process, which, when combined with a belief that students can learn, is a good start. Johns and Espinoza (1992), Peregoy and Boyle (1996), and Diaz-Rico and Weed (1995) suggest the following teaching methods to promote English language development in a natural and meaning-centered approach:

- direct experiences, such as field trips
- simulations of real-life experiences and role-playing

- previewing and reviewing of material schematically (e.g., semantic mapping, webbing)
- substantial oral language opportunities
- uninterrupted, silent, sustained reading
- student journals and learning logs
- technology and audiovisual materials, such as films and photographs
- cooperative learning and collaborative projects
- thematic units that integrate curriculum areas
- maps, graphs, props, concrete materials
- dramatization with gestures and facial expressions
- modeling of clear and understandable language
- encouragement of children to maintain their primary language

A Note from the Teacher

I have become the overhead queen. When I teach, I use an overhead projector for each paper I give the students. They can see exactly what I want. It helps the visual learner and supports the LEP students. Start a notebook for each subject, organize the overheads in plastic sleeves, and use them from year to year.

K. UNGERER

There is a great deal being written about effective methods for working with language minority children. Schall (1995), in profiling four teachers who work with LEP students, adds some other very creative ideas, such as:

- subjecting the LEP and native-English-speaking children to a language foreign to both groups to build empathy;
- making personal history and culture books;
- recruiting native language volunteers or peer mentors;
- labeling objects in the room in all languages represented; and
- having LEP students keep picture journals.

Most of the strategies involve excellent teaching practices: hands-on, active learning in a child-centered environment. Read all you can about specific methods for working with second language learners. References are listed at the end of the chapter.

A FINAL TIP

You will need to seek out all the diagnostic and documentation shortcuts you can so that you can have some fun, not to mention sleep, during your first year of teaching. The importance of carefully gearing your program to children's actual needs, interests, and abilities and of keeping accurate documentation cannot be overstated. During your first year, give yourself permission to use shortcuts to make this time-consuming and uncomfortable aspect of teaching as professional and pleasant as possible.

Reflection Box

In what ways, if any, has the chapter changed my beliefs?

Questions I Still Have . . .

Reflection Box

What practices actually worked for me in my first year?

FURTHER READING

Banks, J., & Banks, C. (1996). *Multicultural education: Issues and perspectives* (3rd ed.). Needham Heights, MA: Allyn & Bacon.

Brandt, R. (Ed.). (1992). Using performance assessment (theme issue). *Educational Leadership, 49*(8).

Davidman, L., & Davidman, P. T. (1996). *Teaching with a multicultural perspective: A practical guide* (2nd ed.). White Plains, NY: Longman.

Lessow-Hurley, J. (1995). *The foundations of dual language instruction.* (2nd ed.). White Plains, NY: Longman.

Lewis, R. B., & Doorlag, D. H. (1995). *Teaching students in the mainstream.* Englewood Cliffs, NJ: Prentice Hall.

McRobbie, J. (1992). *Using portfolios to assess student performance.* San Francisco: Far West Laboratories for Educational Research and Development.

Nieto, S. (1996). *Affirming diversity: The sociopolitical context of multicultural education.* (2nd ed.). White Plains, NY: Longman.

Parke, B. (1989). *The gifted child in the regular classroom.* Boston: Allyn & Bacon.

Pasch, M., Langer, G., Gardner, T., Starko, A., & Moody, C. (1995). *Teaching as decision making* (2nd ed.). White Plains, NY: Longman.

Perrone, V. (Ed.). (1991). *Expanding student assessment.* Alexandria, VA: Association for Supervision and Curriculum Development.

Wang, M. C., & Walberg, H. J. (1985). *Adapting instruction for individual differences.* Berkeley, CA: McCutchan.

REFERENCES

Artesani, M. (1994). Video portfolio assessment. *Teaching PreK–8, 24*(7), 18.

Barnes, S. (1985). A study of classroom pupil evaluation: The missing link in teacher education. *Journal of Teacher Education, 36*(4), 46–49.

Batzle, J. (1992). *Portfolio assessment and evaluation.* Cypress, CA: Creative Teaching Press.

Coelho, E. (1994). *Learning together in a multicultural classroom.* Markham, Ontario: Pippin Publishing.

De Fina, A. (1996). *Portfolio assessment: Getting started.* New York: Scholastic Books.

Diaz-Rico, L., & Weed, K. (1995). *The crosscultural, language and academic development handbook.* Boston: Allyn & Bacon.

Dishon, D., & O'Leary, P. (1994). *A guidebook for cooperative learning: A technique for creating more effective schools.* (2nd ed.). Holmes Beach, FL: Learning Publications.

Gardner, H. (1993). *Frames of mind* (reprint ed.). New York: Basic Books.

Hayes, D. (1997). *Managing technology in the classroom.* Huntington Beach, CA: Teacher Created Materials.

Johns, K., & Espinoza, C. (1992). *Mainstreaming language minority children in reading and writing.* Bloomington, IN: Phi Delta Kappa Educational Foundation.

McDonald, P. (1989). *Cooperation at the computer: A handbook for using software with cooperative learning groups.* Des Plaines, IL: Looking Glass Products.

Manning, M., & Manning, G. (1994). Managing literacy portfolios. *Teaching PreK–8, 24*(7), 84–86.

Parker, C. (1996). Stop and go writing. *Teaching PreK-8, 27*(1), 74.

Peregoy, S., & Boyle, O. (1996). *Reading, writing, & learning in ESL: A resource book for PreK–8 teachers* (2nd ed.). White Plains, NY: Longman.

Schall, J. (1955). Unbeatable ways to reach your LEP students. *Teaching PreK-8, 27*(1), 54–59.

Vavrus, L. (1990). Put portfolios to the test. *Instructor, 100*(1), 48–53.

Vermette, P. (1998). *Making cooperative learning work.* Upper Saddle River, NJ: Prentice Hall.

Viechnicki, K., Barbour, N., Shaklee, B., Rohrer, J., & Ambrose, R. (1993). The impact of portfolio assessment on teacher classroom activities. *Journal of Teacher Education, 44*(5), 371–377.

7

Working with Parents

Reflection Box

What I Believe About

The parent-teacher partnership . . .
Opportunities for parent-teacher communication . . .
Conducting parent conferences . . .
Parent support at school . . .
Parent support at home . . .

If maintaining discipline ranks as the number one anxiety of beginning teachers, establishing and maintaining effective relationships with parents runs a close second. I am not surprised.

Never do I see so few hands raised in my class as when I ask for volunteers to role-play a teacher dealing with an irate parent who storms the classroom demanding to know why his son has been told it is all right for him to be anything he wants to be, even a ballet dancer. Before this situation is played out, all student teachers contribute ideas for the "teacher" to use. When all is said, yelled, and done, the "teacher" has, much to everyone's amazement, dealt with the situation calmly and effectively. This isn't surprising to me either. After all, working with children's parents—whether they be irate, docile, or anywhere in between—requires the same good communication skills and common sense we try to practice all the time when we interact with others. Given Swap's (1993) reminder that increasingly, children live in one-parent homes and that one in four children has one or more stepparents, the term *parents* or *parent* will be used in this chapter for all primary

---

A Note from the Teacher

It was my fourth year of teaching and my first year in a
university demonstration school. The parents were
connected to the university as students or professors. One
nonreader in my sixth grade class had a father who taught
in my doctoral program. "Well, your sixth grader still can't
read," I told this parent with trepidation. I was ready to
accept all the blame for the previous six years. After all, this
father could be my professor next semester! "We don't
want to push him. Don't worry. He'll either learn to read or
he won't." He did, and is now a dad with two readers of his
own.

E. KRONOWITZ

---

caregivers, whether they be biological, adoptive, or foster, stepparents, relatives, guardians, or even probation officers.

Although a person's primary reason for entering the teaching profession is a desire to
work with children, the children's parents play a fundamental role in the educational
process. They are entrusting their precious progeny to you, and it is the best situation for
you and for the children when parents are on your side, working along with you and not at
cross-purposes. The easiest way to engender confidence and respect is to convey in word
and deed that you will treat their child and every child in your care with the same concern
and respect as you would your very own. This attitude will bring out the best that parents
have to give. Engaging the cooperation of the parents in the school setting can provide
you with a critical mass of support during the rough times and enable you to provide the
greatest possible benefit to children.

COMMUNICATING WITH PARENTS

Having a majority of the parents in your corner cheering you on is well worth the time
and effort you take cultivating their support. Parents, when informed about your goals,
program, and procedures, can serve as a valuable backup system—allies away from
school. Moreover, they have a right to be informed about their child's progress—both
strengths and weaknesses. Parental insight and experience will bring to light additional information that may help you better serve the needs of the child. Parents and teachers usually share equally the time children spend awake each day. If the right hand at home
knows what the left hand is doing at school and vice versa, how much better both will be
at understanding and doing the best for the child. Parents and teachers have a lot to offer
and teach one another about a particular child, and a positive communication channel
opened early and used regularly throughout the year is the key to success. *Anticipate that
every communication with parents, whether oral or written, may need interpretation or
translation for those parents whose primary language is not English.*

Many teachers begin their outreach programs even before the school bell rings. One method is to telephone each parent during the week preceding the start of the school year. The call is brief. It includes an introduction, an expression of sincere appreciation for being able to work with the child during the coming year, an invitation to an Open House, and an offer to answer any questions the parent(s) might have. Be brief in making the point—"I care; I want to work with you for your child's sake; let's get together." Few parents could resist this sincere expression of welcome. If telephoning is not your style, you can achieve the same effect with a typed, duplicated letter to each parent before the school year starts. Make sure to have letters translated into the languages represented in your classroom population and send them appropriately to limited-English-speaking parents.

Dear Parent or Guardian,

My name is _____ and I will be your child's third-grade teacher this year. I'm writing to let you know that I look forward to working with you so that your child can develop new talents, skills, and abilities throughout the year. I really love teaching and will do everything I can to make this year a very successful and happy one for your child.

Our Open House is scheduled for the first week in October. If you have any questions or would like to talk with me before then about any of your concerns, please call the school (phone no.). I will return your call as soon as possible. I look forward to meeting you in person.

Ms. Dawn Lewis
Rockville School

While this before-school outreach seems like a great deal of work, weigh the benefits against the costs—time and some effort. One primary teacher sets up an interview with each parent during the first weeks of school. The interviews enable her to gather firsthand information about the children's strengths, abilities, health status, developmental milestones, and other factors. Above all, the very act of scheduling the interviews conveys that the teacher really cares about the children and respects their parents.

You may also want to communicate with children prior to the start of school. Your outreach to them will create an air of expectation and excitement about the first day of school and will convey a special message to parents that you care enough about their youngsters to send possibly the very first letter the child has ever received. You can mail an introductory letter to each child and ask that he or she respond to you by either filling in an attached interest inventory or by drawing a picture and bringing it to class on the first day of school.

First-Day Communications

Your communication with parents should probably begin on the very first day if you haven't started sooner. Parents who are included from the first day may have fewer questions, comply more readily with requests for assistance, and generally feel better about you and the school. The content of first-day notes varies according to how much information is provided by the school itself. Parent handbooks are distributed in some schools; school newsletters often go home the first day as well. Check to see what information is conveyed on a schoolwide basis and tailor your letter accordingly. By the way, your letters can be prepared ahead of time and filed from year to year with only updates added. Some things you may want to mention in your first-day letter are:

- self-introduction
- an expression of willingness to work together
- an early invitation to Open House
- other times to call you, along with the school phone number
- supplies the child needs to bring to school each day
- lunch and milk money collection procedures and snack
- classroom rules and procedures
- homework policy

It is always a good idea to include at the bottom of the letter a cutoff "receipt" that is signed by the parent and returned to you. This will provide evidence to all concerned that the information was conveyed. In other chapters of this text there are sample notes to parents requesting classroom supplies or materials and specifying the discipline policy. Use your judgment about how many different notes to send home to parents at the very beginning of the school year, but however you choose to convey the information, be sure to have the information translated for parents whose primary language is not English. You may choose to organize the information into a classroom handbook with the following headings:

- Self-Introduction
- Handbook Overview
- Benefits of Parent-Teacher Partnership
- Classroom Rules
- Homework Policy
- Supplies Child Needs
- Collection of Money for Lunch and Milk/Snacks
- Discarded Materials That Can Be Used in the Classroom
- Open House/Report Cards/Conference Schedule
- Ways of Reaching Teacher
- Overview of Subject Matter and Skills Your Child Will Learn

You can write this during the summer, keep it on file from year to year, and know that you are off to a good start with parents by providing basic yet needed information. Keep your letters/notes/handbooks short and to the point and avoid using any jargon. The more you convey in writing, the less you will have to review at Open House or in individual conferences with parents. Time spent at the outset is time saved later on. Use newsletters (these can be written by older children on the computer) to keep parents apprised of field trips, fiestas, or plays to which they will be invited, materials needed for an art project, and other information. A once-a-month parent update, in translation as needed, is a good idea.

Open House

As the first few weeks roll by, you'll find yourself with a list of 10 things you forgot to mention in your initial letter home and 20 items you would like parents to collect for future art projects. This realization often coincides with a time-honored tradition in schools known as Open House or Back-to-School night. Generally, after welcoming speeches by the principal and P.T.A. (Parent-Teacher Association) president (with an encouragement to join), parents scatter to the various classrooms, accompanied often, but not always, by their children. This may be your first opportunity to meet a majority of the parents and make a pitch for cooperation.

Teachers feel it is vital to establish a time during the Open House when parents stop milling and wandering around the room and assemble for a brief program. Open Houses should not degenerate into individual parent-teacher conferences. They should be an opportunity to have parents walk around the room, look at children's folders, and even sit in their child's seat. But if you become distracted by one parent, the others will get bored and leave. Make it clear in your invitation to Open House that when the parents arrive in your classroom, following the welcoming speeches (with translation if needed), they can, for example, follow this schedule:

8:00–8:20 P.M.	Sign the guest book
	Walk around the room
	Look at texts, materials, children's portfolios
	Play with the computers, etc.
8:20–8:30 P.M.	Program begins
8:30–8:45 P.M.	Questions and answers

When your program begins, you might want to consider covering the following topics:

- discipline
- homework policy
- curriculum and highlights of the year
- reporting, grading, conferencing
- letting parents know your door is always open

Some creative ways of presenting this information include:

- slides of a typical school day from start to finish
- skits put on by the children showing how they do certain things
- demonstration lessons
- simple explanations
- handouts with any of the above

As for handouts at this time, you may have already used your allotment of these in preparing before-school and first-day written communications to parents. Be reasonable. If time permits, present the information orally, and simply have an outline so visitors can follow along. Be sure that all of the information is conveyed to all parents, since atten-

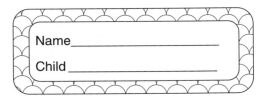

Figure 7.1

dance at Open Houses in some schools may be well below 50 percent. Here are specific suggestions for your first Open House.

Refreshments.   Set up a table with crackers and cheese and some vegetables. Food helps create a warm social atmosphere. Note that in some cultures it is traditional to bring food to functions. Some parents may feel better about attending if they can contribute something, no matter how small. You might extend an invitation, for example, to bring a piece of fruit to cut up and add to a big fruit salad.

Children's Work.   Have representative samples of each child's work displayed around the room and have each child's portfolio (described in Chapter 6) along with a name card on the desk.

Name Tags.   Provide name tags for parents instead of making well-reasoned assumptions about who belongs to whom, which may turn out to be mistakes. Have a space for the names of both parent and child (Figure 7.1).

Schedule.   Write the daily schedule on the board so parents can actually see what the children do all day long.

Body Tracings.   Some teachers have students trace their bodies on butcher paper, color them with tempera paint, cut them out double, stuff and staple them, dress them in clothing brought from home, and prop them up on their chairs.

Sample Texts and Materials.   Have sample texts and materials out for display. Children enjoy showing their books to their parents and showing off a special science kit, math lab, computer program, or video disc.

Questions on Cards.   At the door when parents sign in, you might provide index cards and encourage parents to print their questions on the cards and leave them in a specified box. This will spare parents the embarrassment of asking what they may consider a "dumb" question and encourage those who would totally clam up to open up anonymously. Collect the cards before your program starts, answer the most frequently asked questions on the spot, and announce your intention to deal with the others in newsletters.

Student Guides.   You can make Open House into a learning experience for the children if you prepare them as tour guides, pointing out the classroom landmarks and high points.

One teacher has a guide of the day, every day, whose responsibility it is to greet and show visitors around the room.

Use Worksheet 7.1, Communicating with Parents Time Line, to check off whether you've conveyed the necessary "beginning of school" information to parents and the time frame you intend to use.

Worksheet 7.1

Ongoing Communication

While there is a wealth of information to convey to parents, you can probably handle all of it in one fell swoop with a handbook preceded by a short before-school telephone call and smashing Open House slide show. But would that this were enough! It isn't, in truth, because these strategies deal only with classroom generalities. Communication with parents about their individual child's progress is another aspect of the communication linkage between parents and teacher. Parents need and want to know the general picture, but the specifics of their child's situation are even more important. The following channels are open for more specialized interaction with parents.

Telephone.   This is the quickest and easiest way to talk with a parent about a child's difficulties academically, socially, or emotionally. It's also a good, quick tool for setting up a conference. Finally, don't forget to telephone to let parents know that a child has gained a special recognition or has been progressing steadily since your last conference. Two calls after school each day will give you a three-week cycle of contact with every parent in your room, should you choose this communication medium and both you and the parents have telephone access. You will need a translator to interpret phone messages for parents who speak a different language or feel more at ease in their primary language.

Notes.   Notes serve the same purposes as telephone calls, although the wait time for a response is greater and you'll have to attach a "return receipt" to make sure the note was delivered at all. If you want to be sure the notes get there, mail them. Be careful about the content of the notes you send. Make sure that parents who tend to overreact are given any "bad news" in a positive context. Stress that the child is capable but for some reason isn't performing up to his or her potential. Stress your willingness to plan a solution to the problem together with the parents because you know things can improve. Ask for a face-to-face meeting to address your concerns. Enough said. Don't go into great detail in a note or express negative sentiments. Cool off first. Notes written in haste may come back to haunt you and may cause literal and figurative backlash in the child's home.

Complimentary notes should be frequent and also shared with the pupil before they are sent home. These need not be mailed, as the pupil recipient of such commendations will most likely deliver them Express, Special Delivery, postage paid.

Awards.   Awards (see Figure 7.2) for a variety of academic and social behaviors can be made up beforehand, translated into the child's primary language if needed, and simply filled in as the occasion arises. Parents will be as delighted to receive these as the

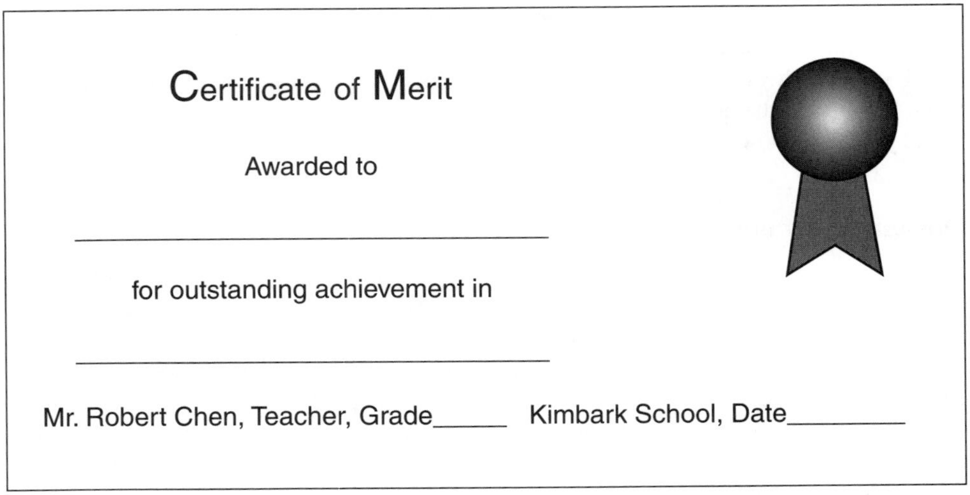

C**ertificate of** M**erit**

Awarded to

_____

for outstanding achievement in

_____

Mr. Robert Chen, Teacher, Grade_____   Kimbark School, Date_____

Figure 7.2

children will be, and any cute design will do, especially if it reflects a favorite "fad" of the time.

Serendipitous Meetings

You will also be able to briefly update parents on children's progress when they arrive to deliver or pick up their children, attend a parent-teacher group function, or come to see a play or performance in the classroom. These encounters will be necessarily brief, but you can convey in a minute or so a word of encouragement or a positive report on progress. It may also be the time to register a need to see the parent again, although it will seem curious to the parent that a serendipitous meeting led to an invitation to confer, as opposed to a well-thought-out, purposely initiated telephone call or note. Remember, parents don't like to hear bad news while shopping for melons in the supermarket or waiting in line at the bank. If seeing a parent outside of school reminds you that you should discuss concerns with this particular parent, make a mental note to contact him or her at a later time. If you can't say something pleasant about the child (who generally is standing right there), save your concerns for a later time, and at a chance meeting simply say, "Hi" and head for the parking lot, making a note to call Mr. or Ms. ——— the next chance you get.

Walking Report Cards

The concept of walking report cards was originated at Sunset View School in Provo, Utah (Cammack & Ives 1997). Parents are invited to school to shadow their children as they go through the day. They sit right beside them, and the day is structured so that parents can get a close-up and personal view of what their children do. While the authors describe a school where all class parents participate, in most classrooms you would have to limit your walking report cards to individual cases, with arrangements made ahead of time so parents could take off time from work.

The Parent-Teacher Conference

In most schools the parent-teacher conference is a semiannual event that coincides with report cards, but additional conferences with parents should be scheduled as needed. The dual goals of such a conference are the exchange of information about an individual child and the formulation of cooperative strategies to deal with any problems.

Prior to the Conference. Here are some suggestions to reflect on when preparing for your conferences:

- Confirm the date, time, and place with the parent.
- Arrange for an interpreter if needed.
- Examine the child's portfolio and have your marking book and any anecdotal records accessible.
- Make a list of points to cover. These should encompass strengths and areas needing improvement at the academic, social, and behavioral level. One teacher suggests thinking ahead of time of three adjectives that really characterize the child. These should be realistic and, it is hoped, positive attributes. Parents won't be surprised, as they probably make the same observations at home as you do at school. Three or four major points are enough for one conference session. Don't overdo it, or you may overwhelm the parent.
- Inform parents ahead of time about the purposes of the conference.
- Have them bring to the conference a list of questions or concerns.
- Establish a waiting area for early arrivals to maintain confidentiality during the conference in progress.
- Dress professionally in an outfit that will not intimidate.
- Prepare a comfortable face-to-face seating area. Make sure the chairs are adult-size—even if you have to raid an upper-grade classroom or the teacher's lounge. A six-foot parent sitting in a first grader's chair will have trouble communicating if his knees are crunched up into his chest.
- Sitting side by side at a table with all of the documentation in front of you is a preferred seating arrangement.

If possible, start the conference by meeting the parent at the door. Have a space available for coats and umbrellas. Be as gracious a host/hostess as you would in your own home. Thank the parent(s) for coming and lead them to the conferencing area. MacDonald (1991) suggests that parent anxiety and any adversarial feelings can be overcome by engaging the parent in small talk at the outset before you launch into more substantive conversation. Start out on a positive note and find something good to say about the child.

The Conference Itself.   During the conference your job will be data gathering, information giving, and analysis and synthesis of the data in order to come to mutually agreed-upon solutions to any problems. This is basically a six-step process:

1. Provide data.
2. Seek information.
3. Listen actively to parents.
4. Synthesize their suggestions with your own.
5. Devise a plan of action.
6. Arrange for follow-up call or meeting.

The data you provide will be comprised of objective data (test scores, academic performance in class) and observational data (behavior in the classroom, social interaction with other children, effort, cooperation, etc.). The data parents provide may include the child's

* talents and abilities
* overall health, fears, and areas of concern to parents
* interests, hobbies, and sports involvement
* attitude toward school
* peer relationships at home
* responsibilities at home
* homework habits
* responses to rules and regulations at home

You can elicit this information as it is relevant through sensitive questioning. Be sure to reflect back both the content and feelings expressed by the parent (s). Be honest yet tactful, and avoid the use of jargon. Charles and Senter (1995) caution that this isn't the time to show off your impressive vocabulary in complex sentences filled with education alphabet soup, better known as acronyms like GATE, SDAIE, and IEP.

A Word About "Good" Kids.   Parents of children who are progressing well in all aspects of their school life want to hear positive comments and should be allotted the same amount of time as parents of the challenging child. Help parents of the "too perfect" children find ways to loosen them up and to encourage greater self-expression. Also, extreme passivity or withdrawal is not any more appropriate than acting-out behavior and should be treated as an area of concern by you and the parents.

Closure.   A good time to end a conference is when either the purposes have been met or you sense that the goals will not be met during the allotted time. At the conclusion of the conference:

* Summarize the major points.
* Clarify what action will be taken, if any.

- Set a date for a follow-up note or conference.
- See the parents to the door.
- Express your sincere thanks for their attendance.
- Make notes about the conference as soon as the parents leave.
- Take a breather before you start talking to the next set of parents.

Schedule conferences with this breathing time in mind. After the conference you may want to send a brief note to each parent, again thanking them for attending and listing the major points covered. This can be a form letter as well.

Some Questions to Consider

Should a Child Attend a Parent-Teacher Conference?   On the negative side, having a child present may subject him or her to humiliation when parents overreact to some unfavorable bit of information. Sometimes children are punished or threatened on the spot by overzealous parents or by parents who want to show you that they are taking what you say seriously.

On the positive side, if your communication with parent(s) and child has been frequent and ongoing, the child who attends the conference won't be in for any surprises. Children also may want to glow with pride in front of their parents when you compliment them on their achievements. Use your best judgment and take direction from school norms. If at some point during the conference you feel a need for private communication, have an activity set up in a far corner of the room and encourage the child to work there. If children must attend conferences because of child-care problems and you plan on excluding them, have an activity set up in the room for them too. Whether children are present at the conference or not, there is always the possibility of retribution at home. Be sensitive to how you present unfavorable reviews. Work with the parents toward positive solutions and make sure the conference ends on an optimistic note.

Should a Teacher Take Notes During the Conference?   Note taking is distracting and can be threatening to parents, who may clam up if they feel their thoughts and feelings will be recorded. Just listen, direct your complete attention to the parent, and you'll remember the important points to jot down in your postconference breather. What you forget was probably forgettable anyway.

How Can You Make Parents Whose Cultural Background and Primary Language Differ from Your Own Feel Comfortable?   Swap (1993) discusses the discomfort and displacement parents who have a cultural background different from the school's population may feel. Find out as much as you can, as early as you can, about the cultural backgrounds of the children in your class and the languages spoken at home. Make sure you have an interpreter present at all conferences and inform the parent in that parent's primary language (through an interpreter, if necessary) that an interpreter will be at the conference to help both of you. Invite the parent to bring someone with them—a relative, a friend, but preferably other than the child or an older sibling—if the school or district either cannot provide an interpreter or they prefer someone they know. Ensure that transportation needs of the parents are met, and try to coordinate conference times with siblings' teachers so that parents need make only one trip to school.

Throughout the school year, encourage all children and their parents to share special customs, holidays, music, crafts, and food from their cultures. Pinpoint on a world map the homelands represented. Everyone will gain a more global perspective this way. Ask veteran teachers familiar with the diversity in your school to alert you to any special considerations you should be aware of when talking with parents who are culturally different from you. Try in large and small ways to increase your own knowledge of the culture and especially the language. Greeting any person with even a few words in his or her primary language builds bonds and shows that you care.

During the conference, listen, show respect, and focus on the child and his or her attributes and abilities. Be aware of parents' body language, and take your cues accordingly. If you make a mistake, simply apologize sincerely. Keep in mind that parents are dealing with someone who is culturally different too! Use Worksheet 7.2, Parent-Teacher Conferencing, to prepare for your upcoming parent-teacher meetings.

Worksheet
7.2

PARENTS AT SCHOOL

Parents are natural teachers. They provide the foundation in the first five years for future learning. Many parents, albeit unsystematically, successfully teach basic motor, language, social, and academic skills to their children. This preparation prior to kindergarten is what enables primary teachers to do their job. After five years of preschool instruction by involved parents, the children come to school on that very first day scrubbed, eager to learn, and ready for the next steps. That first day of school marks a rite of passage not only for children but also for parents. While children are beginning their formal instruction, the parents are decreasing or even ceasing in many cases their informal instruction, leaving the job to those they perceive as more experienced and more capable. They step into the background and relegate to themselves the role of homework overseer. If, however, we reject the notion that schools alone educate children, we accept the premise that there is tremendous potential for harnessing the skills and energy of willing parents throughout the elementary school years. Parents can continue to teach beyond the preschool years with a little bit of help from you.

Parents as Resource Persons

Parents can serve as resource persons in the classroom, sharing their knowledge, skills, and life experiences, or simply sharing artifacts, slides, appropriate videos, computer programs, and so forth. All you have to do is ask. Children also feel proud of their parents when parents arrive to do a demonstration or talk about their jobs. Below is a sample letter you can send to parents of children in your classroom. Naturally, you will have a greater pool to draw from if this is done on a schoolwide basis:

> Dear Parents:
>
> In order to help me provide a rich and exciting program for children, I am compiling a directory of parents who are willing to share their talents and/or resources. Please take some time to fill in the following questionnaire.
>
> Please check any resources below that you would be willing to share or lend to the class. Return this questionnaire with your child. Thank you so much for your willingness to help.
>
> Sincerely,
> Mrs. Rosa Chavez
> Oak Street School

Worksheets
7.3A, 7.3B

Because you may want to duplicate the questionnaire as is, it is included as Worksheet 7.3A, Parents as Resources, and Worksheet 7.3B (the same, in Spanish) in the Appendix.

Class Parents.   Parents can be encouraged to participate in classroom life in other ways as well. Two very special roles for parents are class parents and class volunteers. Class parents (in the old days called class mothers) serve as liaisons between the teacher and the other parents in arranging celebrations, carpooling for field trips, organizing fund-raising for a special excursion, and other activities. They are usually the ones who have the time during the day to go on the trips and the willingness in the evening to make calls to mobilize the others. You can recruit your class parents at the Open House, after fully describing the responsibilities of the position.

Parent Volunteer Corps.   Parents can also be invited to become classroom volunteers. The volunteers should be scheduled for certain days, to avoid having too many adults in the room at any given time. If you have ten shifts, Mondays through Fridays, mornings and afternoons, you can have an army of help deployed evenly throughout the week. Have parents sign up at Open House for slots during the week, making sure that no more than two volunteers are in the room at any one time. Have a sign-up sheet at a designated place in the room along with the posted volunteer schedule. Provide each volunteer with a folder of directions, a seating chart, class rules, basic schedule, and any other relevant information about the classroom. It's always nice to thank volunteers monthly with a letter or certificate and even a buffet lunch hosted by you in the classroom. Some duties for volunteers include:

- marking papers
- filing
- preparing art materials
- helping children cook or do artwork
- putting up bulletin boards
- helping individual children as the parents feel able
- supervising center activities
- reading with individual children for reinforcement
- preparing snacks
- taking dictation from children, binding children's stories into books

Try to find a time to have a volunteer orientation. If this is not possible, spell out in the directions in parents' folders that it is very important to maintain a neutral attitude toward their own child and to work as unobtrusively as possible within the classroom structure, the routine, and the discipline system.

PARENTS AS TEACHERS AT HOME

Traditionally, parents have been asked to supervise homework—that is, schoolwork done in the home. There are several problems inherent in this role as homework overseer. First of all, the parent may not know how to do the work. Second, after a whole day of homemaking or work outside the home, parents may not want to take on yet another job. I know one parent who, forgoing sleep and an early morning jog, gets up at 6:00 A.M. to drill math facts before school. The third inherent problem is that parents may be driven to nagging, threatening, and denying privileges, all of which will ultimately damage the parent-child relationship.

This dilemma is real, and parents are caught between wanting to support the homework policy and, for a variety of reasons, failing at the task. To make their job as teachers easier, I can offer both short-term and longer-term solutions.

Short-Term Solutions

Try to give homework assignments that reinforce previously learned material or that simply provide additional practice. In other words, make sure students are capable of doing the work without parental intervention. Make sure homework assignments are not tedious and lengthy. Why give 100 addition facts on one worksheet if 15 will provide satisfactory practice? Try to tie homework activities into home activities so the parents are not threatened by material they don't understand. Here are examples:

- Write down everything you had for dinner and then categorize the menu on a diagram of the food pyramid.
- Write a one-page review of a television program you watch tonight.
- Take a can of soup from the cupboard. Alphabetize all the ingredients.
- Look up plumbers in the Yellow Pages. Find the three nearest your home.

- Find 20 things in your house that are cubes.
- Take one of your family's favorite recipes. Triple it.
- Write out clear instructions for making a peanut butter and jelly sandwich.
- Plan a menu for dinner. Look up food prices in the local newspaper ads and work out a budget for under $15.
- Keep a graph of the temperatures in the city for two weeks using the local newspaper.
- Prepare a two-minute oral report on a current news item after listening to the news on television or selecting an article from the local paper.

Long-Term Solutions

Parents ultimately can be most effective as home paraprofessionals by reinforcing school learning with the kinds of experiences unavailable at school and by motivating children's natural propensity for learning. This needs to be accomplished so as not to overburden the parent. Lightening the school's load at the expense of the parent is going to backfire. You can become a parent educator by showing parents how to facilitate their child's education through natural, everyday activities that are ongoing in the home.

Parents need first to be clued into the many possibilities for home learning, and then they can take the ball and run with it. You can demonstrate how this is done through written materials or informal meetings with parents. A good activity for a parent is to take a child on a trip to the supermarket. It provides the following opportunities for the youngster to practice skills in:

- estimating total cost
- multiplying and dividing
- reading signs, labels, boxes
- comparative pricing
- recognizing shapes, textures, colors
- learning about different fruits and vegetables
- making change, counting
- learning about nutrition education (looking for additives)
- classifying items in the basket according to common attributes

If parents have a basic idea of the skills needed by their children and are given sufficient training by you in how to incorporate practice of those skills into everyday situations, then you have really created a partnership of learning.

In addition, you can duplicate the suggestions on Worksheet 7.4A, Helping Your Child at Home, or its Spanish-language version, Worksheet 7.4B, for parents. These activities are easy to do and require no teaching experience. They are educational and promote positive interaction between parents and children.

Worksheets 7.4A, 7.4B

A FINAL FLOURISH

Parents, like all of us, need to feel significant, and when invited to participate with you in their child's education, they will jump at the chance. They simply need encouragement to do so. They can participate in big ways, in small ways, in many ways. They are more intimidated by you than you are frightened of them. Extend a hand to them. It will make a difference to you, to them, and to their kids.

Reflection Box

In what ways, if any, has the chapter changed my beliefs?

Questions I Still Have . . .

Reflection Box

What practices actually worked for me in my first year?

FURTHER READING

Brandt, R. (Ed.). (1989). Strengthening partnerships with parents and community (special issue). *Educational Leadership, 47*(2).

Dodge, J. (1995). Making parents your homework partners. *Instructor, 105*(2), 74–77.

Epstein, J. L. (Guest ed.). (1991). Parental involvement (special issue). *Phi Delta Kappan, 72*(5).

Flaxman, E., & Inger, M. (1992). Parents and schooling in the 1990s. *Principal, 72*(2), 16–18.

Jones, L. T. (1991). *Strategies for involving parents in their children's education.* Bloomington, IN: Phi Delta Kappa (Educational Foundation).

Moore, E. (1991). Improving schools through parental involvement. *Principal, 71*(1), 17, 19–20.

Robinson, S. (1997). Parent conference tips. *Teaching PreK–8, 28*(1), 78.

REFERENCES

Cammack, C., & Ives, D. (1997). Walking report cards. *Teaching PreK–8, 28*(1), 68–71.

Charles, C. M., & Senter, G. W. (1995). *Elementary classroom management* (2nd ed.). White Plains, NY: Longman.

MacDonald, R. E. (1991). *A handbook of basic skills and strategies for beginning teachers: Facing the challenge of teaching in today's schools.* White Plains, NY: Longman.

Swap, S. M. (1993). *Developing home-school partnerships: From concepts to practice.* New York: Teachers College Press.

8

Working with School Personnel

Reflection Box

What I Believe About

Getting to know my school and surrounding community . . .
Working with my principal . . .
Working with other teachers . . .
Working with paraprofessionals and paid aides . . .
Preparing for substitute teachers . . .

A school is a community within a community, and if we, like children, have a primary need to belong and gain acceptance, then adapting to these two nested communities will be one of the first personal challenges of the first year. As the new kid on the block, you will need to orient yourself to the physical environment, get to know the key players, and learn the ropes. You will need to scout the community at large so you can feel more comfortable in your home away from home and, most important, establish productive, positive, professional relationships with your administrators, colleagues, aides, substitute teachers, secretaries, and custodial engineers.

YOUR SCHOOL

When you arrive at your school, you will have to find your way to the rest rooms, discover where the custodian hangs out, and go through channels to get your window shades fixed. These are the where, who, and how questions that any teacher faces in a new school setting.

Key Locations

Most schools have campus maps, and you need to ask for one even before school starts. If none is available, take out a piece of paper and start your own survey. Key locations include:

- rest rooms for you
- rest rooms for your students
- water fountains
- the teacher's lounge/refrigerator
- the custodian's space
- the cafeteria
- the resource room
- the computer lab
- the gym
- the library
- the nurse's office
- the audiovisual equipment room
- textbook storage closets
- the assembly room
- the supply room
- the school office
- telephones
- the principal's office
- the school counselor's office
- the mailboxes
- the workroom (laminator, copy machine)
- the school bus depot
- your spot for class lineup
- your spot for emergency lineup
- a place to park your car
- and, of course, your classroom!

Those of you in urban settings need to scope out a parking area that is not in a tow-away zone or negotiate your way to the school from the nearest mass transit stop.

Key People

From time to time you will be seeking the advice of other professionals in the school. First, you need to obtain a faculty and staff roster. Annotate the list as you sit in faculty meetings so you can quickly learn their names and the roles each person performs at the school. Make notes to connect names and faces, and write down any particular skills or talents that come to light. In addition to the principal, the office staff, and custodian, you'll want to find out what other specialists are available to you and the days they serve your school. While you may not find all these lifesavers at your site, services they perform can generally be solicited from your district office on request:

- school nurse or health aide
- community worker

- special-education resource teacher
- psychologist or school counselor
- bilingual resource teacher
- reading specialist
- language and speech specialist
- library aide
- technology resource person
- school secretary
- custodian

A Note from the Teacher

During the workdays before school begins, seek out other teachers and take the initiative to introduce yourself. You will need the support they have to offer later, and they will appreciate your support as well. The first bit of advice an experienced teacher gave me when I started was to get to know the secretary and custodian. They are the two people who will get you everything that you are going to need, so treat them well.

B. MONROE

Get to know the key players at the district office, in the audiovisual center, and also in the resource center. They are all there to serve you so that you can better serve children. Don't be shy; you will reap great benefits from just walking in and introducing yourself. Attend school board meetings from time to time and become familiar with the community leaders and the issues they wrestle with each month.

Key How-to-Do-Its

Now that you can find your way around and can greet by name the key people you will be working with, you are ready to discover how things really get done at your site. Schools are big bureaucracies, and you need to learn the norms and operating procedures as soon as possible. Some districts provide new teachers with a general policy manual. Buy a loose-leaf book and begin to collect all of the policy and procedure documents that cross your desk. Classify them under larger headings and use dividers. Have blank sheets in each section for your own annotated notes. Prepare a list of unanswered questions and get answers to them as soon as possible. Some of these procedural questions might include the following:

- How do I refer a child for special testing?
- What do I do first if I suspect child abuse?
- How do I get into the school on weekends?

- How does the laminating (die press, bookbinding, copy) machine work?
- How do I sign up to use the multiuse or assembly room?
- How do I order media and technology?
- How many times will the principal visit me, and will I have notice?
- How do I get more desks (books, materials, pencils, etc.)?
- How do I get repairs done in the room?
- What do I do when a child gets sick?

Worksheet
8.1

Questions beget questions, and the answers to these and to all other procedural queries should be made a permanent part of your own policy manual. Use Worksheet 8.1, Procedural and Policy Questions, to record the answers as you discover them. There is space for additional questions and answers.

SCOUTING YOUR SCHOOL COMMUNITY

You may or may not live in the same community as your school. If you live in the community surrounding the school, the good news is that you will have a better sense of where your students come from and the types of homes they go to after school. The bad news is that you will run into them in the supermarket or almost anytime you just happen to dash out of the house in your grubby clothes, not expecting to see anyone.

There are three reasons to know something about the surrounding community. First, you want to know as much about your students' lives as possible to better meet their needs. If you have a sense of the quality of life outside of school, you will know how to sustain it, supplement it, or enrich it in the classroom. Second, you need to inform yourself about the recreational, social, cultural, and educational services available outside of the school so you can encourage children and their parents, especially those new to the community, to seek them out and make use of them. Finally, the surrounding community is a source of field trips and free materials gathered from local establishments.

If you live outside of the school community, it is important for you to take a car trip or walking tour around the neighborhood. Look at the condition of the houses and apartments, look for recreation places, playing fields, libraries. Find out about after-school opportunities you can lead children to, such as Scouts, baseball leagues, soccer, tutorial programs, latch-key programs, and summer programs. Find out about health care clinics and other social service agencies. You may have homeless children in your class. Find out where food is available through churches, synagogues, and private agencies. Parents may ask you about social services because not many schools have a community worker, although some do.

Subscribe to or simply buy a few issues of the local newspaper to orient yourself to the community. You can pass on to the children and their parents information you find about artistic and dramatic performances, puppet shows, and recreational opportunities in the local paper. You will also get a sense of the social health of the community by reading the newspaper. You can seek out school personnel who live or have worked for a long time in the community. Frequent the local shops and get to know the merchants. Introduce yourself as a teacher in the local school. Also, talk with children about what they do in the community and share these ideas with other members of the class and their families.

WORKING WITH YOUR PRINCIPAL

You may have been taught to remember the spelling of the word *principal* by an elementary school teacher who told you that the princi**pal** is your pal. You may not have believed it then and you may not believe it now; however, while you and your principal may not become fast friends, to have a successful first year you will need to establish an open, honest, and professional relationship with your principal. You are at least 50 percent responsible for establishing a productive relationship with your principal, and you are 100 percent responsible for meeting the expectations that your principal has for you.

Professionalism

You need to present yourself as a prepared professional who is positive and enthusiastic about the challenges of the first year. You can demonstrate this overtly through your dress and demeanor. Smiling beats complaining, and any first-week difficulties such as over-crowding or too few chairs should be viewed as problems to be solved rather than as tragedies to lament every time you run into your administrator. When requesting modification or changes of any sort, provide an instructional rationale. For example, if you want the piano removed from the room, explain that you need the space for class meetings.

Punctuality rates very high with administrators. This means being on time to school, to meetings, and in turning in any reports or rosters. Maintain an attractive, orderly, and clean room environment at all times. Your room speaks for your program, especially during a quick walk-through by the principal, so make sure the room reflects the enriched program and motivating activities you are promoting with children.

A Note from the Teacher

Being in a foul mood one day I sent four kids to the principal for minor infractions. After school I was called in and given valuable guidance: When you send a student out of the room, you are seen as having less power. Not sending students to the office also keeps principals happy because you are not decorating their office with students.

K. UNGERER

Use great discretion before you send a child to the office for discipline. As a beginning teacher, you want to convey the impression of competence, although you won't be feeling it all the time. Though common in some schools, the practice of using the principal's office for punishment can be an indicator to the administrator that you can't handle the children. On the other hand, don't hesitate to talk to your principal about challenging students and to send them to the office when the need arises.

Communication

Keep your principal informed at all times so that surprises are kept to a minimum. Discuss problem children with your principal well before the parents storm his or her office. Principals don't like to be left in the dark, and they especially don't want to utter or even think the words, "I don't know anything about this." Check over with the principal all the letters or communications you send home to parents. The principal may notice any policy discrepancies and spare you the embarrassment of having to retract what you have written.

Keep your principal informed ahead of time about impending field trips, conferences, inservices, or absences so that substitute coverage can be arranged in plenty of time. Share with your principal all the wonderful activities you are engaging in with children: Give notice of guest speakers and special presentations; send samples of children's work, class newspapers, art projects, and any goodies the children have cooked or baked to the office from time to time; and invite the principal to special happenings, such as plays or debates in your classroom. The children can write the invitations and escort the principal to a good vantage point upon arrival.

Overdoing It

The first-year teacher will be expected by the principal to assume all the responsibilities of any other teacher. If all teachers have yard duty, then you will too. If all teachers have bus duty, then you will too. Since you will be required to attend all staff meetings and many additional new-teacher inservice meetings, don't volunteer too much your first year. Although you are expected to carry your fair share of required duties and responsibilities, veteran teachers warn new teachers to volunteer only for small jobs and to learn to say no politely when asked.

A Note from the Teacher

Public school districts feed your ego to encourage more individual production. When they ask for more work, they often accompany it with a title: mentor, facilitator, representative, coordinator. When asked to volunteer your time, it must be weighed against family responsibilities, stress levels, and time available. (The title is no replacement for sanity.)

K. UNGERER

Many experienced teachers serve on an inordinate number of intraschool committees as well as district committees, but they caution you in your first year to guard your time carefully and use any extra time you discover in your day for your own self-sustenance. However, you still may find that you are asked to serve on a number of committees. Your first year is the time to concentrate on your classroom and teaching. Practice tactful ways to decline invitations for extracurricular involvement.

WORKING WITH OTHER TEACHERS

Perhaps your greatest allies in your school setting are your colleagues. Some of you will have formal mentors; others will be assigned buddies, but all of you will have peers who are ready and willing to help you. They were in your shoes once, and, like most of us, they remember vividly that first year of teaching. They are your first line of assistance, support, and problem solving.

It is important to be friendly to everyone and resist getting pulled into cliques. Try to steer clear of any colleagues you identify as whiners, complainers, or gossips, but remain friendly just the same. There are wonderful opportunities on a staff for collegiality and even deep and lasting friendship. Don't stay in your room during lunch or recess breaks. It is much more important to socialize and break out of the isolation of the classroom. You need that cup of coffee or glass of juice, not only to refresh yourself but also to feel a sense of belonging.

Through this ongoing contact with your colleagues, find out who the experts are in various curriculum areas. Who is adept at computer-based instruction? Who knows every art project ever invented? Who plays guitar and may be willing to swap music for art? To whom can you go for science or social studies ideas? You'll discover this information informally. Don't be shy. Ask for help. Teachers have a poorly deserved reputation for keeping ideas to themselves. In my experience, this simply isn't true. The veterans will most likely be flattered if you ask for ideas or help. One or two colleagues may take you under their wings. Swallow your pride and seek them out. This book could not have been written except for the willingness of experienced teachers to share what they have learned, either by trial and error themselves or from others.

WORKING WITH PARAPROFESSIONALS AND PAID AIDES

Elation and anxiety may set in at the same time when you discover that your school is funded to employ paraprofessionals or paid aides. You are delighted that you will have the additional help, but also you are likely to feel a little nervous about what to do with this extra person in light of your own concerns about beginning the school year.

Ask some questions before you even begin to worry. Aides may talk among themselves, and you don't want to miss the mark with too little or too much initial responsibility. Find out:

- how many hours per day/days per week your aide will be in your classroom;
- what legal constraints exist vis-à-vis a paraprofessional's responsibilities in the classroom;
- what duties aides traditionally perform in your school; and
- what the other teachers at your grade level do with their aides.

Sharing Responsibility

Aides work under the direction of a teacher, but the latitude and degree of responsibility differ from classroom to classroom. This became clear when veterans were asked what roles and responsibilities aides or paraprofessionals generally assume in the classroom. Their responses follow. Try to have your aide spend as much of his or her time as possible working with children in activities such as these and save most clerical duties for volunteers:

- reading with small groups
- assisting individuals during seat work
- conducting drills in small groups
- reinforcing and reviewing reading and math skills

- tutoring individuals/providing enrichment
- overseeing learning center activities
- taking dictation for stories
- assisting children with the computer
- monitoring activities
- correcting papers
- entering grades
- updating records
- filing
- repairing books
- restocking from supply closet
- changing bulletin boards
- preparing materials for lessons
- running off and collating worksheets
- binding children's stories into books
- laminating materials for class use

Orienting Your Paraprofessional

The first step in establishing a good working relationship with your aide involves getting to know this individual as a person. If possible, before school starts, set aside a time to talk face-to-face about your mutual prior experience working with children, your philosophies of education, attitudes toward discipline, and skills you both bring to the classroom.

Describe your program and negotiate what the role and responsibilities of the paraprofessional will be in it. Make the duties clear and write them out. Show the aide around the classroom, or if he or she has been a mainstay at the school and predates you, have the aide show you the ropes. Make sure that you establish an ongoing time during each week to sit down and plan for the following week. Charles and Senter (1995) suggest that you include a discussion of professionalism in your orientation, with such items as appropriate dress, demeanor, promptness, dependability, and avoidance of gossip. Using blank schedules, one per week, will enable you both to see exactly what the aide's duties will be day by day, time slot by time slot.

Discuss your record-keeping system and orient the aide to your marking procedures. Make sure the aide is familiar with the workbooks, texts, equipment, kits, games, technology, and other materials in use in your room. Supplying a duplicate set of manuals will be very helpful. Provide a work station for your aide and a place to store clothing and personal items. Post your aide's name up on the door and chalkboard alongside your own. Make clear to the children that your aide is there as a second teacher and will enforce the same rules and discipline system.

Coaching Your Aide

Form a mutual assistance pact. You can offer your suggestions regarding motivating activities and game formats, every-pupil response techniques, positive discipline strategies, questioning techniques. Your aide can help you orient yourself to the school and community and provide a second opinion.

If you are working with a group of limited-English-proficient youngsters, your aide, if bilingual, can help you bridge the communication gap and help you establish links to the community. Williams and Snipper (1990) caution that if teachers ask the bilingual aide to work with these children exclusively, especially without giving the aide any direction or instruction, the children's academic development may suffer. Further, they point out, the nonnative speakers may feel abandoned by the teacher and feel inferior to the other students who have the "teacher's" attention. If the bilingual aide sometimes acts as interpreter, Williams and Snipper (1990) suggest that the teacher preview the key concepts and lesson format for the aide ahead of time.

If you are working in a special-education, full-inclusion classroom or simply with a mainstreamed population, your aide will prove to be that second pair of eyes, hands, and ears that you will desperately need. Provide coaching in the following areas and others as needed:

- technology and software applications
- questioning and feedback strategies
- motivational techniques and building on children's prior knowledge
- game formats for drill and practice
- every-pupil response techniques
- your discipline plan and positive desist techniques
- the elements of lesson planning
- facilitation of cooperative groups
- shortcuts for checking student work
- the purpose and organization of student portfolios

Worksheet
8.2

If you are lucky, your aide will be a veteran who will know all the school routines, procedures, and ins and outs better than you do. Make this relationship a mutual learning experience. If you relax and maintain open communication channels with your aide, you'll find that two heads will accomplish far more than one. As your relationship with your aide deepens, you'll wonder how you ever managed or could manage alone. Communicate appreciation to your aide frequently and in novel ways. Some teachers present aides with small gifts, award certificates, or recognition luncheons. Prolific thank-yous are also appreciated. Use Worksheet 8.2, Working with an Aide, to prepare yourself for working with a paraprofessional.

PREPARING FOR SUBSTITUTE TEACHERS

Every now and then you will be ill or have an emergency or have a special conference to attend that necessitates calling to your rescue a substitute teacher. This courageous person—unfamiliar with the school, the class, the grade level, the materials, and the content—is supposed to teach your class until you return. The often beleaguered substitute faces, in addition to all the ambiguity that goes along with the position, 30 or so kids who are "out to get" him or her. I have seen children who wear angel wings and halos with their own teachers suddenly turn on substitutes. Thus you need to help out substitutes for their sake, for your children's sake, and for your own sake. You don't want to have to pick up the pieces when you return to school, nor do you want to feel guilty about what might be going on in your absence. There are a few guidelines that you can follow and certain preparations you can make. After that, enjoy the conference, or sit at home sniffling, and hope for the best.

The Substitute Folder

The more information your substitute has about your class, the procedures, and schedule, the better this person will handle the other ambiguities. This information needs to be in concise form, for the substitute may arrive five minutes before class and will not have much time to prepare. Have a red or bright-colored folder clearly marked for substitutes so they can find it without calling out the bloodhounds. That folder should contain the following data.

Class List. Have available in the substitute folder several copies of the class list. On it the substitute can make notations of all sorts and check off the homework.

Seating Chart. A seating chart will help the substitute learn the names or at least call on the children with ease. The seating chart will also help the substitute quickly catch those who decide to pull a switcheroo and sit with a friend for the day.

School Map. Provide a map of the school site for the substitute so that she or he can easily find key school locations. You might circle key locations in red to be even more helpful.

Class Schedule and Comings and Goings. Provide a general class schedule that includes a schedule of out-of-room activities. Be sure to incorporate both days and times. There is often much confusion about comings and goings, and a chorus of voices expressing conflicting accounts of when they have library can be most distressing to an already harried substitute.

Summary of Your Administrative Duties by Day. Substitutes are expected to follow your schedule exactly, but they need to know what your intraschool duties are so they can cover for you. You may have to change this schedule monthly, since your duties may change from month to month.

Discipline and Organization. You want to provide some information to your substitute about your discipline plan. If you don't, the chorus of voices will again take over and tell the sub when and how to give points, hold a class meeting, or put marbles in a jar. The children will not let anything go unnoticed, especially if the stakes are high (incentives or bribes). Your explanation need not be lengthy. You might simply include in your sub folder the letter regarding discipline that you sent home to parents.

Bus Information. You want to make sure that everyone gets on the right bus at the right time in your absence, or you will feel even more guilty than you normally do when you are absent. Provide this information to potential substitutes in a very clear and concise form.

Available Helpers (Buddy Teacher, Aide, Volunteers, Kids).   Have ready for your sub the name of your buddy teacher and his or her room number, the name of your aide and the aide's hours, the schedule of any expected volunteers for the day, and the names of three children who can be counted on to give accurate and up-to-the-minute information about classroom life in general.

Worksheet 8.3

Notations About Students with Special Needs.   Provide information about students with special needs. Some may need to see the nurse for medication or diabetic testing. Others may have adaptive P.E. Still others may have modified work programs and different behavior standards.

You can duplicate Worksheet 8.3, Preparing for Substitutes, which is a concise form for summarizing the vital statistics for your sub.

Lesson Plans and Bags of Tricks

Generally, you will either know in advance that you need a sub (because you have an inservice, feel ill the day before, or have a family obligation) or will have no warning whatsoever when you wake up to an emergency or a severe and quick-onset illness. But in either case, plan you must for an easier day for the sub and an easier day for you upon your return.

In prior-warning situations, you can leave precise, current lesson plans and review work for the class. You can write your plans with the substitute in mind and have all the materials at hand and ready to go. Some teachers, even in an emergency, will quickly write the day's plans and send them to school with a friend or spouse that morning.

In no-warning situations, you will still have your planbook for the sub. The lesson plans that you have already formulated should always be written in a form that would enable any reasonable person to decipher and then teach from them. In addition, have in your sub folder many review sheets and activities for any possible emergency, updating the material every two weeks or so just in case. The sub folder can also contain directions to a box or bag of motivating activities that children enjoy. These may be a favorite book of poems, favorite records, favorite finger plays, and chants for younger children. For older children, have a supply of surefire hits as well. These might include brain teasers, a new book to read to them, a video, a book of riddles, a crossword puzzle, a book of one-minute mysteries, or an engaging art activity. Substitutes often bring their own bags of tricks, but if you provide your own, tailor-made to your class, you will be several steps ahead.

Respect for Substitutes

Although children mistakenly confuse the arrival of a substitute with an invitation to a party, if your classroom discipline policy is based on a premise of self-responsibility, it is more likely that the children will not take too much advantage of the situation. Teachers who hold the reins very tightly and use extrinsic rewards will find their classes running amok when substitutes or even intraschool personnel, who don't use the system exactly as the teacher would, take over the class. Talk to your class about the role of the substitute teacher and explain how that person is really an emergency teacher who saves the day for learning. Discuss specific ways the class can make it easier for this pinch hitter and make a list of them. Should a party occur despite all of your preventive measures, you can impose a logical consequence, such as requiring the culprits to write the substitute a letter of apology or bringing the whole issue up during a class meeting.

A FINAL COMMENT

Isolation (Lortie, 1975) was a factor influencing the high teacher dropout rate addressed in Chapter 1. Schools can be lonely places. They can also be the most friendly, supportive, and warm places. I miss the camaraderie of a school site and seek it out at the Hillside-University Demonstration School, where I am always greeted as a welcome colleague. I attend the lunches, retirement parties, get-togethers, and other social events that all too rarely bring a university faculty together. I even had a secret pal!

Each school faculty member has a part in creating this mutually supportive school climate. You need to make the effort to get to know everyone, since you will be the new-comer. Let the faculty know that you are open to suggestions, advice, and friendship, by word and by deed. *Do not hibernate in your room.* Force yourself, even if you are the shy type, to make a sincere effort at interaction. The benefit to you in terms of acceptance and a feeling of belonging will be manifold.

Reflection Box

In what ways, if any, has the chapter changed my beliefs?

Questions I Still Have . . .

Reflection Box

What practices actually worked for me in my first year?

FURTHER READING

Dubois, M., Gangel, K., Young, L., Heiss, R., Webb, B., & Paprocki, S. (1991). The canvas bag and other substitute survival strategies. *Instructor, 101*(1), 54–57.

Lamont, I., & Hill, J. (1991). Roles and responsibilities of paraprofessionals in the regular elementary classroom. *B. C. Journal of Special Education, 15*(1), 1–24.

Pronin, B. (1983). *Substitute teaching: A handbook for hassle-free subbing.* New York: St. Martin's Press.

Videon, L., (1987). *Take me along: The best substitute teacher's survival guide yet!* Carthage, IL: Fearon Teacher Aids.

REFERENCES

Charles, C. M., & Senter, G. (1995). *Elementary classroom management* (2nd ed.). White Plains, NY: Longman.

Lortie, D. (1975). *School teacher: A sociological study.* Chicago: University of Chicago Press.

Williams, J. D., & Snipper, G. C. (1990). *Literacy and bilingualism.* White Plains, NY: Longman.

9

The First Day

Reflection Box

What I Believe About

Preparation for the first day . . .
Assigning seats and learning names . . .
Meeting parents on the first day . . .
The first day's activities . . .

Teaching is the only profession with a "New Year's Eve" and a first day each and every school year. Other professionals have their first days of work but only once in a career. With this distinction come all of the problems and excitements of "firsts." My New Year's Eve before the first day of a new school year, for example, is spent counting sheep or encouraging my clock to tick faster. I am up all night long, not with party hats or champagne but with butterflies and decaffeinated coffee. In fact, before each first-class session, every quarter at the university, I have to take a deep breath, propel myself into the room, and struggle through the first few awkward moments.

Although the first day gets easier with experience, I can understand why the most pervasive question new teachers ask is, "But what do I actually do the first day of school?" While preceding chapters have explored the ingredients of a successful beginning, you may still have concerns about how to put them all together—concerns about the first encounter of the class kind.

You are certainly not alone. All the methods courses you have taken and all the textbooks you have read probably have not dispelled your concerns and anxieties. Only your own experience will do so, and after the first one, all others will be easier. You will establish your own unique strategy for surviving the first day.

A Note from the Teacher

Waiting anxiously for the school year to begin, I visited the school to meet the principal and see my classroom. I had felt very confident when I completed my student teaching and was excited that I had a contract to teach a kindergarten class—my favorite age level. But as I walked from the office to the classroom with the principal, I burst into tears and told her that I didn't know what I was doing and I didn't even know why I was even there. What a way to make a first impression! The principal smiled, gave me a hug, and told me that I was going to be just fine; and she was right. My first year was a wonderful experience for me and here I am 14 years later still teaching kindergarten and loving every minute of it!

B. MONROE

QUESTIONS TO START THE DAY

Worksheet
9.1

This chapter, while not a substitute for your own experience, is a synthesis of responses to questions most frequently asked by beginners. It will give you enough general and specific information to enable you, at the end, to design your own first-day plans. You will approach the day with more confidence when you can glean from others' experience what might suit you. Two questions are paramount: What one thing can I do to set the stage for learning, and how will I go about establishing a community in the classroom? The remainder of this chapter will shed light on these two questions, but first we will deal with some more specific questions that can be answered more concisely. Before you read the synthesized responses to each question, briefly jot down in the space provided on Worksheet 9.1, First-Day Questions, how you would answer them.

What Should You Wear?

One of my fondest childhood memories of September is shopping for new school clothes and school supplies. Those new composition books and sharpened pencils always extracted silent promises from me to be neat and organized and not scribble or draw on the inside covers of my notebooks. But the real thrill was getting up on the first day of school to finally wear the fresh new clothes that had been set out the night before.

Children in your class-to-be will be going through this ritual the morning of the first day, and so will you. I'll wager you have pondered what you will wear on the first day of student teaching or teaching, as I ponder it each quarter. Teachers recommend dressing as professionally as possible. You need not run out to a color consultant or buy a dress-for-success manual. Follow your own personal preferences but present yourself to students and their parents as a cool and comfortable, well-groomed professional. On the dressy–casual continuum, most teachers land in the center. While some suggest a dressy dress and high heels or suit and tie on the first day, most stress comfort. You will have to take into consideration climate, school norms, and grade level as well as your own personal taste. Sitting on the floor or handling paints and paste may dictate very casual clothing or, better yet, a smock that suits you. Jeans have broken the school barrier, and if they are the norm in your school, as they are in some California schools, fine. But dress up on the first day. Look your professional best. It will give you confidence to cross the threshold and enable you to address the next question.

What Should You Say First?

Somehow we believe that first words are magical and make or break a situation. If we can get the first sentence right, all will go well thereafter. In reality, the children will never remember what you said first, but because it is of primary concern to new teachers, here's what the pros commonly say first.

The Welcomers

"Good Morning. I know we are going to have a good year and lots of fun."

"You are the most important group of first graders I've ever seen. I'm very proud to have you in my class, because we're going to have fun learning."

"Hi, I'm so glad to see all of you. We are going to have a super year."

The Introducers

"I'm Mrs._____, your teacher, and this is Ms._____, our aide, who will help you also."

"I'm Mr._____ and here are Boris and Natasha, our classroom pet rats."

The Managers

"The line is very straight, and I appreciate how quietly everyone entered the room."

"What a nice line. I hope it's this way all year. Please walk in quietly and find a seat."

My Personal Favorites

"I'm happy and excited to be your teacher."

"Mistakes are permitted in this class."

Generally, you're safe if you take one from every category or create your own unique way of breaking the ice. Remember the acronym **WISHES**—*W*elcome, *I*ntroduction, *S*hare *H*opes, *E*stablish *S*tandards. This is your formula for a good start on the first day.

How Much Should You Tell About Yourself?

Beginning teachers are concerned about what to be called by children and how much to tell the children about themselves. In all but the most special circumstances, it is most appropriate to be called by your last name preceded by *Mr.*, *Mrs.*, or *Ms.* In some cases, primary teachers may be called by their first names (e.g., *Mr. Mike* or *Miss Susan*). Some teachers use only their last initials, especially when their names are long and difficult to pronounce.

In all cases, write your name on the chalkboard and pronounce it with the children. During attendance, children can easily learn your name by responding to your salutation "Good morning, Juan" with "Good morning, Mrs. Matsumoto."

Having grown up as I did with the belief that teachers neither visited rest rooms nor shopped in markets, I always make a point of telling my students something about my personal life and professional background. Surprisingly, the majority of teachers do too. They commonly tell their pupils about their families, why they love teaching, why they became a teacher in the first place, their pets, summer vacations, interests, prior career or experiences, hobbies, and any apparent physical disabilities.

A few teachers encourage and respond to student questions about themselves. Some make a biographical poster or bulletin board. On it are photos of families, pets, and pictures of favorite hobbies, sports, foods, and so on. How much you share will depend on your personal style and philosophy. You can share a little at a time as the year progresses as you prefer, but do share something about yourself that first day. Even minimal self-disclosure (the type and name of your pet, your favorite hobby) will ease the tension, satisfy the children's curiosity, and bring you down to earth, where the children can reach out to you. Developing rapport with the children in the class is an essential task that first day. Hopefully, you have enough suggestions for getting through the first two minutes of the day. It's time to sit down and relax.

How Do You Assign Seats?

In the old days there were two ways of assigning seats—alphabetical order and size order. If your name began with the letter Z or you were tall, you were guaranteed a seat in the back. Your saving grace was poor vision, poor hearing, or disruptive behavior. These were the three mitigating conditions that upgraded your seating to first class, front row center. But times have changed. The overwhelming majority of teachers favor self-selection as opposed to prearranged seating, at least the first day.

Allowing children to choose their own seats on the opening day of school is their first exercise in decision making and taking responsibility. We adults are often unhappy about assigned seats in airplanes, in theaters, and at dinner parties. We like to find our spaces and feel comfortable in them. At the movies, the aisle seats are filled first, and either you scramble for the first or last row or fight for center seats midway back. But we all like to choose. And since we are creatures of habit, once we choose, we like to stay put.

Children feel the same way too! Does this mean that once they have chosen their seats they never move? Never say never. Several circumstances are described by teachers who only partially subscribe to the self-selection pattern. They suggested two adaptations:

- Children's choices are modified when special needs arise or seatmates are incompatible. Usually, arrangements are not finalized until the end of the week and still can be modified thereafter.
- Children choose new seats every month—or two or three times per year—for a change of scenery, and their choices are subject to teacher modification should the need arise.

Another popular seating assignment method is random selection by lots. Children draw numbers that correspond to numbers on the desks. These selections are subject to teacher modification, and lots can be redrawn every month or several times per year. In this method there is a certain degree of fairness based on chance, but the risk is that no one may be happy with the outcome, least of all the teacher, who has to deal with the complaints.

At the other end of the continuum from free choice and random selection are the pre-arranged, teacher-determined seating assignments. Although teachers who prearrange seating are in the minority, they base their decisions on three variables: ability, alphabetical order, or desire to integrate the sexes, the races, or ethnic groups. It is important to point out that prearranged seating can be dysfunctional.

In the first case, seating by ability group can stigmatize children and is not necessary, since children can easily change places for special remediation or enrichment. In the second case, ease of learning the names is not a good enough reason for seating in alphabetical order, since last names are not the common form of address and the Z's will always be in the back! A seating chart is a more reasonable way of solving memory lapses anyway. Finally, trying to achieve balance on all important variables (sex, race, ethnicity, size, ability) through seating will drive you batty, so why not let free choice prevail? Step in when necessary to correct obvious imbalances, especially when using cooperative learning strategies that necessitate heterogeneous grouping.

Try to seat nonnative speakers in the front of the room so they can hear you clearly. At the same time, make sure they are sitting near a buddy who speaks their language or near children they choose by themselves, who may be the ones they feel most comfortable around.

If you do prefer assigned places, label the seats or spaces on the floor with name tags and let children enjoy the challenge and excitement of finding their assigned places on the first day. If they can't read, you can shape or color code their names and seat tags to make the task easier.

One final word about seating arrangements. There are those heretics, and I have been one of them, who avoid assigned seats. A classroom organized around learning centers, to which children rotate all day, precludes having assigned seats. During attendance and morning routines, children sit where they like and move to centers using a standard rotation or contract form to guide their choices. Some kindergartens operate this way, with no assigned seats and free-seating choice each and every day. When children have their own cubbies, the tables and chairs in the room become common property and can be used by all. Now that they are in their seats, it's time to ponder the next question.

How Can You Learn the Children's Names?

There is no greater compliment to a child than calling him or her by name at the end of the first day. It requires concentration and extra effort but it can be done. Always check the pronunciation with the child. All children should have the option of going by a nickname or shortened version they prefer. Teachers suggest some tried-and-true methods that will work for you, too, and even by lunchtime dismissal on the first day, you can wish each child a good meal using his or her name. Here are some suggestions:

- One teacher associates the names with faces from photos. In some districts, individual photos are taken at the time of the class picture, and they are attached to the permanent record cards. Take time to make the name–face association before school starts. Children will be shocked and pleased to be recognized. They will think you are a wondrous wizard who has divined their names magically.
- You can borrow a Polaroid-type camera and take instant pictures of the children, table by table or individually. Writing the names below the faces will help you re-

member who's who, and you can memorize the photos during lunch break. Once the photos have served their purpose as memory aids, you can use them to create a lovely welcome bulletin board bearing the caption "We Are All Stars"—with star-shaped frames for the photos.

- Children draw self-portraits on paper plates using mirrors the first day of school, and you can start to associate the artwork with the child, especially if children write their names around the edges of the plates.
- If you have an aide, he or she can work with individuals to create silhouettes that will be posted around the room. The aide can simply tape up a black piece of construction paper, have the child sit in profile between a light source (e.g., filmstrip projector) and the black paper, and trace around the resulting shadow or silhouette. Children can cut, paste on white paper, and label. These are good enough likenesses to enable you to associate names and profiles.
- Name tags and name plates are very popular aids for learning names. Teachers place them on desks or on the front of desks, pin them on the children's clothing, or string them around primary youngsters' necks (upside down so children can read them when they look down). You can have the children make their own and decorate them.
- After children have chosen or have been assigned to seats, one of the most useful devices for learning their names is the seating chart. You can get a jump on the process by having the blank chart or map ready to go. The names just have to be filled in when you take attendance or look at the name tags.
- Some teachers learn the names through simple interaction or games like the ones that follow.

Primary Grades, K–1.   The teacher holds up name cards, and the children recognize their names, retrieve the cards, and place them in the designated spot. The teacher can call the names as well at the beginning, but should encourage recognition solely by visual cues early in the year. The child then says his or her name and one thing about a favorite toy, pet, food, or television program.

Intermediate Grades, 2–3.   Students introduce themselves to the class. They can be given some guidelines and time constraints:

1. Tell us your name.
2. Tell us something about your family, your pets.
3. What do you do after school?
4. What are your favorite television programs?

Children can be given a three-minute egg timer to hold to remind them they can talk under but not over the limit. This places the responsibility for self-monitoring with them and makes it unnecessary for you to interrupt or stop them.

Review alphabetical order by having children come up in small groups and alphabetize themselves, using their tags or cards.

A child who is "It" leaves the room and she is assigned a partner in the room. When the child who is "It" returns, he or she must ask questions to find out who the partner is:

Is my partner a girl or a boy?   Is my partner in the first row?
Does my partner have long hair?   Is my partner wearing blue?

A variation on this name game is to have the class give the child who is "It" hints such as:

Your partner is a girl.	She has long hair.
She sits at the front table.	She is blond.

Upper Grades, 4–6.   Children can interview a partner, following a set of guidelines, and then introduce the partner to the rest of the class. Guidelines can be duplicated, or children can make up the interview questions with you and the outline can be written on the chalkboard. Some suggested guidelines follow:

- partner's favorite subject in school
- partner's least favorite subject
- partner's favorite kind of stories
- partner's pets
- partner's favorite sports, hobbies
- partner's favorite television program
- language(s) spoken at home

Children enjoy playing the scavenger hunt game that requires that they find someone in the class who corresponds to a description on a prewritten sheet of paper.

someone who hates pizza
someone whose favorite color is purple
someone who owns more than three pets
someone who has lived in another state
someone who has lived in another country
someone who speaks two languages
someone who has been to Disneyland or Disney World
someone who has a birthday in September
someone who is wearing a hair ornament

Probably the best way to help children learn each other's names is to practice the name game. Each person introduces all the others preceding, going around the room or up and down the rows in this manner:

Maria:	I'm Maria.
Jason:	This is Maria; I'm Jason.
Pablo:	This is Maria, Jason; I'm Pablo.
Ryan:	This is Maria, Jason, Pablo; I'm Ryan.
Elena:	This is Maria, Jason, Pablo, Ryan; I'm Elena.
Julio:	This is Maria, Jason, Pablo, Ryan, Elena; I'm Julio.

This technique also works very well with adults. Not only does the systematic repetition enable me to learn the names of 25 students in a few minutes, but it also allows everyone else in class to do the same. No name tags are needed for this one!

At almost any grade level, you can play the yarn toss game. Have a large ball of yarn available and seat the students in a circle. The first person says his or her name and something he or she does well, then gently tosses the ball of yarn to someone else in the circle, who follows suit. At the end of the game you have spun a giant web of friendship and hopefully learned some names and some of the special talents of students in the class.

Now that you have introduced yourself, identified the children, and seated them one way or another, you have used up a good 30 minutes to an hour of your first day! Congratulations! Only four to four and a half hours to go. You'll make it, especially if you pick and choose from activities suggested by experienced teachers. Although each teacher does things differently on the first day, there are enough common elements to extract a set of ten guiding principles.

TEN GUIDING PRINCIPLES

Although some of you would like a specific menu of first-day activities, it is more useful to give you the basic ingredients and a dash of confidence to compose your own plan. After all, you are a well-educated professional, able to be as creative as I or the teachers surveyed in terms of specific art ideas or poems or stories to introduce the first day. What you need now is a framework for making decisions about plans for the first day, and here the pros have been most helpful. If you follow these ten commandments of first-day planning, you will be off to a great start. These principles can serve as your criteria when you evaluate your first-day plans later on in the chapter. Here are the ten guiding principles and the corresponding messages they convey to children.

Principle	**Message to Children**
1. Be prepared.	"Teacher knows what she [he] is doing."
2. Motivate kids.	"School is exciting."
3. Establish routines/schedule.	"School is safe and predictable."
4. Establish classroom rules.	"I will learn self-control."
5. Orient children to school/room.	"I am comfortable and belong here."
6. Preview the curriculum.	"I will learn new things."
7. Let children decide and choose.	"We are all in this together."
8. Include a reading experience.	"Reading is wonderful!"
9. Acknowledge every child.	"I am special!"
10. Review and assign easy work.	"I can succeed!"

Be Prepared

Arrive very early yourself. You will feel more confident if you can spend time checking out the room and feeling comfortable in it. Make sure that your name is on the board along with the daily schedule, there is a welcoming sign on the door, all your name tags are carefully prepared, the desks are arranged to your satisfaction, all your instructional materials are ready, and your plans are summarized on an index card for easy reference. I tend to go to the classroom at least 15 minutes before each of my class sessions. Laying out materials and writing the schedule on the board conveys to students that the teacher is well prepared and well organized and will help them pass from a state of uncertainty to a state of knowing and understanding.

Motivate Kids

Some children have waited five years for this first day; some only three summer months; and others, in year-round school, a few weeks. But the motivation and anticipation will be high regardless of the time. Capitalize on it this very first day. Provide a variety of highly motivating experiences. Keep the pace moving and overplan so you never drag anything out to fill time. Children need to go home that very first day with the message that school is exciting. In the case of the primary child, his or her first day can either reinforce good feelings about school or turn around bad ones. Make this a day that students will remember and talk about at home later that day.

I remember a kindergarten teacher who on the very first day of school brought in her hen, an egg that the hen had laid, and some other eggs as well. Children talked about the hen and things made from eggs; they cooked and ate scrambled eggs; they learned the rhyme "Humpty-Dumpty," made "Humpty-Dumpty" collages with the broken egg shells, and wrote a language-experience story about what happened that morning. This was a first school day to remember, and it included math (cooking and measuring) and reading (language experienced) and nutrition and science and oral language development and art and. . . . You may want to provide a thematic beginning as well, but make sure, whatever your activities, that children will respond to the traditional question "What did you do in school today?" with a glowing smile and excited report, instead of a bored "I don't remember," or worse, "Nothing much."

Establish Routines/Schedule

Begin to establish a set of daily routines that first day. Chapter 4 has dealt with routines at length, and you may have had an opportunity during a practicum to observe a variety of routine procedures and the effects of routines on children. Routines are a management tool for saving time and ensuring smooth functioning of the classroom. But they also provide the structure and security that help children meet a basic need. We all make certain predictions about our environment, and when our predictions are verified in reality, we feel good. But when even one of our expectations goes awry (the car won't start, or the alarm doesn't go off, or the shower water is cold instead of hot), we can become disoriented. We need to do certain things by rote so our energies can be spent in more creative endeavors. Introduce some routines on that first day as they are needed; others can be introduced as the week progresses.

In addition to established routines, children (and adults) appreciate a fixed schedule. We are creatures of habit, and when our schedules are disrupted by travel, or by house guests, or by any one of a number of outside factors, we become cranky. My students appreciate knowing how the two- or four-hour time block will be divided, and I always have an activities schedule, including times, on the chalkboard prior to class. They like to see if an exiting activity is coming up, or a videotape, or a simulation game, or maybe they want to mentally check off how much time there is until break. While I don't always stick to the schedule, it's always there as a guide, and students can predict the order of the session. Your students will also want the security of a schedule, and since it is in your head and on paper already, why not let them in on it by writing it along with the alloted times on a special part of the chalkboard?

Your first day should be planned with the context of your eventual daily schedule. While the first day will not be typical, neither should it be *so* different from a usual day that children later are surprised and resistant to a new schedule that seems to come out of left field. Surprises are best introduced and most welcome within predictable routines and an established schedule.

Establish Classroom Rules

You had an opportunity earlier to explore alternative discipline strategies and to add to your already existing repertoire those that seem to suit you. Begin to implement your strategies and create a positive class climate that first day of class. This is the time to talk about and model a discipline system based on mutual respect, responsibility, and dignity. At no time will the children be better behaved than on the first day of class. Capitalize on their first-day formality. Collaboratively establish rules and then show the children you are consistent and fair in enforcing rules. This might be a time to explain the classroom meeting and have your first go at it.

Don't let infractions slide that first day. The children will be checking you out carefully. You can always lighten up as the year progresses, so start out a bit more firm than you plan to be by midyear. Pass all of their tests with flying colors by following the advice in Chapter 5 and using your own good sense. This is also the day to send home the note to parents (in translation, if needed) that describes the class rules and procedures for enforcing them. The children will feel safe and secure in knowing that you will be helping them learn self-control.

Orient Children to School/Room

We all need to get our bearings in a new situation. And even though a change of scenery can be broadening, it is also very scary. On most vacation tours, no matter how tightly or loosely scheduled, a quick orientation tour of every new city encountered is the first order of business. Children are no different in that they need to quickly get their bearings in a new school and/or classroom. The easiest way to orient new students, second language learners, and returning students to their school is to take a walking tour that first morning, pointing out such places of interest as the rest rooms, water fountains, principal's office, and nurse's office. You may need to point out school bus stops, places to line up after lunch, the cafeteria, assigned fire drill locations, and appropriate exits. Let the children know what the bells or other signaling devices mean. With older children you can construct a school map together or organize a treasure hunt to help old-timers orient new children to the school plant.

In the classroom, schedule a walk around the room using just eyes that first day. Children can make mental note of where storage containers are located, where games for free time are stored, and so forth. A good first-day activity for all ages is to make a simple map of the classroom.

Preview the Curriculum

On that very first day, let children in on some of the exciting things they will be learning this year. Preview some of the topics they will cover and introduce them to at least one of their textbooks that first day. Begin work early in the first week on a science or social studies unit and provide opportunity for student input by asking them what they already know about the topic and what they would like to find out. Motivation will be very high. Let children know it's going to be an exciting year and that they will be learning many new things. Telling kindergarten or first grade children that they will learn to read this year, or third grade children that they will learn cursive writing, or sixth graders that they will have pen pals from a foreign country can send them home that first day brimming with high expectations and great anticipation for the coming year.

Let Children Decide and Choose

Share responsibility for decision making with children from the outset. Let them know they will be encouraged to make choices and participate in classroom processes. Participatory experiences that first day might include choosing seats, deciding what game to play at recess, deciding what song they prefer to sing, choosing a library book, writing classroom rules, and so forth.

Include a Reading Experience

Let the children know that very first day that you value reading by incorporating some simple reading or reading-related activity into your plans. You might visit the school library, introduce the librarian, and let each child choose a book. Or you might read a favorite picture storybook to younger children or read to older children the first chapter of a book that later will be read chapter by chapter. Additionally, you might engage kindergarten children in their first language-experience activity and have them read back a story they have dictated and committed to memory. Or you might have a sustained, silent reading period of classroom library books after lunch on that first day. Whatever you choose to do about reading that first day, make it fun! Perhaps you can turn the tide toward reading by showing great wonder and enthusiasm for the world of books yourself.

Acknowledge Every Child

On that first day (and all others) enable each child to feel unique. Let each one know with a verbal or nonverbal response from you that she or he is welcome, valued, and special. It can start with an individual greeting to each child on the way into the room. A greeting in the primary language of second language learners will make the child feel welcome. It continues when you listen to their introductions and learn their names. It is reinforced by your positive remarks and smiling demeanor. It is expanded when you ask them to help you make the rules. It ends with a special good-bye to each child at about 3:00 P.M. and begins again the very next day.

Review and Assign Easy Work

Prepare work for the first day that is slightly below the anticipated level of the class. Why? The children should go home that very first day feeling successful, feeling that they have accomplished something. A few papers can be sent home that very first day with an appropriate happy face or comment by you so parents can see the results of their child's initial efforts. Step in when you see that a given task is too difficult or frustrating for a child. You have the whole year to challenge students and encourage them to work beyond their capacities. But during the first week, make *success* your sole criterion for work given. Encourage children for all of their small steps as well as for their giant leaps.

BUT WHAT DO I ACTUALLY DO ON THE FIRST DAY?

The planning guidelines just enumerated are broad and easy to remember. However, some of you may still be uncertain about specific ideas for first-day activities. For you, I have provided in the pages that follow some sample schedules for primary, intermediate, and upper elementary grades. They are composite schedules of activities actually observed on the first day of school at the Hillside-University Demonstration School. Read and subject them to the test of the ten guiding principles we have discussed. Then it is your turn!

Kindergarten/First Grade

Welcome.   Meet the children and their parents at the door. Don't be surprised if some parents bring video cameras or still cameras to record this milestone. Find a special word (in native languages, if possible) to say to each child, pin on a name tag or have the parent do it, and invite the child to play at an activity center that can be quickly and easily put away later. Reassure parents, answer any questions, and direct parents to the milk money collection envelopes and volunteer sign-up sheets. It is never too early to hook the parents into service. One kindergarten teacher recruits parents from the previous year to help on the first day and during the first week. Encourage the parents to leave as soon as possible, especially parents of crying children. You may want to reassure the crier's parent with a phone call later.

A Note from the Teacher

On the first day of kindergarten I put up a sign outside for parents that reads:

A "first day of kindergarten" good-bye kiss, like a spoonful of medicine, should be given quickly and with a smile, knowing that soon everything will be all better.

A. KOCHER

When you have met all of the children and have shown all of their parents to the door, after writing down on a class list who walks, who rides the bus, and who will be picked up by whom after school, ask the children to clean up, push their seats under the table, and find a place on the rug or a carpet square on which to sit. Introduce yourself and have them pronounce your name. Convey to them your excitement about the school year and how happy you are to be their teacher. Tell them a few of the exciting things they will be learning and doing. Reassure them that you are watching the clock and will have everyone ready when parents return or the bus comes to take them home. This will be a major concern to children on that first day.

Routines.   Take attendance, even though you already know who is here, just to establish the routine. Count the boys together, write "Boys" on the board, and then write the numeral. This is the beginning of reading. I guarantee that when you count the girls and write "Girls" on the board, they will tell you what it says. Conduct appropriate patriotic activities following state or district guidelines.

Class Orientation.   Show the various charts, bulletin boards, and centers to the children. Read labels around the room together. Point out clothing hooks, cubbies, supplies, teacher's desk, pets, and other features. You may want to teach some chants or simple finger plays as they are relevant. When you get to the calendar, for example, teach a seasonal chant or poem; when you get to the weather, teach a simple finger play. Show the children the birthday board and let them know that birthdays will be recognized in class. Tell them about yourself or have a Meet the Teacher bulletin board to show them.

Procedures and Rules.   At this developmental level, it is best to teach rules, procedures, and routines as needed without overloading the children. One teacher tells a puppet the rules. Explain what you mean by the word rule, as this may be a new concept to them. You might want to play Simon Says at this juncture to help students understand the concept of rules. Show the children what you want, praise and encourage their approximations of desired behaviors, and be consistent in following through. You won't have much trouble if you are patient and realize these activities are all firsts for them. They will remember best those rules that are linked to real needs.

For example, discuss bathroom rules first, since some child undoubtedly will need to use the facilities very soon. Show the children the bathrooms, girls and boys separately. Stress the hows and whys of sanitation and hygiene. Stress that children can go when they need to go as long as only one boy and one girl are out of class at a time and that children don't leave when something important is going on in class.

School Orientation.   While fire drill procedures must be practiced as soon as possible, introduce this procedure a little later in the week so as not to frighten the children on their very first day of school. Tour the school together, stopping at key points of interest and to introduce the children to the key people in the school so they can become quickly familiar with the faces of the adults around them.

P.E./Recess.   Take the children outside and show them the equipment and how it is used. Again, discuss taking turns and safety measures. Observe as the children engage in free play. Consider combining recess and learning each other's names. Arrange the children in a circle and have the child who catches the ball when the teacher throws it say his or her name.

Snacks.   If milk is available at snack time, try to teach the children how to open the cartons without spilling them and how to dispose of the straw and paper afterward. One teacher asks her charges to pretend the cartons are glued to the tables. Don't take anything for granted, or they will be crying over spilled milk.

Reading.   Read or tell stories sometime during that first day. Engage children in the reading process by having them describe the pictures, make predictions, and answer simple questions. Some pattern books encourage children actually to read along with you.

Use large-size versions so all can see. Some charming books to read on the first day are *Never Spit on Your Shoes* by Denys Cazet (1990), *This Is the Way We Go to School* by Edith Baer (1990), *Will I Have a Friend?* by Miriam Cohen (1967), and the more recent *Minerva Louise at School* by Janet Stoeke (1996). An excellent poem to use on this important day is Aileen Fisher's "First Day of School" from her book *Always Wondering* (1991).

One teacher proves to children that they can read already, using an oversize teacher-made reader that has in it letters, signs, colors, shapes, pictures, logos, names, trees at different seasons, people's faces in various moods, numbers, and so on. And read it they do on that very first day of school! Every child can read the McDonald's logo, or a stop sign, or a happy face. Make your own first-day reading book. The children will go home feeling as if this reading thing isn't that hard after all. They might write their first language-experience story about the first day of school and read it back together with you.

Centers.   When it's time for work stations or centers, show the children each alternative and explain in simple language how the materials are used, where to play with them, and how and where they are put away. Teach and practice a signal so children will know when to stop playing and start cleaning up and where to go when they are finished cleaning up. Then have children choose any one of the following typical centers: art, math manipulatives, puzzles, house, listening, peg boards, bead stringing, library, blocks, puppets, and flannel board. You can encourage children to work together if you limit the array of materials somewhat. After they have cleaned up their centers, evaluate with them how well they worked and cleaned up. Have your play areas stocked with multiracial and multiethnic dolls and puppets. Seek out picture books reflecting many cultures. Add some bilingual storybooks to your library corner.

Art.   Have the students draw pictures about the first day of kindergarten. Parents will treasure this as a memento, and children will enjoy carrying a paper home that first day.

Wrap-Up.   Sing some songs, play a following-directions record, or do some exercise as a class. Evaluate the session for half-day kindergarten children and ask them what they liked best. Write up the day's events as a simple language-experience story and have them read it back with you. This can be the beginning of a class log. Collect the name tags and preview the next day.

To avoid chaos when the bell rings, organize the class into bus children, walkers, and those who are picked up. This procedure will be one of the harder parts of your day until you make it routine and gain some assistance. Teaming arrangements made with the other kindergarten teachers can work effectively. One teacher can wait with those who are picked up while another takes all the bus children to the vehicles, for example. Have parents line up outside the door and dismiss each child individually after verifying your list. Be very careful about releasing children. Send home a note (translated as needed) with each child outlining class procedures and "need-to-know-immediately" information. At the end of the note, thank the parent for sending such a lovely child to school. If this is full-day kindergarten or first-grade class, the wrap-up occurs at the close of the afternoon.

Afternoon activities might include, in addition to an activity center time and recess, an integrated social studies or science experience. A typical beginning unit in kindergarten is safety. Initiate the unit on that first afternoon. Play red light/green light; make traffic lights out of cereal boxes; read a poem about crossing the street safely; meet the school crossing guard and ask that person questions; role-play crossing the street safely in class; write a first language-experience story about crossing the street safely; draw traffic safety posters for the bulletin board.

Using this pattern for the rest of the week as a basis, you can add a new song, a new finger play, or a new book each day. You can add additional centers and initiate your rotation system. You can continue your mini-unit on safety for the rest of the week, adding activities in all curriculum areas. Other appropriate units for this age group might be Our School, Our Families, Community Helpers, We Are Special, Our Pets. Reading and math readiness can be slowly introduced and integrated into every aspect of the program. Sharing time can be initiated later in the week, and slowly the needed routines will be added and the schedule will fill out until it is chock-full of juicy activities for children.

Intermediate Grades (2–3)

Welcome.   Meet the children at the door or at a designated place on the playground. Invite them to find their name tags and then seats. Let them know you will make any seating adjustments if need be. Introduce yourself. You might ask them to respond to your "Good morning" with a specific response so that they can practice your name. Stress that they are significant and special and that this will be a very good year. Take attendance and encourage the children to correct any mispronunciations or to tell you an alternative form or nickname they prefer. Assign a partner to children who are new to the school. Any latecomers (and there will be latecomers on the first day of school) should be made to feel welcome and be brought into the action immediately.

Routines.   Establish a signal for gaining students' attention before you go very far. Reinforce the signal and the hand-raising rule from the outset. Collect any lunch and milk monies. Conduct appropriate patriotic activities following state or district guidelines. Establish bathroom, water fountain, and pencil sharpening procedures. At appropriate times establish your other procedures and practice them. For example, if you want everyone to push chairs under the table when the students stand up, tell them so and praise them when they do it correctly.

Open the classroom employment agency. Explain how each job functions, how long the job lasts (week or month), and how the helpers will be selected. Use any of the selection methods discussed in Chapter 4.

This might be a time to select the Star of the Week. This is done at random from name cards. Let the student chosen know what special privileges and responsibilities go with the honor, including leading the line and decorating the designated bulletin board with items that reflect the star's interests, talents, and abilities.

Introductions.   Play any of the get-acquainted games or consider a technique one demonstration teacher uses, the Human Treasure Hunt. She makes up a set of cards with directions such as these, one for each student: Find someone who . . .

1. has a birthday this month.
2. has lived in another country.
3. has ridden a horse.
4. is new to this school.
5. rides the bus to school.
6. is wearing new shoes.
7. has flown in an airplane.
8. speaks more than one language.
9. collects something as a hobby.
10. has more than three pets.

The children get a chance to mill around the room for five minutes to find and be found and to get acquainted. When they return to their seats, each child reads his or her card aloud and introduces the classmate who meets the requirement. Afterward, everyone feels much more comfortable. The teacher can talk about his or her life and introduce the Meet the Teacher bulletin board.

Orientation.   Survey the room together. Point out materials storage, cubbies, and areas that are set aside as private spaces for children and teacher. Show them where the class library is, where texts are stored, and where the paper supplies are and how they will be distributed. Briefly discuss the bulletin boards and stress that the room will be decorated with their work and their projects. Introduce any pets and any unusual features of the room.

One teacher gives each child a welcoming present of a pencil box and combines the gift with a system of encouragements. Children keep private track of their efforts on a sticker chart affixed to the top cover of their pencil box. They receive stickers for effort and achievement in behavior and work. The teacher stresses that these charts and the pencil boxes are *totally private.*

Rules.   Discuss rules, agree on them, and write them later on a chart. Include playground rules. Discuss the concept of conflict resolution and let the children know that conflicts will be solved during class meetings. Tell them that class meetings will also be used for planning and for discussion and that during meetings they will have the opportunity to give and to receive compliments to and from their classmates and the teacher. Explain the concept of *agenda* and decide together on a place to write initials when children want to sign on. Decide how often meetings should take place, what time of day is best, and which days of the week include the most people. You may even want to conduct this discussion at your very first class meeting during the wrap-up session in the afternoon.

Recess.   Review fire drill procedures and take a recess break with free choice of activity. Make sure the newcomers (especially new second language learners) leave with their buddies, and stress again how important it is to help new students feel welcome. Allow the children to take short and frequent stretch breaks in the classroom. They are as necessary as a full-blown recess.

Math.   Distribute your math diagnostic test and then play a math game to review simple operations. You can also do some oral math review to get an even quicker evaluation of the summer or year-round break "forgetting factor."

Reading Experience.   Before lunch, read poems about school such as "From School, Some Suggestions" by Bobbi Katz from *Upside Down and Inside Out* (1992) or any of the poems in Kalli Dakos's themed poetry books, *If You're Not Here, Please Raise Your Hand: Poems about School* (1990) or *Don't Read This Book, Whatever You Do: More Poems about School* (1993). Have students write and draw a creative response to one of the poems as a diagnostic measure. Appropriate books for this age group include *The Teacher from the Black Lagoon* by Mike Thaler (1989), *Today Was a Terrible Day* by Patricia Reilly Giff (1980), or *Miss Malarkey Doesn't Live in Room 10* by Judy Finchler (1995), or *Chrysanthemum* and *Lily's Purple Plastic Purse* by Kevin Henkes (1996).

Preview the Curriculum/Art/Social Studies.   After lunch, preview the curriculum in science, social studies, and other content areas. Highlight any field trips or unique experiences students will be having. If you are planning a thematic year, this would be a great time to initiate it. For example, a unit titled "My Journey" might be introduced by having the children draw and share self-portraits. Alternatively, they can construct and decorate time capsules, made out of paper towel rolls, that will be opened at the end of the year. Contents might include: the completed self-portrait, a hand print or tracing, a sample of best handwriting, an interest inventory, the title of a favorite book, television program, game, or sport, the math diagnostic test, a string as long as the child is tall, and a list of three things he or she would like to learn this year.

Wrap-Up.   Evaluate the first day with the children, asking them what they enjoyed most. Collect name tags and preview the next day. Dismiss and distribute first-day notes, translated as needed.

Notice that this sequence of activities has already established a basic schedule, which includes the basic curriculum areas. Use this pattern for the rest of the week, beginning informal reading diagnosis on the second day while children engage in free reading. Incorporate other language arts during this time frame. Reserve afternoons the rest of the week for your integrated social studies or science unit. You can add activities each day, keeping in mind that art and music are wonderful vehicles for social studies/science instruction.

Upper Grades (4–6)

Welcome.   Meet the students at the door or pick them up at the designated spot on the playground. Invite them to find a seat. Introduce yourself. Take attendance, making sure you ask the children to correct any errors. You might want to make some personal observations or comments to each child to help each one feel accepted. Distribute name tags, and assign newcomers a partner. One teacher uses this time to convey his philosophy to the group. He tells them that this will be a wonderful year, that learning will be fun, and that they will be working in groups and even working with other teachers for certain subjects as students do in middle school or junior high. He stresses how important each student is and how the class doesn't function well if anyone is absent physically or mentally.

He reassures the class about two major concerns of older students—too much homework and difficult schoolwork.

A Note from the Teacher

"Whatever you believe about yourself, that is what you will become."

A. GALLARDO

He spends a great deal of time having the students discuss the meaning of the quote and relating it to their lives. By fifth or sixth grade your emphasis should shift from setting down the rules and consequences to developing rapport and building mutual respect, although rules and consequences are the foundation for this positive approach.

Behavior Expectations and Rules. Stress that this will be the best school year for the students and for you. Why? Because you and they are one year more experienced and one year wiser. Some key points you might want to emphasize on that first day, following this teacher's example, are:

We are all unique.
Always try to do your best.
Encourage each other.
You are all needed and wanted here.
Turn mistakes into lessons.
We will treat one another with dignity and respect.
You need to be here in body and spirit.
You need to be responsible and complete all work.

After everyone by show of hands agrees to these expectations, follow with a discussion of logical consequences. Let students know you will allow for mistakes, but when mistakes recur, that you and the student(s) will need to talk about the problem privately and work it out. Subsequent mistakes of the same kind can lead to calls and conferences to enlist parental support in helping resolve the problem. Stress that you prefer logical consequences to punishment and that you will ask parents to avoid unrelated punishment as well. Assure students that you will not humiliate or publicly embarrass them. Ask that they treat you and other classmates with kindness, consideration, and respect in turn. This approach reflects the positive methods of discipline discussed in Chapter 5 (Nelsen, 1996).

Tell students that any conflicts in the room will be solved at class meetings. Describe the purposes of class meetings (conflict resolution, planning, or discussion) and the process for getting on the agenda. Tell them that each class meeting begins with compliments and that they will learn to both give and receive them. Announce a class meeting for later in the day to work out the details of the meeting schedule.

Orientation and Routines.   Collect lunch/milk monies. Follow with a talk about bathroom passes, water fountain rules, trash removal, and any other needed routines. Survey the room together. Point out the private spaces for you and them. Let students know where the supplies are and how they will get them. Show students the class library and their reference materials and any equipment such as a microwave or refrigerator or oven that means cooking and eating! Point out that the bulletin boards are empty because they will be decorating the classroom with their projects. Point out the Student of the Week bulletin board and have the lottery to select the first one. Be sure to tell students what the privileges, rights, and responsibilities of the Student of the Week are, including posting photos, objects, and work they are most proud to display on the bulletin board. The child who is chosen should have a right of refusal if she or he is not quite ready.

Discuss classroom helpers, provide job descriptions orally, and then implement your plan for selecting the student assistants. It is not too soon to begin showing the students that they are indeed part of the class and are needed to help things run smoothly.

Recess.   Dismiss the students for recess, but also give them plenty of in-class socializing breaks of five minutes' duration if they can demonstrate responsibility for stopping at the given signal.

Curriculum Preview.   Go over the daily schedule and let the students know if there will be any teaming arrangements among the upper-grade teachers and how the assignments, including homework, will be given and graded. Preview the curriculum and let them know about the highlights of the year, including the new things they will be learning and any field trips that are in the offing.

Introductions/Language Arts.   You can use any of the get-acquainted games previously mentioned or have student interview one another. Have the class suggest the questions together or use variations on those listed earlier in the chapter.

Math.   You may want to include some math diagnostic work before lunch, or you can use student interest inventories to construct bar or line graphs of favorite sports, music, or other activities. Preview some exciting math games or manipulatives such as tangrams or introduce a new technique such as Venn diagrams. Vow to make math exciting this year.

Lunch.   Dismiss the class, sending new students and their buddies off together.

Reading.   On the first day begin a period of silent, sustained reading with books from the class library. You may want to read as well or start to conduct informal reading inventories with those students new to the school. You might also want to use cloze tests on the first day with the entire group. Alternatively, you can choose an appropriate poem or book and make it the focus of a thematic day. Use poems such as "If I Were in Charge of the World" by Judith Viorst from the book of the same name (1981) or "Homework" by Russell Hoban from *Egg Thoughts* (1972) or choose an appropriate book to begin reading aloud such as *The Biggest Klutz in Fifth Grade* by Bill Wallace (1992) or *Twenty Ways to Lose Your Best Friend* by Marilyn Singer (1990).

Social Studies/Art.   Start with a self-concept miniunit (e.g., "My Journey," Figure 2.3) and consider the following activities:

- Have students write their names vertically, one letter in each space, and then think of an adjective that begins with that letter. Display these on the bulletin board and have students bring in photos to accompany the descriptions or take the photos yourself.
  - **E**legant
  - **L**ovable
  - **I**ntelligent
  - **Z**any
  - **A**rtistic
  - **B**eautiful
  - **E**nergetic
  - **T**alkative
  - **H**appy
- Each child constructs a personal time line of significant events in his or her life. The students can illustrate their time lines, and these make a wonderful bulletin board display that can be added to throughout the year.
- Each student designs a self-descriptive coat of arms (Figure 9.1). These make a colorful and self-concept-building bulletin board as well, especially if the students use colored markers instead of crayons.
- Have students create "Me Collages" from pictures cut from magazines that best reflect who they are (i.e., their interests, abilities, hobbies, pets, and favorite food, sport, season, color, animal, amusement, television program, place, etc.).

Figure 9.1

Wrap-Up.   During the wrap-up you may want to conduct your first class meeting. Decide on the times and the frequency and the days of the week. Plan where the agenda will be posted. Then discuss and evaluate the first day of school and preview the next day. Assign a short homework assignment, such as to find out the country of origin of parents, grandparents, or great-grandparents. These locations will be pinpointed on a world map the next day. Dismiss each child individually and send home a note to parents (translated, if appropriate) discussing your expectations and engaging their help.

FINALLY, YOUR TURN

These composite descriptions of the first day of class will give you some ideas to ponder before you solo. Between now and your debut, arrange to observe a pro on the first day. If that is not feasible, conduct your own survey and ask everyone you meet what he or she does on the first day. Adhere to the principles set forth in this chapter to help you remember key first-day elements. If one thing is certain it is that you will probably forget to do *something* that first day. Remember there will be approximately 179 more days for you to tell children what you forgot to tell them on Day One. But if you start now to get your list of must-do items going, you might be even better prepared than the pros. This is the time to line up an interpreter and someone willing to translate notes home into native languages.

Worksheet 9.2

Worksheet 9.3

Develop your own tentative plan of first-day activities on Worksheet 9.2, Schedule of First-Day Activities. After you have finished outlining your plans, evaluate them using the ten guiding principles. Ask yourself the questions posed on Worksheet 9.3, Evaluating My First Day's Plans. If you cannot answer yes to every question, go back to the drawing board. When you feel relatively secure about the first day, sketch out the plans for the remainder of the week, using Worksheet 9.4, First Week's Schedule.

Once you have established your basic framework, each day after the first should be relatively easy to plan. Add breadth and depth each day until you have a rich and full program for students. If you are using this book during your preservice period, remember your plans can and will change before that first day, but plan you must for a successful first day. Finally, just a couple of days before the grand opening, use Worksheet 9.5, First-Day Inventory, to check once again that you are as prepared as you can be. Now it's time for the plunge!

Worksheet 9.4

Worksheet 9.5

Reflection Box

In what ways, if any, has the chapter changed my beliefs?

Questions I Still Have . . .

Reflection Box

What practices actually worked for me in my first year?

FURTHER READING

Carroll, J. A., McCune, D., & Beveridge, D. (1987). *The welcome back to school book.* Carthage, IL.: Good Apple.

Schell, L., & Burden, P. (1992). *Countdown to the first day.* NEA checklist series. Washington, DC: National Education Association.

Williamson, B. (1988). *A first-year teacher's guidebook for success: A step-by-step educational recipe book from September to June.* Sacramento, CA: Dynamic Teaching.

Wong, H., & Wong, R. (1991). *The first days of school: How to be an effective teacher.* Sunnyvale, CA: Harry R. Wong.

REFERENCES

Baer, E. (1990). *This is the way we go to school.* New York: Scholastic.

Cazet, D. (1990). *Never spit on your shoes.* New York: Orchard Books.

Cohen, M. (1967). *Will I have a friend?* New York: Macmillan.

Dakos, K. (1990). *If you're not here, please raise your hand: Poems about school.* New York: Four Winds Press.

Dakos, K. (1993). *Don't read this book, whatever you do: More poems about school.* New York: Four Winds Press.

Finchler, J. (1995). *Miss Malarkey doesn't live in room 10.* New York: Walker and Company.

Fisher, A. (1991). *Always wondering.* New York: HarperCollins.

Giff, P. (1980). *Today was a terrible day.* New York: Viking Press.

Henkes, K. (1996). *Chrysanthemum* (paperback). New York: Mulberry Books.

Henkes, K. (1996). *Lily's purple plastic purse.* New York: Greenwillow Books.

Hoban, R. (1972). *Egg thoughts and other Frances songs.* New York: HarperCollins.

Katz, B. (1992). *Upside down and inside out: Poems for all your pockets.* Honesdale, PA: Boyds Mills.

Nelsen, J. (1996). *Positive discipline.* New York: Ballantine Books.

Singer, M. (1990). *Twenty ways to lose your best friend.* New York: HarperCollins.

Stoeke, J. (1996). *Minerva Louise at school.* New York: Dutton.

Thaler, M. (1989). *The teacher from the black lagoon.* New York: Scholastic.

Viorst, J. (1981). *If I were in charge of the world and other worries.* New York: Atheneum.

Wallace, B. (1992). *The biggest klutz in fifth grade.* New York: Holiday House.

chapter

10

A Balanced Professional Life

Reflection Box

What I Believe About

Reflecting on my teaching . . .
My professional responsibilities . . .
My professional development plan . . .
Managing stress . . .

A Note from the Teacher

I'm retiring two years from now in the year 2000. That's only semidefinite because every time I think about it, I start to miss the kids already. What will I do? This is my life and my job.

E. RAMSEY

Students, kids, pupils, children, youngsters, learners. They occupy your thoughts and you probably have generated long lists of ideas to make this a fulfilling year for them. But how will you make this a fulfilling year for *you*? Chapters 1 through 9 have focused on what you can do for children. This chapter is for *you* and focuses on what you can do for *you*. It's your road map to a balanced professional and personal life during your first year of

teaching and beyond. Key signposts along the way include reflection, professional development, rejuvenation, and self-forgiveness. Beyond student teaching lies a personal and
professional life in equilibrium.

TOWARD REFLECTIVE PRACTICE

Moir and Stobbe (1995) and colleagues in the California New Teacher Project have identified five phases new teachers commonly experience in the induction year. In a nutshell,
the *Anticipation Phase* is characterized by excitement as you realize, for example, that
you don't have to work as a supermarket checker anymore. Then comes the *Survival
Phase,* a period when you are just happy to keep your head above water. This is followed
by the *Disillusionment Phase,* which speaks for itself, and then the *Rejuvenation Phase*
after a breather, usually a vacation. A *Reflection Phase* follows and leads to another *Anticipation Phase* for the next school year.

According to Grant and Zeichner (1984), one of the most important decisions you
will make is whether or not you will become a *reflective* teacher. What is a reflective
teacher? Interpreting John Dewey's definition of reflective action as opposed to routine
action, Grant and Zeichner (1984) suggest three requisite attitudes for the reflective
teacher. They are *open-mindedness*, a willingness to consider and even to admit that you
are wrong; *responsibility*, a willingness to look at the consequences of your actions; and
wholeheartedness, a willingness to accept all students and to practice what you preach.
The reflective teacher, then, is one who really thinks about what he or she is doing, takes
responsibility for those actions, and goes about the job of educating children with a full
measure of enthusiasm and openness to diversity. Once you decide to be a reflective
teacher instead of a robot, how do you take the first steps?

Berlak and Berlak (1981) suggest that you can begin by examining your current beliefs
(about teaching, children, discipline) and patterns of behavior. Trace your beliefs and practices back to their sources. Did you pick them up in student teaching, in your own childhood, from your own teachers? Next, consider alternative patterns of behavior and their consequences. As you contemplate changing your patterns, talk with colleagues and compare
your beliefs and practices with those of others. The last step is synthesizing your reflections
and taking an active role in broadening your professional identity through studying, asking
questions, dialoguing with other professionals, and engaging in continuous self-reflection.

Clark (1989) brings this to a very concrete level in a seven-point plan for self-
directed development. At the top of the list is recognizing your own implicit theories and
beliefs about teaching. He suggests composing a teaching credo, and you can begin on
Worksheet 10.1, My Educational Credo, to write out your beliefs about teaching, learning, and children. Look at it from time to time throughout your first year of teaching and
revise it as your belief system grows with you. There may be additions, deletions, and revisions. Keep your versions in a journal or notebook.

Clark (1989) also advocates acknowledging your own strengths and relinquishing
the notion that you have to excel at everything. Question the way you always do things,
seek alternatives, and you will be amazed at the results. He recommends that you make a
five-year plan of things you would like to accomplish and that you seek help from all
sources (parents, colleagues, local businesses, professional organizations) to accomplish
them. As you reflect, Clark suggests, find ways to love, respect, and treat yourself well.

Worksheet
10.1

Blow your own horn and take every opportunity (conferences, videos, presentations) to demonstrate your expertise.

Self-reflection may be facilitated by the more objective techniques of videotaping or audiotaping lessons. Children can give you some honest and useful feedback if you ask them. One teacher has the children write down in June the three best things about the year, and she rereads them for confidence on the next first day of school. Another has the current class write letters to the next year's class about their experiences. You may want to design a questionnaire for your students to fill out anonymously at the end of the year. Answers to open-ended questions such as the examples below will provide you with data to ponder before you begin to teach again:

> The best three things about this year were . . .
> The three projects I liked best were . . .
> Five words to describe my teacher are . . .
> This year could have been better if . . .
> If I could change the class rules . . .
> If I could change the class schedule . . .
> We could have used more . . .
> We could have used less . . .
> The most interesting subjects/topics were . . .
> The most boring subjects/topics were . . .

One teacher has the children give her report cards at the end of the year. The design and categories are of their choosing, and it is a creative way to gather material for reflection.

Peer coaching or just talking informally with colleagues will help you think about your practice. Kent (1993) advocates that school-based collaborative teacher reflection be ongoing and that schools become places where teachers are active participants in their own professional development. When teachers come together with school colleagues to openly discuss discrepancies between theory and practice and give voice to their opinions, they become *less isolated, more empowered,* and *intellectually stimulated.*

A simple way of reflecting on your days is to use a diary or journal to write down your beliefs, your successes, your questions, and your ruminations about the day, every day. A very concise form, Worksheet 10.2, Success of the Day, will help you focus on daily successes. Keep these sheets in your desk drawer and write down at least three successes every day. When all seems futile, take out your log and read it from start to finish. That should cheer you up and restore a can-do attitude.

Worksheet 10.2

Katz (1990) suggests that in becoming "lifelong students of your own teaching," you and your colleagues should realize that there are no error-free decisions. She encourages you to use your judgment to make the "least worst" errors and have confidence in your decision making, never considering others' views more seriously than you consider your own.

PROFESSIONALISM AT SCHOOL

When asked what professional advice beginning teachers need most, one veteran offered, "Keep a sleeping bag in the closet." While you need not spend your entire day at school, teachers advise that success the first year is dependent on hard work, long hours, and maintaining professionalism inside and outside of school.

The importance of establishing and maintaining professional relationships with colleagues and school personnel was underscored by teachers in their final words of advice. They suggested that life in school was far more pleasant and productive when relationships with colleagues were positive. They urged new teachers to ask questions of colleagues and to share ideas, lessons, and projects to get two-way communication going. Try to visit other classrooms to see what colleagues are doing, always remaining open to sharing what you are doing as well. Shulman (1988) urges teachers to break through their feelings of isolation at the risk of vulnerability because peer support *can* make a difference. A tremendous support network can operate for you if you reach out and avail yourself of it.

Establishing good working relationships with the office staff, principal, and custodian was another final piece of advice. These individuals are there for support, and knowing whom to ask for what you need will save you a great deal of time, effort, and worry. Besides, a school is a social environment, and you will be far happier getting involved than being a wallflower.

Attend all social functions at the school, from potlucks, to luncheons, to P.T.A. meetings, to skating parties for the children. Your social life will probably not revolve around the school, but while you are there, immerse yourself in its social aspects. You may find a new friend, a mentor perhaps, and you will surely feel better being part of and accepted by the staff.

KEEPING UP WITH PAPERWORK

The more carefully you organize your own assessment and record-keeping procedures at the outset, the less overwhelmed you will feel when inundated by the additional record keeping dictated by your district. Many teachers report that the major frustration in their school day is dealing with the seemingly endless parade of papers across their desks. Here are some ways of making your paperwork load easier to shoulder.

Official School Paperwork

Your district will require quite specialized record keeping, and staying on top of it is a challenge. There are times when you'll want to hire a full-time secretary and a bookkeeper when you look at the papers that have inundated your desk. The school bureaucracy, like all bureaucracies, generates forms for almost all human endeavors. I could not possibly list all the forms you can expect to encounter in your district, and even if I could, I wouldn't want to frighten you away from completing this chapter. Grin and bear it; the paperwork goes with the job! You'll learn all about these forms at staff meetings. Some schools provide new teachers with buddies or mentor teachers. They can lead you through the maze of forms.

Try to set aside a time each day, preferably in the morning before school, to fill in any forms, compose any reports or letters, write your report cards, and do similiar chores. Keep a large calendar on which you mark due dates and special events so you can plan ahead and keep on top of any deadlines. Below are some of the official records you may be asked to keep.

Grade Book and Attendance Book.   Many of your records will be kept in a grade book or marking book as soon as the final class roster is set. Remember to keep careful attendance records, as these are legal documents. Each page in a grade book has room for a roster of student names and columns for recording attendance, test grades, and work completed. It's probably best to use a separate page for attendance and for each of the major curriculum areas. You can save yourself some time by simply duplicating class rosters with columns and with the names already typed in. These sheets can be used for innumerable purposes besides grading and attendance, such as checking off for field trip permission slips, recording lunch money, and checking off for monitors.

Planbook/Lesson Plans.   Practically all schools have a policy regarding the format and length of lesson plans. Some districts require plans to be turned in weekly, some semi-monthly, some not at all. In almost all districts, teachers are required to leave their planbook in school so that a substitute has access to it in case of emergency. Find out about the policy in your school or district regarding lesson plans and when and if they need to be turned in. This is one of the first questions you should ask as a beginning teacher. Turn to colleagues if the format for plans differs significantly from the one you used in former school settings or during student teaching. Remember that your plans will be a reflection of your performance in the classroom, and they will tell the principal a great deal about the program you have established. Follow the herd. Have plans completed in appropriate detail and format and then hand them in on time!

Parent Conference Records.   It is wise to keep records of parent conferences, including name of the child, date, time, and those in attendance along with a summary of the conference and an indication of why it was called. It is also wise to make a record of all telephone calls to parents, including the date, time, and nature of the call. You can easily use five-by eight-inch index cards, one for each child, as a record-keeping device for both conferences and telephone calls, or simply have one sheet for each child for this purpose in your loose-leaf notebook.

Teachers also recommend keeping all correspondence from home, no matter how trivial. If you want to be safe rather than sorry, make copies or use carbon paper when you communicate with the parents as well. You can clear up many a misunderstanding if you can produce the evidence by simply opening up your file cabinet or index card file.

Proficiency Checklists.   Teachers stress how important it is to make accurate and up-to-date entries on proficiency lists, in light of the fact that they are used in some districts to determine promotion to the next grade. Even if they are not used in this way in your district, it is very helpful to use checklists of competencies so you can gear instruction to those skills, concepts, and attitudes required at your grade level. In addition, checklists and proficiency lists enable you to focus on specific remedial efforts for individuals who have not met the objectives or competencies. Finally, reporting to parents and enlisting their aid at home becomes easier if you can be quite specific about which objectives have been mastered by any particular child and which have not.

Children's Paperwork

To keep yourself from lugging home shopping bags full of student papers, use some of the following suggestions when they fit the assignment:

- When students finish their work, have them place papers in the upper right-hand corner of their desk. Walk around and check papers on the spot.
- Have children exchange papers or mark their own.
- Use hand signals, choral responses, and individual sets of flash cards to check understanding without having every response written down.
- Make individual, laminated response cards for each child, give each a grease pencil and wiper, and have the students respond by holding up their plastic cards. Use individual chalkboards if you have them. Floor tiles and grease pencils work well too.
- Use the opaque projector to give answers to worksheet examples or make a transparency of the worksheet and illuminate it on the overhead projector, with the answers filled in all at once or one at a time.
- Recognize that you don't have to test each skill or concept with multiple examples when fewer will suffice. If preprinted worksheets have 25 examples, cut the sheets in half, or tell the children to complete only the odd-numbered ones or the last 10. If you have them do all the examples, you'll have a fair idea of how they have done if you only do spot checking.
- Provide answers on a key or overhead projector to all but the last five examples. These you check yourself, thus determining if the child simply filled in the answers or has really mastered the material.
- Engage parent volunteers to help in the marking.
- Recognize that not every assignment needs careful attention and, additionally, that not every assignment needs to be returned to the children. You can eyeball the work to check for major error patterns, and then place it in the circular file.
- Cochran (1989) suggests that teachers rely more on oral review as a sponge activity instead of on so much written work.
- Another clever idea (Cochran, 1989) is to have children make up their own worksheets on papers folded into eighths. In each box, the children demonstrate mastery of what they have learned during the day. They can, for example, draw a mammal in box 1, write three nouns in box 2, and solve an addition problem in box 3. In just three spaces you have reviewed three subject areas with a third grade class and have very little grading to do at home.
- One teacher suggests having children use answer columns at the right-hand side of their page so that teachers can quickly see the answer.

PROFESSIONAL DEVELOPMENT

Keep reading all you can about teaching and learning, classroom discipline, and management. Some teachers suggest subscriptions to magazines filled with many specific teaching ideas and units. At the end of this chapter you will find a list of elementary-school-oriented periodicals you may want to look for in the resource center or university library and then order for your own professional library.

Continuing Education

You may be required by your state credential laws to continue your education right away. Veterans advise you to take the least demanding courses first and none during the first semester of teaching. Your district will require you to attend new-teacher inservices and meetings that will consume your time during those first few months, and you don't want to overcommit yourself.

The first year of teaching may not be the time to start a new degree program either; however, an extended education course or two to help you bone up on some practical aspect of teaching is a good idea. Take these courses on a need-to-know basis so they are useful to you in your everyday life in the classroom and not just one more obligation. You might want to learn or brush up on second language skills yourself by studying any of the languages spoken by children in your class. Conversation tapes are available in libraries and bookstores, and it would be well worth your effort to communicate with the children in their primary language. Your attempts, however limited, will be welcomed by the children and their parents. Also consider extension courses with titles such as 100 Ways to Enhance Literature (or Creative Writing or Science, etc.) or that focus on bulletin boards or using HyperCard stacks or other technology. Of course, you might just take a course for fun that has absolutely nothing to do with teaching! The Care and Feeding of Your Reptile was one I came across recently.

A Teaching Portfolio

Just as your students will be developing, maintaining, and reflecting on their progress using portfolio assessment, Bozzone (1994) suggests that teachers should keep teaching portfolios as well. You will be able to see your evolution as a professional and have direct evidence, on those "bad" days, that you really are doing some wonderful things. You might include in your portfolio samples of pupil products, videos of performances, or photos of special bulletin boards or displays. You may want to include observations and evaluations by your administrator, letters from parents, notes from children, units you have developed, special lesson plans, a list of professional books and articles you have read, notes and agendas from committee meetings, and lists of conferences and inservices you have attended. From time to time you can reflect on your progress, and share your portfolio with colleagues, mentors, administrators, and parents.

Professional Organizations and Journals

Join local or regional councils of national professional organizations. Read the very informative professional journals they publish. The addresses are listed at the end of the chapter. These local councils provide meeting and inservice opportunities. You may become a local conference presenter yourself. Have business cards (see Figure 10.1) made for yourself to hand out to parents and colleagues as well as at inservice meetings. Your profession? **Teacher** in big bold letters!

Use Worksheet 10.3, Professional Development Log, to keep a log of your professional activities during your first year and beyond.

Worksheet
10.3

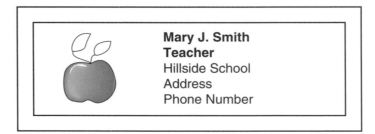

Mary J. Smith
Teacher
Hillside School
Address
Phone Number

Figure 10.1

STRESS AND REJUVENATION

A great deal has been written about teacher burnout and teacher stress. I hear from student teachers that they are burned out, and I chuckle because they haven't even been lit yet. The word *burnout* should be reserved for a teacher who at least has a credential in hand!

Wangberg (1984) describes several causes for the feelings of emotional exhaustion, depersonalization, and failure that we associate with the term *burnout*. Societal-level causes include the low respect and low pay associated with teaching. Institutional factors include increased accountability, a sense of isolation, lack of real decision-making power, lack of autonomy, and poor physical working conditions in schools. Personal factors include poor health choices (e.g., smoking and drinking), neglect of one's own emotional needs and well-being, and the unrealistic expectations of "superteacher" syndrome.

Relieving Societal Stress

Although there is not much you can do about the pay scale either in your district or nationwide, you can do your part to promote respect for teachers by recognizing, as Landsmann (1988) states, that "it only takes a few waves to start a sea of change." She suggests assuming your rightful role as teacher and not letting anyone undermine it. She encourages teachers to sell themselves (and thus their profession) by speaking at service clubs and attracting publicity in the local papers for school events and happenings.

To sell your profession, be the best possible teacher you can be. Make a continuing list of your strengths or improvements to sell yourself to yourself first. The word will get around. Parents are your best partners, and they can promote you in the community if you extend your hand. Write articles for the newspaper. Offer to appear on local cable television programs to talk about helping children with homework, or start an after-school tutorial program. Network with other teachers to brainstorm ways of sprucing up your profession's image in the community. Remember always that, whatever the public perception, you are engaged in *significant* work that makes a difference in the lives of children.

Relieving School Stress

At school, until the school-based management and teacher empowerment movements come to full fruition to give teachers more decision-making power and autonomy, it is best to limit your efforts to what is currently under your control. You can do something about the stressors of increased accountability, isolation, and poor physical working conditions.

Set realistic expectations for yourself and the children. Keep careful and up-to-date records and communicate often with parents and your administrator about your progress with the class as a whole and with individuals. View the child holistically and recognize that test scores are only one facet of the child's development. Ask yourself when you are feeling low, Where was the child at the beginning of school? Where is he (or she) now? Justify your program with confidence.

Counter the sense of isolation by establishing collegial relationships at school and by making a promise to yourself to socialize during lunch and recess no matter how much work you have. You need to get out of your classroom and see grown-ups. Establish a lunchtime walking group or go out to lunch for a change of routine. Team with other teachers, plan with other teachers, jog with other teachers. Organize a support group of new teachers that meets once a week during lunch or at someone's house. Just get out of your room and socialize! Make frequent contact with a mentor or a buddy who has been officially designated or simply find a friend at school to whom you can talk.

You may not be able to do anything about too few rest rooms, peeling paint, or poorly designed furniture, but you can relieve stress by designing a learning environment you want to live in for six hours each day. Pay great attention to decoration, furniture arrangement, bulletin boards, and add personal touches, such as a sofa, lamps, or bean bag chairs. Clean up, organize, and redecorate your room from time to time. Throw things out that are dog-eared or no longer useful. Play soft music during work time. The room environment is key to how teachers feel about coming to school each day. Your room reflects you as well as it does the children.

Devise ways to break the routine for you and your students. Have a backward day, during which the schedule goes in reverse and so do students' shirts. Other themed days teachers have tried and thoroughly enjoyed include an all-day read-a-thon, crazy-hat day, wearing-slippers day, students-teach-the-class day, bring-your-stuffed-animal-to-school day, and wearing-certain-color day. Do some silly things like jumping rope with the kids or playing basketball with them at recess. Bring in a Frisbee and toss it around with them. Take them out for an unexpected walking field trip on the first day of spring. Create new projects, such as a classroom window garden or a class newspaper. Cook with them unexpectedly. The list of routine breakers is endless.

Bozzone (1995) suggests taking a few minutes out of the day for your own R and R ritual, which includes deep breathing and easy stretching and muscle-flexing exercises. Or take a few minutes during recess to engage in visual imagery techniques. Regulate your breathing and take a mental trip to a quiet, secluded, peaceful place you have been to or hope to visit. A few minutes in Tahiti or on a hike in the woods during a break will put you in a better frame of mind.

Relieving Personal Stress

The bad news is that some teachers don't give as much to themselves as they give to their students. They set unrealistic expectations for themselves, and they often don't take care of their health. The good news is that you can relieve the stress from personal sources by being good to yourself in any number of ways.

A Note from the Teacher

New teachers spend every waking moment on school-related tasks: lesson plans, grading, preparing materials for lessons, and so on. You need to take one day each weekend for yourself and your family instead of devoting both days to work. On Friday evenings, I enjoy lighting a candle and sipping a glass of sparkling cider as I soak in a bubble bath. Even just 20 minutes for myself makes me feel refreshed and renewed.

B. MONROE

Each of you has some special ways you are good to yourself, and it is a useful idea to write them down and post them on your mirror so you can face them every day. Mental well-being is as important as physical health, and you need to find some opportunities to be good to yourself. Here are some other low-cost suggestions from teachers to get you started on your own personal rejuvenation plan.

- Plan a weekend away (or stay home and hibernate).
- Buy yourself flowers.
- Read a book you "don't have time for."
- Play with your pet.
- Buy a new article of clothing.
- Spend some time alone.
- Take a walk.
- Bake or cook.
- Listen to music.
- Go to the gym.
- Give yourself a facial.
- Have your house or apartment cleaned.

- Get a babysitter.
- Keep a journal.
- Play a board game.

For you it might be a movie, a sporting event, a pedicure, a minivacation on Saturday, or dinner out with a friend. You might have to negotiate responsibilities at home for more free time. School has a way of consuming teachers, especially new ones, so learn to make yourself a priority. Give yourself time between school and arrival home to unwind or, if not, take a few minutes upon arrival to make the transition. Try to complete most paperwork at school, even if it means staying there to do it. You don't want to be burdened with papers every night. Establish a schedule that gives you some free nights, even your first year, and use the grading shortcuts cited in this chapter.

Sundays can be especially depressing if you wait until the last minute to plan for the week. Try to parcel out your planning over the weekend so you can get it done and have some free, unstructured time to pursue your own interests and hobbies or to just to catch up on family or sleep!

Stress caused by poor health can be countered through a program of exercise, nutrition, meditation or relaxation techniques, vitamins, and any number of ways of relaxing and having fun. If you drink excessively or smoke or if you don't get enough sleep and exercise, you are risking your health and, as a result, your classroom effectiveness. Some references are included at the end of the chapter for those of you who want to know more about how to reduce stress and keep the unwanted nighttime "what-ifs" and "I can'ts" at bay.

The "superteacher syndrome" is a debilitating condition that new teachers confuse with responsibility and accountability. Should you catch this obsession with perfectionism, beware that it promotes competition instead of cooperation and reduces new teachers to quivering, self-proclaimed failures. You will make mistakes. We all make mistakes. You can either learn from your mistakes or be paralyzed by them. The quest to be perfect, to be a superteacher, can be replaced with attitudes such as these expressed by experienced teachers. Recite them ten times each day:

A Note from the Teacher

I will be as forgiving of myself as I am of students.
I will be realistic and won't dwell on mistakes.
This too shall pass.
Everything is a learning experience.
It seemed like the best thing to do at the time.
Mistakes are learning opportunities.
I'll do my best every day; then I won't worry.

Many teachers who offered advice to beginners underscored repeatedly that the first year is a continuous learning experience. Seen in that light, it becomes a little less frightening. Teachers were all in agreement that there will be good days and bad days, and they urged beginning teachers to be self-forgiving of mistakes. Don't try to implement in the first week every teaching strategy and idea learned in teacher-training courses. Ease up on yourself, and everything will fall into place. At all costs, don't overextend yourself at the outset. You'll tire yourself out and be ready for a vacation two weeks into the school year.

Another antidote to stress and frustration is flexibility in dealing with the many challenges that keep you from accomplishing all you feel you should. One respondent cautioned, "Don't complain. Turn obstacles into opportunities."

Worksheet
10.4

On Worksheet 10.4, Rejuvenation Calendar, a blank calendar for duplication, record all the rejuvenating activities you engage in each month. Make sure that each month it is filled with revitalizing activities so you can be of sound mind and body for the children in your class; they rely on your well-being more than you know.

A FINAL NOTE

When all is said and done, there is so much else that could have been said. This book will help you take the first tentative steps across the threshold of your new teaching career. Your experience will mold and shape you, and you will continue to grow and learn with each successive year. Teaching is a dynamic interaction between you and the children, one that will mutually change your lives in big ways and in small ways. Let the children guide your development as you guide theirs. Take the advice contained in this book and in other books, as well as the advice offered by colleagues and in courses, and incorporate what works for you. Finally, you have to trust yourself and internalize your own unique teaching style from all the well-intentioned advice you receive. Your professional development is a process that can't be short-circuited and will continue as long as you call yourself teacher. Listen, learn, ask questions, but ultimately, during your first year of teaching and beyond, your personal teaching style will emerge and you'll find your own way.

Reflection Box

In what ways, if any, has the chapter changed my beliefs?

Questions I Still Have . . .

Reflection Box

What practices actually worked for me in my first year?

FURTHER READING

Blumenfeld, L. (1994). *The big book of relaxation.* Roslyn, NY: The Relaxation Company.

Gold, Y., & Roth, R. (1993). *Teachers managing stress and preventing burnout: The professional health solution.* London: Falmer Press.

Metcalf, C. W., & Felible, R. (1993). *Lighten up: Survival skills for people under pressure.* Reading, MA: Addison-Wesley.

Miller, L. H., Smith, A., & Rothstein, L. (1994). *The stress solution.* New York: Pocket Books.

Moskowitz, R. (1993). *How to organize your work & your life* (2nd ed.). New York: Doubleday.

Ryan, K. (Ed.). (1992). *The roller coaster year: Essays by and for beginning teachers.* New York: HarperCollins.

PROFESSIONAL JOURNALS

General Teaching Ideas

Instructor	Scholastic P.O. Box 53894 Boulder, CO 80321-3894 (1-800-544-2917)
Teaching Pre K–8	P.O. Box 54808 Boulder, CO 80322-4808 (1-800-678-8793)

Elementary Subject Areas

Social Studies and the Young Learner *Social Education*	National Council for the Social Studies 3501 Newark Street N.W. Washington, DC 20016
Teaching Children Mathematics	National Council of Teachers of Mathematics 1906 Association Drive Reston, VA 22091
Science and Children	National Science Teachers Association 1742 Connecticut Avenue N.W. Washington, DC 20009-1171
Language Arts	National Council of Teachers of English 1111 Kenyon Road Urbana, IL 61801
The Reading Teacher	International Reading Association 800 Barksdale Road P.O. Box 8139 Newark, DE 19714-8139

Issues, Practices, and Programs

Educational Leadership   Association for Supervision and
                                                Curriculum Development
                                            1250 North Pitt Street
                                            Alexandria, VA 22314

Phi Delta Kappan   Phi Delta Kappa
                                            Eighth and Union Streets
                                            P.O. Box 789
                                            Bloomington, IN 47402

REFERENCES

Berlak, A., & Berlak, H. (1981). *Dilemmas of schooling.* London: Methuen.

Bozzone, M. (1994). The professional portfolio: Why you should start one now. *Instructor, 103*(9), 48–50.

Bozzone, M. (1995). A teacher's stress survival guide. *Instructor, 104*(5), 55–59.

Clark, C. (1989). Taking charge. *Instructor, 99*(3), 26–28.

Cochran, J. (1989). Escape from paperwork. *Instructor, 99*(4), 76–77.

Grant, C., & Zeichner, K. (1984). On becoming a reflective teacher. In C. Grant (Ed.), *Preparing for reflective teaching* (pp. 1–8). Boston: Allyn & Bacon.

Katz, L. (1990). Reflect on your role as a teacher. *Instructor, 100*(1), 47.

Kent, K. (1993). The need for school-based teacher reflection. *Teacher Education Quarterly, 20*(1), 83–91.

Landsmann, L. (1988). 10 resolutions for teachers. *Phi Delta Kappan, 69*(5), 373–374.

Moir, E., & Stobbe, C. (1995). Professional growth for new teachers: Support and assessment through collegial partnerships. *Teacher Education Quarterly, 22*(4), 83–91.

Shulman, J. (1988). Look to a colleague. *Instructor, 98*(5), 32–34.

Wangberg, E. (1984). The complex issue of teacher stress and job satisfaction. *Contemporary Education, 56*(1), 11–15.

Appendix: Worksheets

Worksheet 1.1
Job Search Checklist

1. Visit your career/job placement center. Ask about the following services:

placement files	☐
employment listings	☐
upcoming job fairs	☐
on-campus recruiting	☐
workshops on résumé writing	☐
workshops on interviewing	☐
publications, newsletters, brochures	☐
salary schedules for school districts	☐
requirements for certification in other states	☐
directories of public and private schools	☐

2. Consider using some or all of these job search strategies:

call or write for applications from school districts	☐
make personal contacts during student teaching	☐
seek observations by and letters of recommendation from school and district administrators	☐
join professional education organizations such as Pi Lamda Theta or Kappa Delta Pi	☐
volunteer in schools	☐
use employment listings	☐
attend local/regional professional conferences	☐
look at directories of public and private schools	☐
attend job fairs	☐

3. Put together a résumé and consider these factors:

use a chronological format	☐
use a computer and laser printer	☐
use heavy white paper	☐
make it easy to read	☐
keep it short and to the point	☐
include the following headings:	
Name, address, phone	☐
Credential(s) held	☐
Professional Objective	☐

Education ☐

Professional Experience (Don't forget student
    teaching) ☐

Other Experience ☐

Special Skills and Talents ☐

Professional Organizations (future teachers club,
    student membership in International Reading
    Association, etc.) ☐

4. Prepare a cover letter to go along with your résumé. ☐

5. Prepare for an interview well ahead of time by:

analyzing your strengths and weaknesses ☐
learning about the school district and the school ☐
preparing a professional portfolio ☐
preparing appropriate questions to ask to show
    interest ☐
thinking about and preparing answers to the inter-
    view questions that follow this checklist ☐

6. At the interview present yourself in a positive light by:

dressing professionally ☐
paying close attention to grooming ☐
bringing your portfolio and/or résumé ☐
listening attentively ☐
making eye contact ☐
being aware of two-way nonverbal communication ☐
expanding on answers ☐
selling yourself ☐
emphasizing the positive ☐
taking time to compose answers ☐
having some questions to ask such as: ☐
    Is there an orientation for new teachers?
    Will I have a mentor or buddy assigned to me?
    Is there a districtwide discipline policy?
    What special services are there in the district?
    When can I expect to hear from you?

7. Write a thank-you letter immediately after the interview expressing:

pleasure in meeting the interviewer(s) ☐
enjoyment of the discussion ☐
continuing interest in the position ☐
anticipation of hearing from the prospective employer ☐

8. Consider writing or outlining answers to the following questions, which are somewhat typical. Collect other questions from your friends, colleagues, and teachers.

Why did you choose this district?
Tell me about yourself.
What did you learn from student teaching?
Which curriculum areas are your strengths? Which ones are your weaknesses?
What are your strengths and weaknesses?
Why did you become a teacher?
What grade levels are you more prepared to teach?
How will you provide for diversity in your classroom?
What is multicultural education?
What accomplishment are you most proud of?
What is your experience with . . . (second language learners, bilingual students, special-education students, the gifted, etc.)?
What is your idea of the ideal classroom environment?
What do you expect to include in an effective lesson?
How do you teach . . . (reading, math, social studies, science, etc.)?
How would you conduct the first day of school?
What is your philosophy of discipline?
How do you go about individualizing instruction?
How do you organize for cooperative learning?
Talk about thematic teaching and any integrated units you have planned.
What would I see if I came into your room at midyear?
What is authentic assessment, and how do you organize student portfolios?
What would be a good question to ask you? Make one up and answer it.

	Yes
District policy and procedures	☐
Guidebook for new teachers	☐
School procedural manual	☐
School manual for parents	☐
District or school discipline policy	☐

Curriculum Guides/
Proficiency Lists

	District Yes	State Yes
Reading	☐	☐
Math	☐	☐
Language Arts/Spelling	☐	☐
Science	☐	☐
Social Studies	☐	☐
Art	☐	☐
P.E.	☐	☐
Music	☐	☐
Health	☐	☐

Teacher's Manuals/
Student Texts

	Yes
Reading	☐
Math	☐
Language Arts/Spelling	☐
Science	☐
Social Studies	☐
Art	☐
P.E.	☐
Music	☐
Health	☐

**Resource Material/Kits/
Computer and Laser Disc Applications**   Yes

Reading   ☐
Math   ☐
Language Arts/Spelling   ☐
Science   ☐
Social Studies   ☐
Art   ☐
P.E.   ☐
Music   ☐
Health   ☐

Other:

Topic

Concepts:

Skills:

Attitudes:

Learning Activities

Art		Social Studies

Math		Language Arts

Resources: Books, Materials, Technology

P.E.		Music

Health		Science

Worksheet 2.3
Unit Evaluation Criteria

Unit Evaluation Criteria

	Yes	No
Rationale		
Is the unit topic consistent with the formal curriculum?	☐	☐
Is the unit topic significant?	☐	☐
Is the topic of interest to children?	☐	☐
Is the topic developmentally appropriate?	☐	☐
Content		
Is the content coverage sufficient?	☐	☐
Is the content focused?	☐	☐
Is the content age-appropriate?	☐	☐
Are multicultural perspectives included?	☐	☐
Objectives		
Do the objectives include higher order thinking skills?	☐	☐
Are the objectives written in proper form?	☐	☐
Are there sufficient objectives to cover the content?	☐	☐
Are there objectives for skills:		
Critical thinking skills?	☐	☐
Communication skills?	☐	☐
Cooperation skills?	☐	☐
Research skills?	☐	☐
Basic math and reading skills?	☐	☐
Learning Activities		
Is there an initiating event to motivate the children?	☐	☐
Are there enough activities to meet each objective?	☐	☐
Are multiple objectives met by each activity?	☐	☐
Are there a variety of strategies used?	☐	☐
Are there opportunities for pupil-teacher planning?	☐	☐
Are other curriculum areas integrated in the unit?	☐	☐
Are the activities more active than passive?	☐	☐
Do the activities address all learning styles?	☐	☐
Are there opportunities for research and group work?	☐	☐
Is there a culminating event that ties the unit together?	☐	☐

Evaluation

	Yes	No
Does the unit have built-in pupil assessment measures:		
pre-/post-unit attitude and knowledge survey?	☐	☐
observational data collection?	☐	☐
pupil work samples or journals?	☐	☐
Are there enough alternatives so I can change direction if the unit needs to be altered?	☐	☐
Is the evaluation component tied to the objectives?	☐	☐
Are the evaluation measures varied?	☐	☐

Resources and Materials

	Yes	No
Are there enough resources for me to use?	☐	☐
books?	☐	☐
A.V. (tapes, films, filmstrips, videos, records)?	☐	☐
technology?	☐	☐
field trips?	☐	☐
resource people as speakers?	☐	☐
artifacts or realia?	☐	☐

The Unit Overall

	Yes	No
Is it fun?	☐	☐
Is it cohesive?	☐	☐
Is it coherent?	☐	☐
Is it varied?	☐	☐
Is it child-sized?	☐	☐
Is it focused?	☐	☐
Is it teachable?	☐	☐

Other Criteria:

Worksheet 2.4
Weekly Plan

Week_____Year____

Theme_____

(Place curriculum areas you are integrating—for example, math and science or language arts and social studies—in close proximity so you can work across the blocks.)

	Language	Social Studies	Art	Math	Science	Music	P.E.	Health
Monday ___/___(date)								
Tuesday ___/___								
Wednesday ___/___								
Thursday ___/___								
Friday ___/___								

Notes: Duty: Meetings: Things to Do: Calls:

Worksheet 2.5
Daily Lesson Plan

Daily Lesson Plan

Date

Time/Subject	Activity/Procedures	Materials or Page #s

A.V. Equipment	Homework Assignment	Announcements	Resources
Calls to Parents	Special Events/Assemblies		Things to Do

Worksheet 3.1
Inventory of School Supplies and Materials

General Supplies	Yes	No	Storage Location
tacks	☐	☐	
clips	☐	☐	
rubber bands	☐	☐	
glue	☐	☐	
rubber cement	☐	☐	
paste	☐	☐	
tape	☐	☐	
stapler/staples	☐	☐	
tissues	☐	☐	
scissors	☐	☐	
markers	☐	☐	
crayons	☐	☐	
chalk (white & colored)	☐	☐	
rulers	☐	☐	
ink, stamp pads	☐	☐	
laminating machine	☐	☐	
die cut press	☐	☐	
dry mount press	☐	☐	
bookbinding machine	☐	☐	
newspaper	☐	☐	
newsprint	☐	☐	
pens, pencils	☐	☐	
tissue paper	☐	☐	
cardboard	☐	☐	
paper towels	☐	☐	
cleansers/detergent	☐	☐	
buckets	☐	☐	
rags	☐	☐	
soap	☐	☐	
sponges	☐	☐	
scrub brushes	☐	☐	
pipe cleaners	☐	☐	

Math

	Yes	No	Storage Location
flannel boards	☐	☐	
pocket charts	☐	☐	
Cuisinaire rods	☐	☐	
rulers	☐	☐	
scales	☐	☐	
measuring containers: spoons, cups	☐	☐	
clocks	☐	☐	
number lines	☐	☐	
aids for teaching fractions	☐	☐	
aids for teaching decimals	☐	☐	
math games	☐	☐	
thermometers	☐	☐	
skill cards	☐	☐	
meter sticks	☐	☐	
tape measures	☐	☐	
graph paper	☐	☐	
cubes/base ten materials	☐	☐	
beads	☐	☐	
weights	☐	☐	
balance	☐	☐	
height measures	☐	☐	
dice	☐	☐	
calipers	☐	☐	

Reading/Language Arts

	Yes	No	Storage Location
handwriting/alphabet charts	☐	☐	
big books	☐	☐	
skill kits	☐	☐	
reading and language games	☐	☐	
picture book filmstrips	☐	☐	
paperback books	☐	☐	
writing paper of all sizes	☐	☐	
large chart paper	☐	☐	
cassette tapes of stories	☐	☐	

Science

	Yes	No	Storage Location
test tubes	☐	☐	
lab coats	☐	☐	
microscopes	☐	☐	
magnifying glasses	☐	☐	
thermometers	☐	☐	
eye droppers	☐	☐	
spoons	☐	☐	
measuring containers	☐	☐	

194

	Yes	No	Storage Location

measuring and weight scales ☐ ☐
compasses ☐ ☐
telescope ☐ ☐
lamps, flashlights ☐ ☐
filmstrips ☐ ☐
rock sets ☐ ☐
water table ☐ ☐
magnets ☐ ☐
cooking equipment ☐ ☐

Social Studies

globes ☐ ☐
U.S. maps ☐ ☐
state maps ☐ ☐
world map ☐ ☐
road maps ☐ ☐
city maps ☐ ☐
map puzzles ☐ ☐
travel posters ☐ ☐
photographs of presidents ☐ ☐

Music

records for singing ☐ ☐
listening earphones ☐ ☐
tape recorder ☐ ☐
record or CD player ☐ ☐
autoharp ☐ ☐
bells ☐ ☐
piano ☐ ☐
guitar ☐ ☐
other musical instruments ☐ ☐

Art

yarn ☐ ☐
calligraphy pens ☐ ☐
tempera paints ☐ ☐
watercolors ☐ ☐
brushes ☐ ☐
easels ☐ ☐
smocks ☐ ☐
construction paper ☐ ☐
foam rubber ☐ ☐
plaster ☐ ☐

	Yes	No	Storage Location
clay and glazes	☐	☐	
kiln	☐	☐	
potter's wheel	☐	☐	
looms	☐	☐	
glitter	☐	☐	
wood remnants	☐	☐	
styrofoam	☐	☐	
cloth	☐	☐	

Physical Education

	Yes	No	Storage Location
soccer balls	☐	☐	
softball equipment	☐	☐	
jump ropes	☐	☐	
volleyballs and net	☐	☐	
jacks	☐	☐	
marbles	☐	☐	
tether balls	☐	☐	
hula hoops	☐	☐	
tricycles	☐	☐	
roller skates	☐	☐	

Media

	Yes	No	Storage Location
film projector	☐	☐	
slide projector	☐	☐	
overhead projector	☐	☐	
opaque projector	☐	☐	
tape recorders	☐	☐	
screens	☐	☐	
cameras	☐	☐	
earphone sets	☐	☐	
computers/software	☐	☐	
video camera and VCR	☐	☐	
laser disc player	☐	☐	
compact disc player	☐	☐	

Kindergarten

	Yes	No	Storage Location
blocks (large and small)	☐	☐	
puppets	☐	☐	
dress-up corner materials	☐	☐	
house corner materials	☐	☐	
picture books	☐	☐	
puzzles	☐	☐	
primary instructional posters	☐	☐	

	Yes	No	Storage Location
primary chart paper	☐	☐	
children's records and tapes	☐	☐	
dough and cookie cutters	☐	☐	
typewriter	☐	☐	
sand table	☐	☐	
water table	☐	☐	
beads	☐	☐	
peg boards	☐	☐	
sequencing materials	☐	☐	
stuffed animals, multiracial dolls	☐	☐	
wooden trucks, cars	☐	☐	
outdoor equipment	☐	☐	
climbing bars	☐	☐	
swings	☐	☐	
wagons	☐	☐	
Nerf balls	☐	☐	

Other:

Worksheet 3.2
Wish List of Items from Parents

Art   Science

Social Studies   Music

Math   Cooking

General Supplies   Other

Worksheet 3.3
Things I Can't Beg or Borrow
But May Need to Order

ITEM   JUSTIFICATION

Worksheet 3.4
Scrounging Directory

Store   Telephone/Address   Materials Obtained

Worksheet 3.5
The Local Field Trip Directory

Field Trip	Telephone # Address	Contact Person	Notes

Worksheet 4.1
Sketch of Ideal Classroom Environment

Worksheet 4.2
Initial Bulletin Board Ideas

The ones I will create:

1. General Ideas   Notes

- ☐ star of the week
- ☐ calendar
- ☐ weather chart
- ☐ student work
- ☐ rules
- ☐ monitors chart
- ☐ handwriting
- ☐ Pledge of Allegiance
- ☐ birthday board
- ☐ tooth chart
- ☐ welcome back
- ☐ teacher introduction
- ☐ reading
- ☐ current events

_____

_____

2. Instructional Ideas

	Location		Distribution		
	Desk	Central	Pupil	Monitor	Teacher
paper					
art paper					
pencils/pens					
scissors					
paste					
rulers					
crayons					
texts:					
math					
social studies					
science					
language					
readers					
health					
library books					
lunch boxes					
clothing					
other ( )					

Generally, these are my procedures for distribution of materials:

I. Materials and Equipment

Materials distribution
Materials collection

II. Entrances, Exits

Entering room
Leaving the room
Bathroom
Water fountain

III. Movement Within the Room

Pencil sharpener
Wastebasket
To groups

IV. Instructional Routines

Morning exercises
Noise control
Asking and answering questions
Getting help
Free time
Computer access
Ending the day

V. Other Routines

Procedures I Will Use

☐ Class Leader/President/Line Leader
☐ Vice President
☐ Secretary
☐ Attendance Taker
☐ Messenger/Office Runner
☐ P.E. Monitor
☐ Clean-Up Director
☐ Paper Passer
☐ Board Eraser
☐ Pet Feeder
☐ Plant Tender
☐ Door Monitor
☐ Lunch Counter
☐ Flag Salute Leader
☐ Calendar Updater
☐ Library Assistant
☐ Row Leaders/Table Monitors

_____

_____

The method I will use to select and rotate monitorial duties:

Worksheet 5.1
Discipline Clarification Activity

Rank from 1–8 alone and then in a group.

Me   Group

_____ _____ Discipline is manipulation and isn't appropriate for children.

_____ _____ I'll figure discipline out as I go along.

_____ _____ I believe in talking out discipline problems with individuals.

_____ _____ Children should participate in setting up classroom rules and working out classroom problems.

_____ _____ Discipline is helping children make the right choices.

_____ _____ Children should experience the logical consequences of their behavior.

_____ _____ Children respond best to rewards and punishments.

_____ _____ A classroom is a dictatorship, and I make the rules.

Worksheet 5.2
Discipline System Criteria

MY DISCIPLINE PLAN IS:

	Yes	No
Reasonable	☐	☐
Respectful	☐	☐
Dignified	☐	☐
Consistent with school plan	☐	☐
Age-appropriate	☐	☐
Flexible	☐	☐
Time efficient	☐	☐
Easy to administer	☐	☐
Stress-free	☐	☐
Easy to communicate	☐	☐
Consistent with my philosophy and beliefs	☐	☐

Worksheet 5.3
Setting the Stage for Discipline Checklist

	Yes	No
I. Physical Environment		
A. Room is properly ventilated.	☐	☐
B. Room is well lit.	☐	☐
C. Room is an attractive and stimulating environment.	☐	☐
D. Room is clean and uncluttered.	☐	☐
E. Private spaces are provided.	☐	☐
F. Children can see and be seen from all angles.	☐	☐
G. Seating arrangement promotes good management.	☐	☐
II. Meeting Individual Differences		
A. Assignments are differentiated for slower and faster learners.	☐	☐
B. Children are grouped according to needs, interests, abilities.	☐	☐
C. Children have some choices.	☐	☐
D. Teacher expectations are realistic.	☐	☐
E. Instruction is geared to pupil interests.	☐	☐
III. Planning		
A. Success is built in.	☐	☐
B. Activities are worthwhile and meaningful.	☐	☐
C. All materials are ready.	☐	☐
D. Procedures are clear.	☐	☐
E. Each day is overplanned, and sponges are used when needed.	☐	☐

IV. Instruction

A. Attention is focused prior to beginning instruction. ☐ ☐
B. Lessons are well paced. ☐ ☐
C. Attention is monitored. ☐ ☐
D. Lessons are varied, and pupils are involved. ☐ ☐
E. Overlapping is practiced. ☐ ☐
F. Transitions are smooth. ☐ ☐
G. Lessons are brought to closure. ☐ ☐
H. Procedural questions are encouraged. ☐ ☐

V. Organization

A. Procedures and routines are set. ☐ ☐
B. Signals for attention are consistently reinforced. ☐ ☐
C. Materials are equally and efficiently distributed. ☐ ☐

VI. Other

Worksheet 5.4
Discipline Letter to Parents

Dear Parent or Guardian:

Worksheet 6.2
Pupil Self-Evaluation

creative writing (poetry and prose) ☐
essays ☐
letters ☐
journal entries ☐
art in all media ☐
cooperative group products ☐

attitude inventories ☐
interviews ☐
autobiographies ☐
interest inventories ☐
proficiency lists ☐
diagnostic tests ☐

cloze tests ☐
reading lists ☐
peer comments/review ☐
teacher reflective comments ☐
parent reflective comments ☐
principal comments ☐

anecdotal records ☐
parent conference notes ☐
videos of performances ☐
computer discs of writings ☐
audiotapes of child reading ☐
_____ ☐
_____ ☐

Worksheet 7.1
Communicating with Parents Time Line

Information to Convey

	Before	1st Days	Open House
1. Self-introduction			
2. Invitation to partnership			
3. Discipline and classroom rules			
4. How to reach me			
5. Supplies			
6. Homework policy			
7. Your goals and objectives/philosophy			
8. Highlights of the curriculum			
9. Grading/conferencing/reporting practices			
10. Materials they can collect and save for me			
11. Snacks, lunch, and milk money			
12. Other			

Worksheet 7.2
Parent-Teacher Conferencing

Planning   Yes

   1. Have I confirmed the date and time
      with parents and arranged for an interpreter, if needed? ☐
   2. Are my records, marking book, and folder of
      child's work ready? ☐
   3. Have I made a list of points to cover? ☐
   4. Do I have a seating arrangement that provides
      face-to-face contact in adult-size chairs? ☐
   5. Am I dressed comfortably in nonintimidating clothing? ☐
   6. Do I have a place for coats, umbrellas, etc.? ☐
   7. Is there a waiting area for parents and/or children or
      younger siblings? ☐

The Conference

   8. Did I greet the parents warmly at the door? ☐
   9. Did I start the conference on a positive note? ☐
  10. Did I provide data to the parent and collect data,
      especially data relevant to a perceived problem? ☐
  11. Did I listen actively to the parents and reflect back
      to them both content and feelings? ☐
  12. Did I enlist their help in seeking solutions to any
      problems? ☐
  13. Did I incorporate their ideas into a final plan for action? ☐
  14. Did I arrange for a follow-up meeting or note? ☐
  15. Did I summarize the main points covered? ☐
  16. Did I terminate the conference at an appropriate point? ☐
  17. Did I see the parents to the door and thank them for
      coming? ☐

Postconference

  18. Did I take time to make notes about the conference? ☐
  19. Did I give myself breathing time between conferences? ☐
  20. Did I send follow-up notes to parents summarizing the
      major points covered? ☐

Name
Address
Daytime phone

I. Informal talks to classes:

About your job (specify)
About your travels (specify)
About your hobby (specify)
About your country of origin if born elsewhere (specify)
About special interests (specify)
Other (specify)

II. Films, videos, laser discs, slides, photo albums, records, compact discs you would be willing to share (please specify)

III. Crafts, souvenirs, costumes from your native country or travels, rock collections, shell collections, poster sets, etc.

IV. Demonstrations: Please list below any special talents you would be willing to demonstrate to the class:

cooking (ethnic foods)   voice
crafts (specify)   gymnastics/exercise
dance   model building
musical instruments   hobbies or collections
pets   gardening techniques
other

V. Computer technology: HyperCard stacks, educational software and hardware.

Worksheet 7.3B
Parents as Resources
Los padres como recursos

Nombre
Domicilio
Número de teléfono de día

I. Charlas en clase:

Acerca de su trabajo (explique)
Acerca de sus viajes (explique)
Acerca de sus pasatiempos (explique)
Acerca de su pais de origen si nació en otro lugar (explique)
Acerca de sus intereses especiales (explique)
Algo más (explique)

II. Películas, videos, discos láser, diapositivas, álbumes de fotografías, discos, discos compactos que le interesaría compartir (explique)

III. Artes, recuerdos, trajes de su país nativo o de viajes, colecciones de piedras, colecciones de conchas, láminas, etc.

IV. Demostraciones: Haga una lista de algunos talentos especiales que le gustaría demostrar en clase:

cocina (comidas regionales)   voz
artes manuales (explique)   gimnasia/ejercicios
baile   construcción de modelos
instrumentos musicales   pasatiempos o colecciones
mascotas   técnicas de jardinería
algo más

V. Tecnología de computadoras: HyperCard stacks, programas educativos para computadoras, y aparatos de computadoras

1. Read to your child every night and develop a library.
2. Watch television with your child, asking questions about the characters, the plot, the setting. Encourage guessing during quiz shows.
3. Encourage your child to read comics in the newspapers. Cut the strips apart and have your child rearrange them in sequence.
4. Play games that encourage thinking: dominoes, bingo, card games, backgammon, Scrabble, Boggle, Monopoly.
5. Have your child count everything in sight.
6. Have your child identify and classify everything in the house according to shape, beginning sound, color, texture, etc.
7. Have your child arrange selected items in sequence according to size and weight.
8. Provide a variety of reading material: newspapers, labels on cans, boxes, time tables, mail, telephone books, menus in restaurants, signs in stores, road signs.
9. Encourage your child to write to out-of-town relatives.
10. Talk with your child, answering questions whenever possible.
11. Help your child acquire new interests and hobbies.
12. Encourage your child to follow maps and keep diaries on trips.
13. Post your child's work in a prominent place (refrigerator/bulletin board).
14. Visit the library with your child and subscribe to children's magazines.
15. Attend plays, concerts, puppet shows with your child.
16. Encourage creative expression through art (clay, paint, markers).
17. Work on projects with your child (creating an aquarium, building a bird feeder, cultivating a garden, baking cookies, painting the fence).
18. Encourage your child to start a collection (rocks, leaves, dried flowers, stamps, shells, buttons, coins).
19. Encourage physical activity, active play, and sports.
20. Borrow from the library records, videos, and tapes especially for your child.
21. Encourage siblings to help one another.

1. Lea a su niño/a cada noche y forme una biblioteca.

2. Mire televisión con su niño/a, hagale preguntas acerca de los personajes, desarrollo de la obra, ambiente. Anímelo/a a adivinar cuando vea programas de preguntas y respuestas.

3. Anime a su niño/a a leer las tiras cómicas de los periódicos, recorte las escenas y dígale que las vuelva a poner en orden.

4. Juegue juegos que alienten a pensar: dominós, bingo, backgammon, Scrabble, Boggle, Monopoly.

5. Pida a su niño/a que cuente todo lo que vea.

6. Pida a su niño/a que identifique y clasifique las cosas de la casa según el tamaño, el primer sonido, el color, la textura, etc.

7. Pida a su niño/a que ponga algunas cosas en orden según su tamaño y peso.

8. Déle variedad de materials para leer: periódicos, etiquetas de latas, cajas, horarios, cartas, guías de teléfono, menús de restaurantes, letreros de tiendas, señales del camino.

9. Anime a su niño/a a escribir a parientes que vivan fuera de su ciudad.

10. Hable con su niño/a y conteste sus preguntas cuando sea posible.

11. Ayude a que su niño/a adquiera intereses y pasatiempos nuevos.

12. Anime a su niño/a a seguir mapas y llevar un diario cuando haga un viaje.

13. Ponga el trabajo de su niño/a en un lugar prominente (refrigerador, etc.).

14. Visite la biblioteca y subscríbase a revistas de niños/as.

15. Vaya al teatro, a conciertos, y espectáculos de títeres con su niño/a.

16. Anime a que su niño/a exprese su creatividad por medio del arte (plastilina, pintura, marcadores).

17. Trabaje en proyectos con su niño/a (haciendo un acuario, construyendo un comedero para pájaros, cultivando un jardín, haciendo galletas, pintando la cerca).

18. Anime a que su niño/a coleccione algo (piedras, hojas, flores secas, estampillas, conchas, botones, monedas).

19. Anime a su niño/a a que participe en actividades físicas y deportes.

20. Saque de la biblioteca discos, videos, y grabaciones especialmente para su niño/a.

21. Anime a que los hermanos se ayuden entre sí.

1. How do I refer a child for special testing?

2. What do I do first if I suspect child abuse?

3. How do I get into the school on weekends?

4. How does the laminating (die press, bookbinding, copy) machine work?

5. How do I sign up to use the multiuse or assembly room?

6. How do I order media and technology?

7. How many times will the principal visit me, and will I have notice?

8. How do I get more desks (books, materials, pencils, etc.)?

9. How do I get repairs done in the room?

10. What do I do when a child gets sick?

11.

12.

13.

14.

15.

16.

17.

18.

Worksheet 8.2
Working with an Aide

	Yes	No
Preparing to Meet My Aide		
1. Do I know the hours/days per week my aide will be with me?	☐	☐
2. Do I know the legal constraints governing the aide's responsibilities in the classroom?	☐	☐
3. Have I drawn up a list of responsibilities for my aide? Are they consistent with what other aides in the school are asked to do?	☐	☐
Orienting My Aide		
4. Have I discussed my aide's prior experience working with children, and his/her philosophy and attitude toward discipline?	☐	☐
5. Have I described my program and schedule clearly?	☐	☐
6. Have I oriented my aide to the classroom, materials, and supplies?	☐	☐
7. Have I discussed record keeping and marking procedures?	☐	☐
8. Have I given my aide duplicate copies of all texts and familiarized my aide with other instructional materials?	☐	☐
9. Have I established a weekly or biweekly planning time?	☐	☐
10. Have I provided a suitable work station for my aide?	☐	☐
Coaching My Aide		
Have I coached my aide in:		
11. questioning skills?	☐	☐
12. motivation strategies?	☐	☐
13. drill techniques?	☐	☐
14. discipline procedures/routines?	☐	☐
15. lesson planning/grading shortcuts?	☐	☐
16. cooperative learning?	☐	☐
17. portfolio assessment?	☐	☐

224

Appreciation

		Yes	No
18.	Do I provide sincere acknowledgment for my aide's efforts?	☐	☐

I. Class List, Seating Chart, School Map, and Lesson Plans are attached.

II. Daily Schedules (attached)

Assembly	Day	Time	Place
Library	Day	Time	Place
Computer Lab	Day	Time	Place
P.E.	Day	Time	Place
	Day	Time	Place
	Day	Time	Place

Resource Room

Student	Day	Time	Place
Student	Day	Time	Place
Student	Day	Time	Place
Student	Day	Time	Place
Student	Day	Time	Place

Other (Band, Lunch Monitors, etc.)

Student	Day	Time	Place
Student	Day	Time	Place
Student	Day	Time	Place
Student	Day	Time	Place
Student	Day	Time	Place

III. Teacher Duties (bus, recess, lunch, etc.)

Day	Time	Place
Day	Time	Place

IV. Synopsis of Discipline System. (Further explanation attached.)

V. Procedures

Attendance
Free Time
Getting Help
Lunch Tickets
Bathroom
Water
Entrances/Exits
Emergency Procedures

VI. Bus Children and Time(s) to Dismiss Them

VII. Helpers

Buddy Teacher	Room
Student Helpers	
Aide	Times and Days
Parent Volunteers	Times and Days
	Times and Days
	Times and Days
	Times and Days

VIII. Special Needs Students

IX. Where to Find

Grade Book
Lesson Plans
Manuals
Art Supplies

1. How will I set the stage for learning on the very first day?

2. How will I go about establishing a community in the classroom?

3. What should I wear on the first day?

4. What is the first thing I should say?

5. How much should I tell about my personal life?

6. How do I assign seats?

7. How can I learn the students' names?

8. What do I actually do on the first day of school?

Other Questions:

Worksheet 9.2
Schedule of First-Day Activities

TIME   ACTIVITY

Worksheet 9.3
Evaluating My First Day's Plans

	YES	NO
1. Are my plans complete, flexible? Did I overplan?	☐	☐
2. Are my activities motivating?	☐	☐
3. Do I introduce routines and plan within my eventual schedule?	☐	☐
4. Do I introduce rule making and behavior expectations?	☐	☐
5. Do I provide for school and classroom orientation?	☐	☐
6. Do I preview the curriculum for the children?	☐	☐
7. Do I have opportunities for children to choose and decide?	☐	☐
8. Do I include a reading experience?	☐	☐
9. Do I have plans to acknowledge each child?	☐	☐
10. Will children feel successful after the first day of school?	☐	☐
11. WILL THEY WANT TO RETURN THE NEXT DAY?		

Other Criteria:

Week_____Year_____								
Monday ___ / ___(date								
Tuesday ___ / ___								
Wednesday ___ / ___								
Thursday ___ / ___								
Friday ___ / ___								

Notes:　　Duty:　　Meetings:　　Things to Do:　　Calls:

	YES	NO
1. Is my name on the chalkboard?	☐	☐
2. Is there a welcome sign on the outside door?	☐	☐
3. Are name tags prepared?	☐	☐
4. Are bulletin boards ready to go?	☐	☐
5. Is the flag pressed and in place?	☐	☐
6. Is the pledge and patriotic song neatly lettered on a chart?	☐	☐
7. Is the daily schedule on the chalkboard?	☐	☐
8. Do I have all cubbies and coat hooks labeled?	☐	☐
9. Do I have a seating chart ready to be filled in?	☐	☐
10. Do I have enough textbooks for every child?	☐	☐
11. Do I have extra furniture for any unexpected newcomers?	☐	☐
12. Is the room cheerful, bright, attractive?	☐	☐
13. Have I established a seating method?	☐	☐
14. Have I determined how to introduce myself?	☐	☐
15. Have I selected a method for learning their names?	☐	☐
16. Do I have my own outline of activities prepared on an index card, along with lesson plans?	☐	☐
17. Do I have all my materials laid out in the order they are used?	☐	☐

Other Questions:

I BELIEVE:

Worksheet 10.2
Successes of the Day

HIGHLIGHTS OF MY DAY

Date   Instruction   Management

Worksheet 10.3
Professional Development Log

Inservices and Conferences I Attended

Date   Topic   Most Important Ideas

Journals/Professional Books

Professional Organizations

Worksheet 10.4
Rejuvenation Calendar

Month_____

Sun	Mon	Tues	Wed	Thurs	Fri	Sat

CODE

P = Physical Activity
M = Meditation or Quiet Time
N = Nutritious Meals
S = Socializing
E = Entertainment
O = Other (specify)

Index